Social security for the eXcluded majority

Case studies of developing countries

Social security for the eXcluded majority

Case studies of developing countries

Edited by
Wouter van Ginneken

INTERNATIONAL LABOUR OFFICE
GENEVA

van Ginneken, Wouter
Social security for the excluded majority: Case studies of developing countries
Geneva, International Labour Office, 1999

/Social security/, /Informal sector/, /Benin/, /China/, /El Salvador/, /India/, /Tanzania/.02.03.1

ISBN 92-2-110856-2

ILO Cataloguing in Publication Data

Printed and bound in Great Britain by Biddles Ltd, Guildford and King's Lynn

PREFACE

This study is the result of an ILO work programme on social safety nets, social assistance and the prevention of poverty that was carried out from 1996 to 1997. The programme had two objectives: first to examine the reasons why statutory social security schemes do not reach larger proportions of the labour force; and second, to develop a more informed base for the consideration, design and implementation of tax-financed social assistance and contributory social insurance schemes. As a complementary goal, the programme began to develop new technical cooperation activities, with the aim of strengthening the capacity of governments, social security agencies, social partners, NGOs and insurance companies to design and implement social security schemes for the informal sector.

The basic reasons for low social security coverage in most low-income developing countries are complex. Usually a large proportion of the labour force lies outside the formal sector and does not have a regular job whose earnings can be monitored and on which mandatory contributions can be collected from both the worker and the employer. This weakens the participatory basis on which most formal sector social security schemes are predicated. Often the formal sector schemes open up participation to informal sector workers on a voluntary basis. But many workers outside the formal sector are not able or willing to take up this possibility. They are generally poor, and it would mean contributing a relatively high percentage of their income (the equivalent of the worker's plus the employer's contribution) to finance social security benefits that do not meet their priority needs. These frequently differ from those of workers in the formal sector. In general, workers outside the formal sector give preference to more immediate concerns, such as health and education, or to death and disability benefits, rather than to pensions or unemployment benefits. Informal sector workers may not be familiar with, and/or distrust, the way the statutory social insurance schemes are managed.

There is clearly a large and unmet need for social protection, and the introduction and case studies in this book provide a clear illustration of its magnitude and the ways in which the problem is being tackled in a range of countries. One possibility is to create new benefit schemes within the context of statutory social insurance schemes, for example on disability and survivorship, that would meet the priorities of informal sector workers. Another possibility is to extend the scope of social assistance schemes, which are usually financed out of general revenues. However, the principal problem with this approach is that the countries with the greatest need for social protection in the informal sector are also those whose public finances are most severely constrained: they simply do not have the resources or tax base to provide much in the way of anti-poverty support. Finally, a frequently tried approach is the development of area- and occupation-based social protection programmes, founded on organizations which have emerged at the local level and in the informal economy. Many of them are still experimental, and they rely greatly on the cooperation and solidarity of various social actors. But they may offer the best hope of a way forward to a world in which social protection can be extended to the vast majority of the population.

Colin Gillion
Director
ILO Social Security Department
March 1999

CONTENTS

List of tables

ACKNOWLEDGEMENTS

Work on this study was carried out between 1996 and 1998. I received much encouragement and support from Colin Gillion, the Director of ILO's Social Security Department, as well as from Jean-Victor Gruat and Emmanuel Reynaud, who headed the Standards, Planning and Development Branch during that period.

I would also like to thank the authors of the individual chapters who were generally patient in accommodating the many comments and queries that were addressed to them. A special word of thanks goes to my colleague Mr. Chanyou Zhu from the ILO Office in Beijing who coordinated and edited the study on China and had it translated. I am also most grateful to Ricardo Córdova – the Director of the FundaUngo Foundation in San Salvador who coordinated the study on El Salvador.

The study benefited enormously from the comments by ILO colleagues Roger Beattie, José Burle de Figueiredo, Christian Jacquier, Carmen Solorio and John Woodall. Finally, I am indebted to the three external reviewers whose comments resulted in significant changes in Chapter 1 as well as in the addition of Chapter 8 on policy recommendations.

GLOSSARY OF ABBREVIATIONS

This glossary is divided into six sections. The first contains the abbreviations that are used throughout the book; the five others correspond to the country case studies on Benin, China, El Salvador and the United Republic of Tanzania.

General abbreviations

AIDS	Acquired immune deficiency syndrome
CDR	Crude death rate
DANIDA	Danish International Development Agency
EOBI	Employees' Old-age Benefits Institution (Pakistan)
ESR	Erythrocyte sedimentation rate
GDP	Gross domestic product
HDI	Human development index
HFA	"Health for All by the Year 2000"
IADB	Inter-American Development Bank
IFM	Institute of Financial Management
IILS	International Institute for Labour Studies
ILO	International Labour Organization *or* International Labour Office
ILO INTERDEP	ILO Interdepartmental Project on the Urban Informal Sector (1994–95)
ILO PROMICRO	ILO Project for the Promotion of Micro-enterprises (Central America)
ILO-SAAT	ILO South Asian Advisory Team
IMR	Infant mortality rate
ISSA	International Social Security Association
MCH	Maternal and Child Health

MOH   Ministry of Health
NGO   Non-governmental organization
NHP   National Health Policy
NMBS   National Maternity Benefit Scheme
PAYG   Pay-As-You-Go
PHC   Primary Health Centre *or* Primary Health Care
RHC   Rural Health Centre
SME   Small and medium-sized enterprises
UNDP   United Nations Development Programme
UNICEF   United Nations Children's Fund
USAID   United States Agency for International Development
WHO   World Health Organization

Benin

CADER   Regional Action Centres for Rural Development
CREDESA   Regional Centre for Development and Health
DAS   Department of Social Affairs
FNRB   National Retirement Pension Fund
GTZ   German Technical Cooperation Agency
OBSS   Benin Office of Social Security
PDSP   Pahou Sanitary Development Project
SONAR   National Insurance and Reinsurance Company

China

TVE   Township and village enterprise

El Salvador

ACACSEMERSA   Savings and Loans Cooperative Association for the
                Women of Municipal Market No. 2, Santa Ana
ANDA   National Water and Drainage Authority
ANTEL   National Telecommunications Health Network
CEL   Rio Lema Hydroelectric Executive Board's Health Service
EDUCO   Community Participation in Education
FIS   Social Investment Fund

FSV	Social Housing Fund
FUMA	Maquilishuat Foundation
INPEP	National Pensions Institute for Public Employees
INSAFOCOOP	National Register of Cooperatives of the Salvadorian Institute for Cooperative Development
IPSFA	Institute of Social Security for the Armed Forces
ISSS	Salvadorian Institute of Social Security
MIPLAN	Ministry of Planning
MOH	Ministry of Public Health and Social Assistance
PACTEM	Promotion of Urban Self-Help Organizations
PROSAMI	Mother and Child Health Programme
SETEFE	External Financing Technical Department
SRN	Department for National Reconstruction

India

ACCORD	Action for Community Organization, Rehabilitation and Development
AMS	Adivasi Munnetra Sangam
ASSEFA	Association for Sarva Seva Farms
CDF	Cooperative Development Foundation
EPF	Employees' Provident Fund
ESI	Employees' State Insurance
ESIS	Employees' State Insurance Scheme
GEPF	Government Employees' Provident Fund
GIS	Group insurance scheme
IRDP	Integrated Rural Development Programme
LALGI	Landless Agricultural Labourers' Group Insurance
LIC	Life Insurance Company of India
NABARD	National Bank for Agriculture and Rural Development
NCAER	National Council for Applied Economic Research
NSAP	National Social Assistance Programme
RBI	Reserve Bank of India
RMK	Rashtriya Mahila Kosh
SEWA	Self-Employed Women's Association
SHG	Self-help group
SPARC	Society for Promotion of Area Resource Centres

United Republic of Tanzania

ACP	AIDS Control Programme
CDD	Control of Diarrhoea Diseases
DASICO	Dar es Salaam Small Industries Cooperative Society
EDP	Essential Drugs Programme
EPI	Expanded Programme on Immunization
FPU	Family Planning Unit
ICHF	Igunga Community Health Fund
LAPF	Local Authorities Provident Fund
MOL	Ministry of Local Government and Cooperatives
MSD	Medical Stores Department
NIC	National Insurance Corporation
NPF	National Provident Fund
NSSF	National Social Security Fund
PMO	Prime Minister's Office
PPF	Parastatal Pension Fund
REPOA	Research on Poverty Alleviation
RMA	Rural Medical Aid
SACCO	Savings and credit cooperative
SHPS	School Health in Primary School
TDL	Tanzania Distilleries Limited
T.sh.	Tanzanian shillings
TTI	Tanganyika Textiles Industries
TZR	Tanzania-Zambia Railway Authority
UMASIDA	Health Fund for Informal Sector Workers in Dar es Salaam
UPATU	Rotating savings and credit group
UPE	Universal Primary Education
VHP	Village Health Post

OVERCOMING SOCIAL EXCLUSION 1

Wouter van Ginneken, Senior Economist, Social Security Department, ILO

One of the key global problems facing social security now is the fact that more than half of the world's population (workers and their dependants) are excluded from any type of statutory social security protection. They are covered neither by a contribution-based social insurance scheme nor by tax-financed social assistance. In sub-Saharan Africa and South Asia, statutory social security coverage is estimated at 5 to 10 per cent of the working population and decreasing. In India for example, not more than 10 per cent of workers were in the formal sector in the mid-1990s, compared to more than 13 per cent in the mid-1980s. In Latin America, coverage lies roughly between 10 and 80 per cent, and is mainly stagnating. In South-East and East Asia, coverage can vary between 10 and 100 per cent, and is generally increasing. In most transition countries of Europe, coverage varies between 50 and 80 per cent, while most developed countries have reached practically 100 per cent.

It was against this background that, during the 1996–97 period, the ILO's Social Security Department undertook an action programme on the role of social security in the fight against poverty. The first objective of this programme was to examine the reasons why statutory social security schemes did not reach larger proportions of the labour force. Secondly, it aimed to establish a more informed base for the consideration, design and implementation of tax-financed social assistance and self-financed social insurance schemes. In addition, the action programme started to develop new technical cooperation activities, with the intention of strengthening the capacity of governments, social security agencies, social partners, NGOs and insurance companies, in their efforts to design and implement social security schemes for the informal sector (van Ginneken, 1997).

The choice of countries for which case studies were included in this book was mainly based on two criteria. The first was their geographical diversity, so as to ensure maximum contrast between experiences and situations. The second was their relatively low level of economic development, because it is a general characteristic of those countries where social security coverage is lowest. A third reason for choosing the five particular countries for inclusion was as a result of requests from countries and of activities that the ILO had already been undertaking in this field.[1] In the United Republic of Tanzania, the ILO is already experimenting with pilot projects on social security for the informal sector, while in three others – Benin, El Salvador and India – it is planning to do so.

Countries at a low level of economic development (see table 1.1) are characterized by high levels of poverty and illiteracy, with the result that the vast majority of the population cannot afford to contribute to statutory social insurance schemes. In Benin and the United Republic of Tanzania less than 5 per cent of the working population contributes to statutory pension schemes, and the figure is around 10 per cent for India, and about 25 per cent for China and El Salvador. In most cases, the percentage of the working population contributing to statutory health insurance is considerably lower. In India, for example, it is not more than 4 per cent.

This situation of low coverage reflects a failure by countries and the international community to meet their obligations under article 9 of the International Covenant on Economic, Social and Cultural Rights which "recognizes the right of everyone to social security, including social insurance". It also goes against a commitment contained in the Philadelphia Declaration of 1944, by which the ILO Conference recognized the ILO's "solemn obligation ... to further among the nations of the world programmes which will achieve ... (f) the extension of social security measures to provide a basic income to all in need of such protection and comprehensive medical care".

In the industrialized countries the expansion of social security over the past 30 to 40 years has been a success (ILO, 1993). The incidence of poverty among the elderly is now not greater than for the population as a whole. Access to good quality health care is almost universal, and income support for those who are out of work has meant that unemployment no longer leads inevitably to unacceptable levels of hardship. Nevertheless, there is no reason for complacency, because social security systems will not only have to respond to new social security needs and find new forms of financing (ILO, 1995), but will also be severely challenged simply to maintain their achievements so far.

---

[1] India was chosen because, at the request of the Ministry of Labour, the ILO undertook a UNDP-financed mission on "Social protection for the unorganized sector" in 1995 and produced a report with extensive recommendations (ILO-SAAT, 1996) as well as a publication containing the main background papers (van Ginneken, 1998). The United Republic of Tanzania was included in the country case studies, because the ILO Social Security Department has been behind the setting up of the UMASIDA health insurance scheme for informal sector workers in Dar es Salaam (see Chapter 5). The choice of Benin was partly because it played the lead role in the follow-up activities on social protection after the ILO meeting on the consequences of the devaluation of the CFA Franc for Francophone African countries (ILO, 1997). El Salvador was selected to represent Central America, where the level of economic development is relatively low. Finally, a case study on China was included because it is the largest developing country in transition to a market economy.

Table 1.1 Economic and quality of life indicators, selected (groups of) countries, mid-1990s

	GNP per capita (1997)		Population under national poverty line (%)	Adult illiteracy (1995) (%)		Life expectancy at birth (years) (1996)	
	US dollars	PPP	(early 1990s)	Men	Women	Men	Women
Benin	380	1 260	33.0	51	74	52	57
China	860	3 570	8.4	10	27	68	71
El Salvador	1 810	2 810	48.3	27	30	66	72
India	390	1 650	40.9	35	62	62	63
Tanzania (United Rep.)	210	—	51.1	21	43	49	52
Low income countries	350	1 400	n.a.	35	59	58	60
Middle income countries	1 230	3 760	n.a.	12	25	66	71
High income countries	25 700	22 770	n.a.	<5[a]	<5[a]	74	81

PPP: Purchasing power parity.

[a] UNESCO estimates illiteracy to be less than 5 per cent.

Source: World Bank, 1998, pp. 190-93.

In its standard-setting and most of its technical cooperation activities on social security, the ILO had traditionally expected that all workers would sooner or later end up in secure formal sector employment. However, experience in developing countries – and more recently in the transition and developed countries – has shown quite the contrary, and this situation is unlikely to change in the foreseeable future. Even in countries with high economic growth, increasing numbers of workers are in less secure employment, such as the self-employed, casual labour and homeworkers. Clearly, the extension of statutory social security programmes cannot be the simple answer to satisfying the social security needs of the growing numbers of workers (and their families) outside the formal sector. Informal sector workers need to (and have) set up schemes that are better suited to their needs and contributory capacity. In addition, special social assistance measures are necessary for the most vulnerable groups outside the labour force, including the disabled and old people who cannot count on family support, who cannot be reached by other social policies and who have not been able to make provisions for their own pensions.

The exclusion of informal sector workers and other vulnerable groups from social security protection is part of a larger process of social exclusion that can be seen both as an attribute of individuals and as a property of societies (IILS, 1996).

As an attribute of individuals, social exclusion can mean not only material deprivation or poverty, but also the lack of social ties to a family, the community, voluntary organizations, or even the nation. Social exclusion is experienced by individuals and households as a lack of control over their own work and life situation. Many informal sector workers are in this position, because they live from one day to the next and are faced with the risk of various calamities that can throw them into a state of permanent indebtedness. Moreover, they lack the long-term planning horizon of formal sector workers who – as a result of their stable income patterns – can afford to save for their retirement. From the point of view of society, social exclusion can be thought of as institutions and/or rules that enable and constrain the access of different types of people to various goods, services and resources. These institutional processes will be highlighted in section 2 of this chapter.

The issue of the exclusion of those who are not in regular wage employment from the statutory social security system remains a vexing one, which deserves more discussion in the literature. Although it is not a new topic, it has not been resolved by policy-makers. In the current political climate, when social security is under increasing critical scrutiny, steps need to be taken to deal with this problem. This book aims to facilitate an appropriate policy response.

Section 1 of this chapter defines the concepts of social security and of the informal sector, and will review some basic characteristics of the countries included in this study. Section 2 examines the main reasons for exclusion from social security protection. Based on the case studies, section 3 then documents the various existing and alternative approaches to extending statutory social insurance. Section 4 highlights some of the emerging opportunities for contributory social insurance schemes in the informal sector, and attempts to draw some first lessons from these experiences. Section 5 identifies the various vulnerable groups that need social assistance, and reviews some experiences from the case studies. Section 6 concludes that experimentation with pilot projects is vital for finding new ways to extend social security protection, while section 7 outlines the main conclusions.

1. Introducing the concepts and the case-study countries

The ILO's research on the informal sector has demonstrated that a wider concept of social security is needed in order to understand the realities faced by informal sector workers, who constitute the majority of the world labour force. The traditional concept of social security is included in various ILO standards. According to the Income Security Recommendation, 1944 (No. 67), income security schemes should relieve want and prevent destitution by restoring, up to a reasonable level, income which is lost by reason of inability to work (including old age) or to obtain remunerative work, or by reason of the death of the bread-winner. Income security should be organized as far as possible on the basis of compulsory social insurance, and provision for needs not covered by compulsory social insurance should be made by social assistance. In the same vein, the Medical Care Recommendation, 1944, (No. 64), suggests that medical care should be provided either through a social insurance medical care service with supplementary provision by way of social assistance, or through a public medical service. The Social Security (Minimum Standards) Convention, 1952 (No. 102), identifies nine areas for social insurance, i.e. medical care as well as benefits in case of sickness, unemployment, old age, employment injury, family circumstances, maternity, invalidity and widowhood.

For the purposes of this book we shall use the following – wider – definition (van Ginneken, 1996 and 1998):

(a) The provision of benefits to households and individuals
(b) through public or collective arrangements
(c) to protect against low or declining living standards
(d) arising from a number of basic risks and needs.

The first element in this definition establishes that people derive individual rights from social security. The second element defines the social element of social security, i.e. that it is provided through public or collective – and often voluntary – arrangements. Social security schemes are called statutory when they are established by legislation. The third element makes it clear that social security aims at protection, and that its role should not be confused with policies for the promotion of employment and social services. Finally, it makes the point that social security is not only concerned with cash benefits and medical care, but also with benefits in kind and other basic needs areas such as basic education, housing and possibly food security.

In this book, social security is defined as being composed of social insurance and social assistance. *Social assistance* is defined as benefits in cash or in kind that are financed by the State (national and/or local), and that are mostly provided on the basis of a means or income test. The concept also includes universal benefit schemes, i.e. those which are tax-based but do not use a means test. Following the wider definition of social security, we shall also adopt a wide definition of social insurance. Thus, *social insurance* is social security that is financed by contributions and is based on the insurance principle. The essence of insurance is understood here to be the elimination of the uncertain risk of loss for the individual or household, by combining a larger number of similarly exposed individuals or households into a common fund that makes good the loss caused to any one member. In general, the common fund is financed by individual contributions, but it may also be replenished by the State – partially or even totally. As noted earlier, the salient, social, characteristic of a social insurance scheme is that it is operated through public or collective arrangements. But this does not prevent social insurance schemes from being administered by private insurance companies or through an intermediary. In the definition used here, social insurance does not have to be compulsory; it can also be voluntary.

There is a wide variety of definitions of the informal sector. In principle, informal sector workers are employed in (micro-) enterprises that have the following characteristics (ILO, 1994):

- the owner is personally liable for gains and losses (the enterprise is unincorporated);
- there is an absence of full and written accounts;
- the enterprise has less than 10 employees at a time.

Workers outside the formal sector are generally employed in small, often family-based enterprises. When they own their business, they are usually better off than other workers in the informal (and sometimes even the formal) sector. When they are wage workers, they usually have low incomes. Most informal sector workers and their families live in poverty, and a large proportion of them are women.

Our definition of the informal sector also covers workers affected by the informalization of labour relations with their employers, which often means the absence of written labour contracts. Such informality does not only affect wage earners and other groups such as homeworkers in the informal sector, but also casual workers who work – directly or indirectly – for so-called formal sector enterprises.

Finally, we also include in this analysis some population groups, such as widows, orphans and old people, who are neither protected by the employment income of their family nor by any other family support.

2. Reasons for exclusion

Among the five countries included in this publication there is a great diversity in social security systems, mainly due to different cultural and historical backgrounds, as well as to a variety of levels of economic development. However, there are also several similarities which apply to most developing countries. Civil servants are usually covered separately by the Government, which – in the case of pensions – pays all the contributions and – in case of health insurance – provides health services free of charge. All other formal – private and parastatal – sector

Table 1.2 Contributions to statutory social insurance (in percentages of earnings and/or payroll), selected countries, 1997

	Benin	China	El Salvador	India	Tanzania (U.R.)
Old-age*, disability and death	10	23–25	7.5	22	20
Sickness and maternity*	0.2	11*	} 3	} 6.5*	0
Work injury	1–4	el			el
Family allowances	8.8	0	0	0	0
Unemployment	0	1	0	0	0
Total	20–23	35–37	10.5	28.5	20

el: Employers' liability.
* including medical cost insurance.
Source: Updated from: SSA, 1997, various pages.

workers are often covered for old-age, survivors, and disability pensions, which represent the main benefits, followed by medical cost insurance (see table 1.2). In most countries these workers are incorporated into one scheme, although some groups of workers in the parastatal sector may be covered by a few special schemes. The benefits for all these workers are financed from employers' and workers' contributions, sometimes supplemented by Government subsidies. In some countries, such as China, El Salvador and India, there are also schemes financed exclusively by employers, such as for maternity, gratuity (severance) and employment injury benefits. In four of the five countries, contributions to social insurance exceed 20 per cent of the payroll – well beyond the contributory capacity of most informal sector workers.

There is an extensive literature on the lack of social security coverage in developing countries. With regard to social assistance, Midgley (1984a) maintains that even though the benefits paid may appear derisory when compared with those paid in industrialized countries, they do supplement the incomes of the poor. Nevertheless, he admits to four sets of problems that limit the usefulness of social assistance in developing countries, i.e. lack of government resources, of appropriate policy-making and of administrative capacity, as well as the stigmatization of claimants.

With regard to statutory social insurance, the discussion from the end of the 1960s until the mid-1980s revolved mainly around the question of inequality. Paukert (1968) demonstrated that such social insurance schemes in developing countries accentuated the favourable income position of formal sector workers, in particular because of the large amounts of government subsidies to such schemes. Midgley (1984b) added to this that the transfer of resources, however small, from those who have no income security to those who do, reinforces the privileges which wage and salaried employees enjoy, in particlar the elite in the civil service and the military.

To achieve an egalitarian system of social security, Midgley (1984b) proposed various reforms and innovations that in many ways are similar to the propositions made in this book. He was in favour of restricting social security privileges and extending social security benefits; of strengthening traditional social security institutions and protecting rural people through agricultural social security; and of fostering social security cooperatives and developing appropriate forms of social assistance.

In the 1990s Guhan (1994) argued that the "contingency approach" of social security cannot be transferred from developed to developing counties, where poverty is caused by many structural factors. Mesa-Lago (1994) showed for Latin American countries that low coverage is largely the result of three main factors – (i) the heavy contributory burden; (ii) the high cost of detecting, inspecting and collecting from the large numbers of self-employed, of domestic servants and of wage earners in microenterprises; and (iii) the fact that benefits available for this group are usually very small and reduce incentives for affiliation even more. These factors are further aggravated for rural areas, where the population is very dispersed; accessibility is low because of poor or non-existent public service infrastructure; and there are various cultural (e.g. linguistic) and socio-economic barriers (lower living standards).

Later studies (Bailey, 1994; van Ginneken, 1996 and 1999; Midgley and Tracy, 1996) and technical cooperation reports (ILO-SAAT, 1996) have also analysed the reasons for the low level of social security protection in developing countries. A common conclusion is that many workers outside the formal sector are unable or unwilling to contribute a relatively high percentage of their incomes to finance social security benefits that do not meet their priority needs. In addition, they may not be familiar with, and/or distrust, the way the statutory social security scheme is managed. There are also a host of factors that restrict access to the statutory social security schemes, such as legal restrictions, administrative bottlenecks and non-compliance. Finally, the environment of structural adjustment has had a mainly negative impact on social security coverage.

2.1 The impact of structural adjustment

The structural adjustment policies pursued recently in most developing countries have contributed to a decline in the small percentage of the working population in the formal sector. The successive waves of structural adjustment programmes have also led to wage cuts in the public and private sectors, thereby eroding the financial base of statutory social insurance schemes. Simultaneously, many such schemes in developing countries have suffered from bad management, partly because of too much government interference, which has often strongly reduced the trust of members in the scheme. In addition, structural adjustment programmes have often resulted in severe cuts in social budgets. In Benin for example, health expenditure's share in the total government budget dropped from 8.8 to 3.3 per cent between 1987 and 1992. As most governments can no longer guarantee access to free health and education, there is greater demand for group arrangements to finance and organize these social services. It is often more efficient to be part of a group insurance scheme than to have to face health and education expenditures individually.

Structural adjustment, socio-economic changes and the generally low level of economic development have also produced large vulnerable groups that cannot contribute to social insurance schemes and cannot be reached by other social policies. The most vulnerable groups outside the labour force are the disabled and old people who cannot count on family support, and who have not been able to make provisions for their own pensions. Some countries, such as China and India, have taken specific social assistance measures to meet the needs of these groups.

Finally, the positive message of this section is that there is an increasing number of associations of informal sector workers that are – or are capable of – financing and/or organizing their own social security protection. The positive result of structural adjustment has been the emergence of a more vibrant private sector with greater income-earning capabilities. In many developing countries there is a great variety of organizations engaged in social security, such as mutual benefit societies, "tontines", savings and loans societies, informal sector associations and NGOs, some examples of which will be examined in Chapters 5 and 6.

2.2 Social security priorities: Health, pensions and education

Some developing countries, such as China and India, have set up social assistance schemes that are aimed at people in financial need, who cannot be reached by policies for productive employment, and who cannot – and/or have not been able to – contribute to self-financed social insurance schemes. Social assistance schemes often provide pension benefits in cash or in kind, and may either apply to wide societal groups such as children, disabled and retired people, or be limited to certain occupational groups. The principal advantage of such social assistance pension benefits is that they can be targeted to those who are most in need, but they require sophisticated administration to determine who is really deserving and to ensure that the benefits reach the target population effectively. Thus, the costs of delivering the benefits are often high and, without an efficient and accountable control and monitoring system, leakages or corruption are likely. The size of these schemes depends on the resources, the management capacity and the priorities of the countries concerned.

Workers outside the formal sector are generally employed in small, often family-based enterprises. When they own their business, they are usually not integrated into the formal economy, but if so, they are often associated under very unfavourable terms. When they are wage workers, they usually have informal labour relations with their employers, and have no written labour contracts. Such informality not only affects wage earners and other groups, such as homeworkers in the informal sector, but also casual labourers who work – directly or indirectly – for formal sector enterprises.

Most formal sector workers have steady and high income patterns, and are therefore in a position to contribute regularly to social security. They generally have a long-term planning horizon, and given their regular earnings, they can provide for their retirement. This is not the case for most informal sector workers, who may not wish to save for retirement, since – if they reach retirement at all – they hope to be supported by their children. Moreover, if they have the resources, they may prefer to invest in their business, in land or in housing. However, most informal sector workers "are psychologically engrossed in their problems of immediate survival to such an extent that any concern or motivation to provide for a distant eventuality gets almost obliterated" (Singh, 1994). They live from one day to the next and are faced with catastrophic risks that can throw them into a state of permanent indebtedness. These catastrophic risks can be grouped into the following four categories:

- calamities (e.g. flood, fire, civil unrest and famine);
- loss of earning power (disability, ill-health, loss of assets, economic recession);
- life-cycle crises (death and family breakdown);
- sudden and large expenditures (e.g. hospital bills, major social occasions).

Social security schemes cannot protect informal sector workers against all these risks and calamities. Most informal sector households already spend a considerable part of their budget on vital life areas such as health and education. It is exactly in these areas that collective action can improve the cost-effectiveness of their expenditure. Moreover, many people in the informal sector seek protection against death and disability.

Generally speaking, the principal social security priorities for informal sector workers are as follows:

- improving the effectiveness of health-care expenditure;
- death, survivor and disability benefits;
- smoothing out expenditure on basic education;
- maternity and childcare benefits.

Perceived social security needs also vary according to the types of informal sector workers and their families, as well as according to the various risks that they run. Therefore, help with housing costs is often a high priority for urban residents where housing prices are high; social assistance is a high priority for old-age pensioners, orphans and widows who cannot be reached with employment and labour market policies; food security measures (social assistance) are appropriate in famine and civil unrest situations.

2.3 Contributory capacity: Low, irregular and unreliable

The statutory sector contribution rate for social insurance is usually 20 per cent or more of the total payroll (see table 1.2), as is the case, for example, in Benin, China, India and the United Republic of Tanzania. Formal sector wage workers share these contributions with their employers; however, self-employed workers are often not prepared to pay the full (workers' and employers') contribution by themselves. Chapter 4 on the United Republic of Tanzania also shows that the high contribution rate for the National Provident Fund (NPF) was an important deterrent against informal sector workers joining the scheme.

Informal sector workers often have irregular earning patterns, since their employment is unpredictable and irregular. Casual and seasonal wage employment, for example, depends on the availability of jobs in specific periods. When there is no work, employment is immediately terminated, hence incomes are lost. Self-employment is often dependent on the business cycle and the state of the various product and services markets. The irregularity of informal sector employment makes it unreliable as a source of income for social insurance contributions. Moreover, the findings of the 1995 Dar es Salaam Informal Sector Survey indicate that supplementary income opportunities from which contributions could be made for financing social security provision are not reliable either (see table 4.7 in Chapter 4).

Another way of looking at the unreliability of income sources to deal with social contingencies is to ask informal sector workers how they would finance long-term sickness, large medical expenses and old-age pensions. Again, Chapter 4 (see table 4.8) shows that for large medical expenses and long-term sickness, most respondents in Dar es Salaam mentioned that they would raise money to meet those costs through their own family savings and assistance from relatives. However, neither of these can be considered a reliable source of funding. With regard to family savings, there may be many other competing demands. The willingness and ability of relatives to contribute from their own pockets inevitably varies from time to time and place to place, so that this type of support for the cost of social needs is neither reliable nor sufficiently effective.

11

The same respondents were also requested to indicate what kind of provision they had made for old age. The majority had acquired land as a form of security for old age, whereas about one-third had made monetary savings. Land may not be a reliable means to sustain a person during old age unless some funding is made available to turn it into a productive asset for future income generation. We have already seen above some of the limitations of personal savings as a source of social security funding. Other respondents indicated that ownership of a house for renting out represents a provision for old age. This may be a reliable source of income, but only if a continuous flow of rent can be ensured.

2.4 Legal restrictions

Most statutory social insurance schemes in developing countries have adopted a very cautious approach to the extension of coverage beyond the formal sector. Not only does this often result in the exclusion of the self-employed, family workers, domestic employees and casual workers, but it has also meant that restrictions have often been imposed on coverage for people in regular employment. Here the considerations are principally administrative. It has long been the practice for new social security schemes based on social insurance principles to adopt a policy of the gradual extension of coverage, so that account is taken of the limited administrative capacity of the system and of employers. The view is taken that it is better to ensure that the scheme operates satisfactorily on a restricted basis, and then to extend it gradually. Thus, coverage may be restricted by size of employer, on the understanding that the larger employers are more likely to comply with the obligations of the scheme.

An alternative approach adopted in some developing countries is to restrict the scheme on a geographical basis (as in Mozambique) or with regard to certain occupational groups. For instance, the Indian Employees' State Insurance (ESI) scheme, covering mainly health and sickness benefits, is restricted to only about 600 industrial centres where sufficient medical services are available and where the strength of insurable employment is greater than 1,000 employees (see Chapter 2). In some countries (an example is the EOBI scheme in Pakistan), social security was – at least initially – focused on the lower paid or on manual workers, and higher-paid workers or managers were specifically excluded from coverage, in the belief that such persons could make their own arrangements or were likely to be adequately covered by their employers' arrangements. Similar provisions apply to the Malaysian social insurance scheme. The Employees' Provident Fund in India applies a combination of provisions to restrict membership. First, the employment must fall within the scope of one of 177 prescribed occupations; secondly, the establishment must have at least 20 workers; and thirdly, until 1997, the establishment had to have been operating for at least three years (termed an "infancy period").

2.5 Administrative bottlenecks

The case study on China shows that within the informal sector, employees in private enterprises and urban self-employed workers amount to 20.5 million – about one-fifth of the number of formal sector workers. The informal sector workers are scattered in nearly 9 million employing units, with an average of one to five employees in each employing unit. Absorbing so many scattered employees in the social security scheme will result in high overhead costs, as it will double and redouble the workload of the existing social insurance organizations.

Therefore, the tendency in most countries has been for the restrictions based on legislation to be removed only slowly, because amendment of the legislation is a slow process which often has to be negotiated. Many social security administrations in developing countries find it difficult to cope with the volume of administrative tasks associated with the operation of a social insurance scheme, which requires the maintenance of accurate lifetime records for insured persons. These problems are intensified by the administration's dependence on the cooperation of employers and insured persons in providing the necessary data accurately and regularly. There is therefore a close connection between the extension of coverage and the administrative capacity of employers and the social security agencies.

Other factors affecting the extension process are a general lack of awareness among the excluded groups (see Chapter 4), or perhaps even reluctance where the scheme is perceived either to be inefficient or not in their best interests. Some people (both employers and workers) feel overwhelmed by the bureaucratic obligations associated with registration under the statutory social security scheme, or may fear that entry into the "public system" will have other unwelcome implications.

3. Extension and reform of statutory social insurance

As noted before, in many low-income developing countries less than 10 per cent of the working population and their dependants are covered by statutory social insurance, and this mainly concerns the areas of pensions and health care. As a general rule, and at the present stage of economic development, extension and reform of the statutory social insurance system could reach perhaps another 10 per cent of the working population, i.e. most regular and some casual wage workers in the informal sector. Some of the presently unprotected section of the working population and their families could be covered if legal restrictions and administrative bottlenecks were removed. Some other groups could be covered through the reform of the benefit and contribution structures of statutory social insurance schemes. This section will therefore first examine the opportunities for legal extension and administrative reform, and then investigate how the benefit and contribution structures of pensions and health insurance schemes can be reformed so as to extend social insurance protection to hitherto uncovered groups.

3.1 Extending existing social insurance schemes

In some developing countries the process of economic growth has resulted in the transfer of a large part of the labour force to the formal sector. In addition, in such countries the government had – and used – sufficient resources to subsidize the extension of the statutory social insurance schemes. This has happened in various countries in East and South-East Asia. The most striking example is the Republic of Korea, which achieved universal health insurance coverage in 1989, within about 12 years of the commencement of compulsory medical insurance in 1977 (Park, 1992).

Some case studies described in this book have shown that existing social insurance schemes can be extended successfully. Chapter 2 (on India), for instance, documents the successful coverage of about 400,000 mainly home-based beedi workers under the Employees' Provident Fund Act. The crucial factor here has been the issuing of identity cards. This indicates that a procedural mechanism can assume a significant role in making statutory benefits accessible to categories of informal sector workers. In China (see Chapter 3) there are various opportunities for the existing pension schemes covering state-owned and collective enterprises to be extended to foreign investment enterprises, to private enterprises, and to some township and village enterprises (TVEs) with stable labour relations.

An important precondition for such extension to take place is the removal of various legal obstacles that were documented in the previous section. But the most important accompanying measure is the improvement and streamlining of the existing administrative structure. Chapter 4 (on the United Republic of Tanzania) for instance recommends the following four improvements:

- Benefit payment procedures need to be streamlined so as to shorten the period involved in claiming benefits and to decentralize benefit payment procedures.
- Record-keeping needs to be improved, and statements of account should be sent to members regularly.

- The National Social Security Fund (NSSF) authorities must establish a system whereby information about all aspects of the scheme is collected, processed, analysed, stored accurately and securely, and shared with its members.
- NSSF scheme members need to be visited to resolve social security-related problems. Such visits would not only provide an opportunity to understand and address the problems faced by members, but could also be used as one way of disseminating information about NSSF operations.

Generally speaking, the administration of social security systems is often unable to deal with the special circumstances of the self-employed and casual wage workers (Jenkins, 1993). When statutory social insurance is extended to smaller enterprises, each new employer has to be identified, registered, educated and persuaded to comply with all the rules of the scheme, in so far as they relate to the registration of existing and new employees, and to the mode and timing of the payment of contributions. In the case of casual workers, contributions are difficult to collect, and maintaining up-to-date and correct records is administratively complicated, as such persons work intermittently and irregularly for different employers. There is also some conflict with the underlying concept used for the calculation of benefits, i.e. that of "replacement" income, in situations where the income to be replaced cannot always be determined clearly.

Other administrative reforms may improve compliance and enforcement, for example by developing cooperation with other public agencies, such as tax agencies, to identify individuals and businesses that should be covered by the social security scheme. Moreover, improved governance – supported by effective public relations and educational activities to increase awareness as to rights and obligations – needs to be underpinned by compliance and enforcement procedures and powers that reinforce the mandatory character of the scheme.

3.2 Reforming pension schemes

One of the greatest challenges facing pension schemes is the extent to which pensions should be funded or financed on a PAYG basis. This is one of the main topics of a major ILO book on social security pensions (ILO, forthcoming), which comes to the conclusion that it is important to diversify the various sources of financing so as to minimize the risks that could affect future pension benefits. It also observes that the traditional "pay-as-you-go" form of financing basically links pension benefits to the outcomes of the labour market, and in particular to wage growth. The funded form of financing links pension benefits to the capital market,

15

and in particular to the rate of return on stocks and bonds. Both forms of financing have their advantages and disadavantages, both in theory and in practice. The book recommends that "pay-as-you-go" is generally more appropriate for financing mandatory systems providing minimum and some earnings-related pension benefits, whereas the "funded" system is more suitable for voluntary and some mandatory schemes providing earnings-related pension benefits.

It is interesting to observe that out of the five countries included in this publication, four have recently reformed their pension schemes. China and El Salvador have converted at least part of their pension system into a funded scheme with individual accounts. Their reform was based on a desire to strengthen the link between contributions and benefits, and on the belief that pension benefits would grow faster in a funded scheme. On the other hand, India and the United Republic of Tanzania converted at least part of their provident fund into a PAYG social insurance pension scheme. These countries wanted to increase solidarity within the scheme, and to ensure that all pensioners would receive regular payments of pension benefits.

It is not clear whether and to what extent the transition to a funded scheme would contribute to the extension of coverage. The study on El Salvador (Chapter 6) claims that the new Pensions Savings System offers – through voluntary and optional entry – opportunities for greater coverage for the self-employed, non-resident Salvadorians and farm workers. However, it also admits that funded as well as PAYG systems are hampered by the same obstacles as mentioned in section 2, i.e. of a legal and administrative nature. Furthermore, Midgley and Sherraden (1996) warn that if there is a shift in social security policy towards asset accounts, it is quite possible – and even likely – that the poor will be hurt more than they are helped by these changes to the welfare state. Thus, they plead for active and progressive principles for including the entire population in social development and economic growth. More specifically, they see the need, as a first step, for the creation of accounts at the youngest possible age, preferably at birth, which would constitute the base for a wide range of creative funding strategies to build assets for the poor.

Both funded and PAYG pension systems are faced with largely the same problem with regard to the extension of coverage. Each system can therefore learn from the fact that attempts by governments to integrate self-employed workers into the formal pension insurance programmes have met with very mixed success (ILO, forthcoming). Some groups that are part of, or close to, the formal sector may be induced to join such schemes, but the self-employed are usually not prepared to pay "double", that is the employers' plus the workers' contribution. Some special schemes for these workers tend to have more success, particularly if the Government is willing to subsidize them. If individual self-employed workers are not willing to join, however, they have much greater opportunities for non-compliance than employees working in formal sector enterprises. In various developing countries, Governments have also attempted to create special schemes for casual and homeworkers outside the formal sector. These have had some success, in particular if such schemes can be supported by earmarked taxes.

All case studies in this book show that a revision of the benefit and contribution structure can facilitate the entry of the self-employed and informal sector workers. It is in China where this has been demonstrated most convincingly. In particular, a clear distinction has been drawn between the mandatory pension schemes for urban workers and the pension scheme for rural workers, which is government-supported and provides for the voluntary participation of farmers. However, there are also considerable variations in the benefit and contribution structures of pension schemes for different groups of workers in urban areas.

Consider, for example, workers who move from rural to urban areas. Farmers who obtain jobs in urban areas are highly mobile, but have little stability of employment. For such workers, lump-sum payments may well represent the most suitable form of "retirement" benefit. Despite the general consensus in favour of benefits payable in the form of pensions through insurance schemes, neither workers nor employers would feel satisfied with these – the latter would consider that they were required, unreasonably, to subsidize the "city dwellers", while the workers themselves would not be entitled to any real benefits. As a result, sectors such as the coal and building industries, and areas like Shenzhen and other coastal cities employing a great number of rural workers, have started to adopt a flexible measure different from the standard pension insurance scheme. Rural migrant workers who leave the enterprise or the city are paid a lump sum equal to 60 to 70 per cent of the total insurance premium contributed by themselves and the employing units. For rural migrant workers who leave one city and find jobs in another city, the insurance premium is transferred to that city, while for those who return to rural areas, the insurance premium is transferred to the insurance management organization covering that particular area, if one exists.

Another way to adapt pensions to the priorities and contributory capacities of different groups of workers would be to design benefit packages for the self-employed and the informal sector, which would range from a basic core of social protection obligatory for all gainfully occupied persons, through to a more comprehensive provision that would be optional but subject to certain tests of membership. As noted in section 2.1, survivors' and disability benefits would be the first candidates for such a core package. Statutory social insurance schemes would have a comparative advantage to deal with such benefits, because insurance against these risks requires a large pool of contributors.

3.3 Health insurance reform

The chapters on Benin, India and the United Republic of Tanzania document the significantly reduced access of informal sector workers to free and good quality health care. For these three countries in particular, this situation has resulted in a low health status of the population and a low service level of medical care (see table 1.3). This decline was mainly the result of structural adjustment measures that led to sharply declining government health expenditures. It is unlikely that many informal sector workers will be able and/or willing to pay the high contributions to the existing statutory health insurance schemes. In section 4 we shall therefore review the opportunities for contributory health insurance schemes to meet the health needs of the majority of informal sector workers. In this subsection we shall give some examples of ways in which the cost-effectiveness of statutory health insurance schemes can be improved.

In El Salvador (see Chapter 6) the majority of people are dependent on self-treatment, i.e. a situation where the patient starts a course of medical treatment, without previous consultation with a relevant professional or technician. About 5 per cent of the population relies on the private medical sector, and about 20 per cent has access to health care provided by either the Salvadorian Institute of Social Security (ISSS) or the Ministry of Public Health and Social Assistance (MOH). Chapter 6 shows that there is a considerable difference between the costs and productivity of the latter two providers. Productivity in ISSS hospitals – as measured by the number of consultations per hour – is about 50 per cent higher than in MOH hospitals. On the other hand, the cost of MOH medical hospitalization is only one-quarter of that in ISSS hospitals. Also, for most other hospital interventions the MOH cost is much lower than that in ISSS hospitals.

China has carried out some of the most interesting experiments with new forms of health insurance financing. The Pay-As-You-Go (PAYG) premiums for the statutory urban health insurance schemes have now reached the high level of 8–9 per cent of the payroll. As an experiment, enterprises in the cities of Zhenjiang and Jiujiang have introduced a system by which the workers' half of the contributions are paid into individual savings accounts, and the employers' half into a social pooling fund. Payment of health-care costs is first of all paid from the individual accounts and from self-payment. When, however, the total medical care costs for the year exceed the sum of the amount in the individual accounts plus 5 per cent of the total wage of an employee, the balance is paid mainly by the social pooling fund and partially by individual employees themselves in cash. If the maximum medical care costs exceed a ceiling (for example, five times the annual employees' wage bill), they are covered by a supplementary medical insurance. The new health system has heightened awareness of both the provider and the consumer of medical services. Hospitals have rationalized their treatment and diagnosis patterns and

Table 1.3. Health indicators, selected (groups of) countries, mid-1990s

	Infant mortality rate (per 1 000 live births)	One-year-olds fully immunized (%) against		Underweight children under age 5 (%)	Malaria	Doctors	Nurses
		Tuberculosis	Measles		(per 100 000 people)		
	1996	1995-96	1995-96	1990-97	1994	1993	1993
Benin	84	90	74	...	10 398	6	33
China	38	97	97	16	6	115	88
El Salvador	34	100	97	11	51	91	38
India	73	96	81	53	243	48	...
Tanzania (United Rep.)	93	96	81	27	27 343	4	46
Developing countries	65	89	79	30	954	76	85
Industrialized countries	13	92	86	...	...	287	780

... not available.

Source: UNDP, 1998, pp. 156-59.

adopted a list of basic medicines, while consumers have tended to reduce the use of services, since they had to pay a somewhat larger part of the costs themselves. The application of this system has led to much lower health cost increases – about 10 per cent in 1996 compared with more than 20 per cent between 1994 and 1996. In May 1996 it was decided to extend this experiment to a further 57 cities.

3.4 Extending statutory social insurance

The issue of extending the personal coverage of statutory social insurance schemes deserves to attract greater priority and further study in many countries. There are great gaps in our knowledge with regard to the social security priorities and contributory capacities of the non-covered population, as well as about the various mechanisms that could be used to extend coverage through the adaptation of existing statutory social security programmes. There is scope for innovation and experiment based on a general recognition that there is no one solution.

Given the variety of countries, in relation to their level of economic development as well as to that of social security institutions, it is difficult to propose general policy conclusions. It may be possible to distinguish two types of developing countries. The first consists of middle-income countries, some of which have well-developed social security institutions. Such countries could aim at covering the population as a whole through the extension of the statutory social insurance programme. Secondly, there is the large group of low-income countries, where a rapid increase in coverage has to be achieved through setting up social insurance schemes directly financed and managed by informal sector workers. However, for both types of countries some of the following conclusions may be suggested:

- Consider a revision of the scheme to facilitate partial membership by the self-employed, domestic workers, agricultural workers and those with a regular income from informal sector activities.
- Strengthen the administrative capacity of the social security schemes, particularly in compliance, record-keeping and financial management.
- Undertake education and public awareness programmes to improve the image of the social security system.
- Extend coverage within a prescribed timetable to all persons working as employees, except special groups such as domestic servants, family workers and casual workers.
- Open up new "windows" and offer benefits that suit the needs and contributory capacity of non-covered groups.

4. Promoting contributory schemes

Informal sector workers are increasingly setting up their own schemes in order to meet their priority social security needs. The mechanism used in these schemes is generally the provision of mutual support through the pooling of resources based on the principles of insurance, help being extended to those in need within the overall framework of certain basic regulatory conditions. In this system, it is the group itself that decides on the size and the source of contributions that group members are meant to make. The collection and management of contributions – as well as the disbursement of benefits – are again matters for the group to consider and arrange.

The analysis of such schemes (van Ginneken, 1996) has shown that there are two fundamental requirements for establishing such self-financed (or contributory) social insurance schemes:

(i)   the existence of an association based on trust; and
(ii)   administration that is capable of collecting contributions and paying benefits.

Various groups can provide the foundation for self-financed schemes. First there is a large array of traditional arrangements and institutions that can be used for this purpose. New private social security arrangements such as mutual aid schemes have also emerged, sometimes replacing the traditional social security systems.

4.1 Indigenous social security arrangements

In most developing countries the population has depended on traditional social solidarity relations to meet their social security needs. They consist of those indigenous cultural mechanisms which obligate individuals, groups and communities to provide assistance to others in time of need. In most African countries for instance, and especially in rural areas, social relations of production are still principally of the classic kind in which an element of reciprocal obligations ensures that each member of a clan can, in the last resort, count on an irreducible guarantee of social security (Kane, 1997). Traditional systems also consist of institutional mechanisms which foster cooperative endeavour and are developmental rather than protective in nature. They encourage activities which prevent need or which otherwise enhance collaboration and solidarity. It should not automatically be assumed that indigenous arrangements always function effectively and meet people's needs adequately (Midgley, 1994).

New private arrangements have therefore emerged, such as cooperatives or mutual benefit societies, benefit burial societies and rotating credit societies. Cooperatives or mutual benefit societies generally operate at the community level. Apart from the large-scale, formal, cooperatives that are regulated by governments, there are many small, spontaneous organizations of local people which operate in both urban and rural areas and have social security functions. These associations not only maintain income flows in times of difficulty, but may have preventive and promotional functions as well.

A common form of cooperative association is mutual benefit burial societies which accumulate regular contributions paid by their members. The accumulated funds are then used to pay for funerals and other ceremonies at the time of death. These ceremonies often require substantial expenditure, and can lead to debt and create hardship.

Another popular cooperative association is rotating credit societies, which are most prevalent in sub-Saharan Africa where the financial and insurance markets are still underdeveloped. They are practised among not only informal but also formal sector workers.

In Benin (see Chapter 7) – and in most West African countries – the so-called "tontines" (rotating credit societies) are considered as both a financial institution and a means of mutual aid. They seem above all to be a way of encouraging saving, and can be perceived as a form of social insurance. There are also mutual benefit societies, which collect money from their members and return it in the form of investment and operating loans for their businesses, or as social development loans. These "tontines", mutual benefit societies and cooperatives combine social solidarity and economic efficiency, without, however, being governed by the profit motive. One should also take note of a tightening of neighbourly bonds and mutual aid between members, for these organizations rely on mutual trust and a territorial base.

In the United Republic of Tanzania (Chapter 4) there are two main categories of private social security arrangements. The first category is commonly known as "UPATU" – which simply means a "rotating savings and credit group." These are similar to the "tontines" in West Africa and are mainly found among urban communities; in 1995 more than 10 per cent of informal sector entrepreneurs in Dar es Salaam were covered by these "UPATUs". A second category represents groups that are organized along cooperative principles. The United Republic of Tanzania has 906 Savings and Credit Cooperatives (SACCOs): 440 cooperatives for formal sector workers and 466 for the informal sector. Under this arrangement, members make contributions to the cooperative's fund, which provides loans that may be used for meeting children's education and health care. Unlike UPATUs, groups in this category have a constitution and elaborate organizational structures, with an elected chairperson, secretary and treasurer to manage the scheme.

As shown by Chapter 6 on El Salvador, there is a whole range of social institutions (such as the extended family) and organizations in the informal sector that are seeking through self-financing to provide protection against various circumstances. The risks covered by such organizations and institutions include disability, old age, death, illness and maternity. In addition, other types of need can be incorporated, such as housing, education, funeral expenses and assistance to families on the death of a relative.

4.2 Health insurance

As noted in section 2.2, health insurance is the most urgent social security priority for informal sector workers. The majority of contributory health insurance schemes provide primary health-care services rather than coverage against hospital care costs. As shown in some of the recent literature (ILO-SAAT, 1996; Bennett et al., 1998), informal sector health insurance schemes can be classified into either high-cost, low-frequency events (hospital care), or low-cost, high-frequency events (primary health care) and are designated as Type I and Type II schemes respectively in table 1.4. Both types of schemes have different implications for variables, such as the frequency of service utilization and possibilities for cost control.

Health insurance schemes covering hospital costs (and which are often also hospital-based) have been proposed (see for instance Shaw and Griffin, 1995) as one of the strategies for generating additional revenues for health financing. These schemes have generally been set up in a context of reduced government and/or donor financing, and are basically aimed at putting hospital financing on a sound

Table 1.4   Two ends of the health cost risk-sharing spectrum

Type of scheme	Type I	Type II
Costs insured	Hospital care	Primary health care
Cost per intervention	High	Low
Frequency of utilization	Low	High
Ownership	Hospital	Community or association
Coverage	District	Community or association
Basis for premium setting	Actuarial study	Ability to pay

Source: Adapted from Bennett et al., 1998, p. 10.

footing. The great disadvantage of most of these schemes is their inability to prevent cost escalation. Costs often rise rapidly, because these schemes tend to suffer from adverse selection, as patients tend to enrol when they know that they will need hospital care. In addition, hospital-based schemes often lead to overprescription and overprovision of services. Finally, such schemes provide relatively high-cost primary and secondary health-care services.

Governments in many developing countries claim to provide free or subsidized access to basic health care for low-income families. But in practice, all workers – even those with incomes under the poverty line – can spend between 5 and 10 per cent of their budget on health services (see Chapter 2), so that they are potential candidates for participating in health insurance schemes. As a result, informal sector workers are usually more inclined to contribute to small-scale health schemes focused on the provision of primary and some secondary health-care services for which they face relatively small but periodical expenses.These schemes usually achieve low population coverage, because the participants would not trust the large-scale operation of such schemes.

In a recent article, Dror and Jacquier (1999) characterize these small-scale health insurance schemes using the concept of micro-insurance which conveys two major connotations: (i) the insurance is independently managed by groups and units at the local level; and (ii) the local unit is structured in such a way as to link up with multiple small area- and occupation-based units into larger structures that can enhance both the insurance function and the support structures needed for improved governance. Such local micro-insurance structures have the advantages of cohesion, direct participation and low administrative costs.

The main advantage of health insurance schemes for informal sector workers is that they improve health expenditure efficiency or the relation between quality and cost of health services. There are basically three reasons why informal sector workers would prefer group schemes to individual spending and financing (van Ginneken, 1998):

(i)   by regular contributions, the problem of indebtedness brought about by high medical bills can be improved;

(ii)   the financial power of the group may enable administrators to negotiate services of better quality or representing better value for money from private health-care providers; and

(iii)   the group may be willing to spend on preventive and health promotion activities so as to keep down the cost of curative services.

Some of the health insurance schemes reviewed in the various chapters reflect the variety of circumstances and priorities. The SEWA health insurance scheme in India (see Chapter 2) concentrates on hospital cost insurance, and is part of a comprehensive social security scheme that also covers the contingencies of death, disablement and maternity, as well as loss of working tools, house and property. The ACCORD scheme for tribal people in Gudalur, Tamil Nadu is a hospital-based scheme (Eswara Prasad, 1998), with its consequent problems of sustaining contributions. The Maquilishuat Foundation (FUMA) in El Salvador concentrates on mother and child care in poor, often rural, areas. The great advantage of such programmes is that they also deal with disease prevention and health promotion. However, Chapter 6 shows that the degree of self-financing is very low, so that its future depends mainly on the availability of outside money.

The example of rural health insurance in China (Chapter 3) is interesting, in that it combines elements of insurance to cover hospital and primary health-care costs funded by a combination of private and public contributions. In rural areas, about 10 per cent of the population is covered by the so-called "cooperative medical care system", which is mainly financed by rural residents, supplemented by the collective economy and supported by (various levels of) government. In the rural areas of South Jiangsu, for instance, the cooperative medical care system is mostly of the "risk type", i.e. only medical care costs for major diseases are reimbursed. This scheme is run by local people and subsidized by the State, while the fund is raised jointly by the county, the township and the village. Each villager contributes an average of 10 to 20 yuan a year. The village public welfare fund provides a subsidy equivalent to an average annual per capita amount of 1.5 to 2 yuan. In underdeveloped areas, both contribution and reimbursement usually start from a low rate which reflects local conditions. In Kaifeng county, Henan, for instance, the fund is financed with an average per-capita amount of 2 to 6 yuan a year. A moderately tight control on the reimbursement rate is exercised to maintain a balance between income and expenditure, and to ensure that the cooperative medical care system is functioning in a sustainable manner.

The experience with the UMASIDA scheme in Dar es Salaam (see Chapter 5) is a clear example of a demand-oriented scheme providing access to primary and some secondary health care. Monthly contributions amount to 600 T.sh. (one US dollar) per worker, supplemented by another US dollar for covering the family. In 1997 the scheme covered about 1,500 workers (plus about 4,500 family members) who are part of five informal sector associations, and in 1998 it was extended to five more associations in the Temeke District of Dar es Salaam. The contracted private practitioners provide primary health care, consultation, laboratory services, and all needed drugs for treatment. Only drugs from the WHO Essential Drugs List are reimbursed. The Government health-care units provide some secondary and tertiary services as well as complicated medical investigations. One novel mechanism applied in this scheme is the use of the so-called circulating invoice, which all beneficiaries must present at points of service, and which have to be filled out by the care provider. The information in these invoices on morbidity and treatment are checked and used for determining the amount of reimbursement. This information can also be used for the design of preventive and health promotion activities at work and at home. In future, the UMASIDA scheme could grow into a professional organization with a "beehive" structure, that would enable informal sector workers' organizations to affiliate rapidly.

4.3 Pensions

As noted in section 3.2, the extension of coverage to the self-employed is easier to achieve in respect of those persons who have a well-established business or profession which is readily identifiable, and which produces a sufficiently high level of regular income for contributing to social security. Even for this group, it may be difficult to reconcile the contributory basis within a scheme which is dominated by the circumstances of employees, and in respect of whom contributions are also paid by employers. In addition, self-employed persons may prefer to invest in their own business as a form of future social protection, or may see better opportunities for investing any spare resources. As a result, some informal sector entrepreneurs insure themselves with private sector companies (see Chapter 4). Many other self-employed workers prefer to set up their own pension schemes, which often include people who have chosen not to participate in statutory social insurance pension schemes.

The example of China (see Chapter 3) shows that specific pension schemes for farmers can be designed which are voluntary and adapted to the needs and circumstances of the rural population (including coverage for rural migrants to urban areas). In the rural pension insurance schemes, farmers themselves contribute most of the insurance premiums, in addition to some subsidies from the collective economy. The State offers policy support. The contributions made by farmers themselves and the subsidies provided by the collective economy are put into individual accounts. The rate of pension benefits is determined by the accumulated total amount in the individual accounts and by the relevant regulations. The insurance fund is now both regulated and managed at the county level.

In India (see Chapter 2) there are various pension schemes that are fully financed by individual contributions. One example is the pension scheme by the Cooperative Development Foundation (CDF), an institute designed to strengthen cooperatives, which works mainly with thrift and credit groups in Andhra Pradesh, as well as in Tamil Nadu, Karnataka and Kerala. For social security, a death relief fund has been constituted by the CDF covering about 25,000 members. This scheme provides a form of life insurance, i.e. a payment on the death of a member. The protection extends to the relief of all liability of surviving family members to repay any outstanding loans which the deceased member had taken from the thrift cooperatives. On reaching the age of 60 years, or on withdrawing from the scheme, the deposit amount is returned with a 2 per cent bonus (Gupta, 1994).

In India the benefits of social insurance have also been available to different categories of vulnerable groups under the various group insurance schemes (GIS) subsidized by the Social Security Fund under the Life Insurance Corporation. The most prominent example is the Rural Group Life Insurance Scheme introduced on 15 August 1995, in which insurance is available between the ages of 20 and 60 years for an assured amount of Rs.5,000 (US$125), the premium being around Rs.60 per annum.

4.4 A preliminary assessment

The activities organized by and for informal sector workers are generally based on a comprehensive concept of development and social security. Organizations such as NGOs and cooperatives have a good understanding of the particular needs and priorities of their client groups, and have jointly developed with them institutions and policies that are quite different from those the Government is used to and/or can cope with. As noted in section 1, this broader concept of social security includes not only the nine contingencies traditionally defined by the ILO, but also preventive steps in both the social and economic fields. In the social field, NGO action integrates traditional social security measures with complementary measures in the field of (primary) health care, childcare, housing and targeted social action. In the economic field, more security can be achieved through self-help and self-employment, resulting in an enhancement of income and the creation of productive assets. Such initiatives usually operate within the context of a credit scheme which has already had experience with the collection of contributions and the administration of benefits.

However, a preliminary assessment of self-financed schemes is that they have so far reached only a very small proportion of the poor and of informal sector workers. This is because self-financed schemes are not available in most areas, and when they are, the poor (especially women) have little or no knowledge about them. Most schemes of this type are limited to small groups of workers, so that the administration costs are relatively high.

One important implementation and design issue is to define social insurance packages that are affordable and meet the priorities of workers. But there are a number of other issues that need to be analysed so as to establish conditions for replicating and extending such schemes. Some of these issues are:

- dependence on the input and charisma of one person or group of people;
- dependence on money from outside for the scheme's long-term financial viability;
- an evaluation of the implicit costs and the capacity of the scheme's administrators, who are usually not remunerated;
- the possibility of pooling resources among different schemes;
- a possible link-up with private insurance companies and/or social insurance agencies.

5. Cost-effective social assistance

Many developing countries have set up statutory social assistance schemes aimed at people in need, who cannot be reached by employment or other social policies, and who have not been able to protect themselves through social insurance. Such schemes are predominantly contingency based, as they limit means-tested support in cash or in kind to specific needy groups, such as widows, orphans and old people without income and family support. As shown by the examples of Benin and the United Republic of Tanzania, in many developing countries the role of the non-governmental sector is important, because it can play a leading part in protecting and integrating marginalized groups in urban and rural areas. These organizations are involved in health, education and nutrition, as well as financial and material help.

Social assistance is also an important part of family obligations in most, if not all, cultures. Governments can strengthen such family support systems by paying benefits to family or kin members who care for needy relatives. Statutory social assistance programmes have conventionally emphasized the notion of relatives' responsibility to require people to care for dependent relatives. However, the notion of relatives' responsibility has relied on a punitive rather than incentive approach, and it fails to recognize that in many poor countries, relatives are themselves often too poor to assume additional responsibilities (Midgley, 1994).

Governments can also formulate policies that strengthen community obligations to provide support, and which seek to integrate community responses with statutory provisions (Midgley, 1994). Various governments of predominantly Islamic nations have sought to organize the collection and distribution of *zakat** and to modify the voluntaristic nature of this institution. Saudi Arabia, for example, introduced in 1962 a system which requires the payment of 50 per cent of *zakat* to the state programme, which distributes it according to its own statutory criteria. The other 50 per cent can then be disbursed according to individual preferences under Islamic law.

Among the government social assistance programmes reviewed in the various case studies, the example of India is worth mentioning. In mid-1995 the Government of India introduced the National Social Assistance Programme (NSAP) covering – among others – more than 10 million old-age pensioners. It consists of three cash benefits: a pension of Rs. 75 per month for people older than 65 years, with low incomes and generally without relatives; a lump-sum payment of Rs. 5,000 for families whose prime income-earner dies before the age of 60; and a payment of Rs. 300 per pregnancy, up to the first two live births.

In Mongolia, local "Assistance Councils" provide social assistance benefits in kind, such as winter clothing and boots for children who would otherwise not be able to go to school. They also provide free lunches and discounts on rent and fuel costs for the disabled and elderly who either have no family support or have not been able to insure themselves during their working life (van Ginneken, 1995).

In its transition to a market economy, China has also recently modernized its social assistance system. The minimum livelihood protection scheme for urban residents provides supplementary subsidies from the government to poor urban households whose average per-capita income is lower than the minimum livelihood protection line. It provides relief to 3 million people out of a total of 13 million poor people in urban areas. In rural areas the Government has started to experiment with a minimum livelihood protection system that provides a combination of benefits in cash and in kind. In the mid-1990s more than 3 million poor people in rural areas received regular relief allowances and subsidies.

There are various difficulties associated with the administration of a social assistance scheme. These commence with the design of the system and the basis for distinguishing those among the many who are poor who should be potentially entitled to help, and then determining to what extent account should be taken of

---

* An obligatory payment of alms per capita and on wealth, for onward distribution to the less fortunate, which constitutes one of the five pillars of Islam.

support provided (or expected) from other members of the household and family. A recent field study on the application of the Indian old-age social assistance scheme in Gujarat, Orissa and Uttar Pradesh (Sankaran, 1998) showed various cases of patronage, for example at the selection stage, and of abuse, in particular with regard to cash payments. It also highlighted the various problems in determining a suitable means test.

Thus, in assessing the cost-effectiveness of social assistance schemes, some of the following questions need to be addressed:

- What are the responsibilities of the central and local government in the financing, administering and fixing of the social assistance benefits?
- What should be the criterion for the means test (income, land, assets) and at what level should eligibility be determined (local government, local community)?
- How can one design corruption-free delivery mechanisms?
- How can the implicit administrative costs incurred by the Government be estimated?
- How should comparisons be made about the cost-effectiveness of social assistance in relation to other social policy interventions, such as food for work, employment guarantee schemes, etc.?

6. The need for experimentation

The case studies in this book demonstrate that the vast majority of the population in developing countries is excluded from social security protection. Over the past 50 years, the bulk of technical cooperation – both by the ILO and most other international agencies – has concentrated on extending social security coverage to formal sector workers. We have now reached the stage where the emphasis on "top-down" policy design has to give way to "bottom-up" and participatory approaches. We must recognize that we do not know, and that only careful experiments – in conjunction with the informal sector workers themselves – will teach us where to go. Various issues play a role here: the choice of core benefits, the advantages and disadvantages of occupational- versus area-based approaches, and the broadening of the traditional social security partnership.

6.1 The core benefits: Health, pensions and education

In most developing countries, the role of the State in the provision of health and education has been seriously curtailed. This has been the result not only of (relative) declines in government expenditure, mainly as a result of prolonged structural adjustment, but also of a different perception of what the role of the State should be. In health, governments and international donors have emphasized spending on public health programmes, such as immunization, family planning, water supply and sanitation. At the same time, tertiary care still occupies a large part of the national health budgets. So, in many developing countries, particularly in sub-Saharan Africa and South Asia, governments cannot guarantee free access to primary health-care services. In education, the situation is probably worse, particularly in many sub-Saharan African countries, where primary school enrolment has gone down over the past ten to 15 years. As a result, households themselves have had to pay for these basic services, thereby increasing the necessity and opportunity for the collective financing (and managing) of such services.

With regard to pensions, the question is more complicated. Informal sector workers usually consider that contributing to old-age pension schemes would be a secondary priority. They generally prefer to invest their savings in their own business – or even in the education of their children. Further, if they wish to contribute to old-age pensions, they are not very motivated to join statutory pension insurance schemes which are financed by both employers' and workers' contributions, often on a Pay-As-You-Go basis. The example of informal sector entrepreneurs in Dar es Salaam shows that they prefer to contribute to pension savings schemes run by private sector companies. On the other hand, informal sector workers are more prepared to contribute to survivor and disability pension schemes, because death or disability of the primary income-earners can throw the family into a permanent state of poverty and indebtedness. In some countries, such as India and China, the Government tends to subsidize such schemes.

The State is faced with an obligation to provide social assistance to old-age pensioners who have not been able to contribute to their own pensions and who cannot count on any family support. The same is true for widows and orphans. Thus, various governments in developing countries focus their social assistance measures on these and other vulnerable groups.

6.2 Area-, occupation- and gender-based social insurance schemes

There are various characteristics on the basis of which groups of informal sector workers can organize themselves for employment and incomes, as well as for the provision of social insurance protection. People can organize themselves because they share the same occupation, live in the same area or belong to the same gender, cultural or religious group, for example. Each of these characteristics has its own advantages and disadvantages with regard to group factors such as trust, leadership, as well as financial and organizational capacity. These characteristics also have a major impact on the extent and speed with which self-financed social insurance schemes can be replicated. Table 1.5 reviews the impact of their organizational base on the success of such social insurance schemes.

As noted in section 4, there are two main factors in the success of contributory mechanisms: the existence of an association based on trust (group cohesion) and an administration capable of collecting contributions and administering benefits. At that point, we neither made further distinctions about the organizational base of such associations nor discussed the issue of replicability. The latter issue is important because the aim of any pilot projects is to demonstrate not only that successful schemes can be set up, but also that they can reach and be replicated to larger groups of the population.

In most countries, work-based organizations have been at the origin of social insurance programmes. Informal sector workers – to the extent that they are organized at all – are principally organized in occupation- or sector-based associations and cooperatives. Their first priority is to improve their economic base, in terms of credit, marketing and production technology, but when that is ensured, their organizations can often constitute a foundation for the establishment of social insurance schemes. This is also frequently true for women's organizations, whose purpose often includes raising consciousness with regard to the position of women in the family, work and society. Finally, some of these organizations have set up savings and/or credit bodies which significantly improve the chances of successfully organizing social insurance schemes. It seems likely that women are generally more interested in and committed to the provision of health care and education to their family, rather than in occupation-based (and often male-dominated) schemes, which tend to consider disability and survivor pensions as a greater priority. Most work-based schemes are characterized by a high level of group cohesion, but they take a long time to mature. As a result, they are not easily replicable, even though – in the case of savings and loans societies – they could reach out to larger segments of the population with short-term loans for financing children's education (uniforms, fees, school-books, etc.).

Organizations based on the place of residence are usually less cohesive, even though we have to put a question mark against communities. In rural areas, communities are often close-knit, but in towns and cities they may display less cohesion because of the floating character of most of the urban population. Moreover, political, social and economic stratification may diminish the cohesion of communities. At the area (district) level the social cohesion is likely to be even lower, but the quality of local government strongly influences whether some form of consensus, incentives and accountability can be established. The area-based approach is very suitable for social health-care financing, since it can

Table 1.5 The impact of the organizational base on contributory social insurance schemes

	Organizational base				
	Place of work			Place of residence	
	Occupation	Women	Savings and credit scheme	Community	Area
Benefits					
Health	0	+	+	+	+
Survivors, disability	+	0	+	+	+
Education	0	+	+	0	+
Group scheme characteristics					
Replicability/outreach	0	0	0/+	0	+
Group cohesion	+	+	+	?	0

+ = positive impact; 0 = no impact; ? = uncertain impact.

take into account the provision of not only curative but also preventive and promotional activities. In addition, participation by local government can also increase the extent and speed of replication of pilot experiences. Experiments with area-based schemes should therefore be given high priority.

6.3 Galvanizing the social security partners into action

The widening of the social security concept, as developed in section 1, implies the broadening of the social security partnership. While for the formal sector it is logical to use the national tripartite formula of employers, workers and governments, this partnership has to be broadened to make social security a reality for informal sector workers. As noted in the previous section, a larger role will have to be played by local government, by associations that directly represent informal sector workers (such as cooperatives, mutual benefit societies and communities), and by intermediary organizations that work on behalf of informal sector workers (such as workers' and employers' organizations as well as NGOs). In addition, there is room for greater participation by private insurance companies who – when correctly regulated and supervised – can provide a useful contribution in the form of efficient administration and management of social insurance schemes. One of the purposes of pilot projects is therefore also to experiment with different forms of partnerships.

Enthusiasm, good management and planning will to a large extent determine whether or not the pilot projects and their extension to other areas and situations will be successful, and whether an integrated social security policy can be designed. This enthusiasm will have to be fed by well-documented experiences which show that success is possible. Such positive experiences can be disseminated through workshops at various levels and to various partners. Informal sector associations, NGOs, cooperatives and mutual benefit societies would be more interested in the administrative aspects of running small social insurance schemes. Governments, social security agencies and the social partners would have greater interest in policy and research seminars.

7. Conclusions

More than half of the world's workforce is excluded from coverage by statutory social security, and the proportion is often much higher in developing countries. The deficiency is greatest in sub-Saharan Africa and South Asia, where fewer than 10 per cent of workers are covered. In other parts of the developing world the coverage is typically between 10 and 50 per cent of the workforce.

The fundamental reason for exclusion from coverage is that many workers outside the formal sector are unable or unwilling to contribute a relatively high percentage of their incomes to financing social security benefits that do not meet their priority needs. In general, they prioritize more immediate needs, such as health and education, in particular because structural adjustment measures have reduced or eliminated access to free health care and primary education. Within the range of pension benefits, they seek protection in case of death and disability, rather than for old age. In addition, they may not be familiar with, and/or distrust, the way the statutory social security scheme is managed. As a result, various groups of workers outside the formal sector have set up schemes that better meet their priority needs and contributory capacity. Moreover, there are also a host of factors that restrict access to the statutory social security schemes, such as legal restrictions, administrative bottlenecks and problems with compliance.

There is a need for new approaches to social assistance aimed at people in financial need, who cannot be reached by policies for productive employment and who cannot – and/or have not been able to – contribute to social insurance schemes. Where possible, statutory programmes should be grafted on to existing family and community support systems. The advantage of social assistance benefits is that they can be targeted at those who are most in need, such as children, the disabled and retired people. However, a sophisticated administration is required to determine who really meets the relevant criteria, and to make sure that the benefits reach the target population effectively. Thus, the costs of administering the benefits are often high, and if the administration is not well organized, it can lead to leakages and corruption. Naturally, the size of these schemes must depend on the resources, the administrative capacity and the priorities of the countries concerned.

Beyond the tax-financed social assistance schemes, various policy options are discussed in the case studies. Approaches adopted by governments to integrate self-employed workers into the statutory pension insurance programmes had a very mixed record. Some groups that are part of, or close to, the formal sector may be induced to join such schemes, but the self-employed are usually not prepared to pay "double", that is the employers' plus the workers' contributions. Special schemes for these workers tend to be more successful, particularly if the Government is willing to subsidize them. If individual self-employed workers are unwilling to join, however, they have much greater opportunities for non-compliance than employees working in formal sector enterprises. In various developing countries, governments have also attempted to create special schemes for casual labour and homeworkers outside the formal sector. These have reached larger groups of workers, in particular if such schemes can be supported by earmarked taxes.

Over the past decade, many contributory, and often self-managed, schemes for informal sector workers have emerged. These are based mainly on cooperatives and mutual benefit societies, but also on indigenous social security arrangements, such as burial and rotating credit societies. Social insurance organized by and for informal sector workers is generally based on a comprehensive concept of development and social security. Organizations such as NGOs and cooperatives have a good understanding of the particular needs and priorities of informal sector workers, and have developed institutions and policies with them that are quite different from those the governments have been used to.

Over the past 50 years, the bulk of technical cooperation – both in the ILO and in most other international agencies – has concentrated on extending social security coverage to formal sector workers. We have now reached the stage where the emphasis on "top-down" policy design has to give way to a participatory ("bottom-up") approach. For example, pilot activities would include setting up and/or monitoring special social insurance schemes for informal sector workers and social assistance schemes, as well as extending statutory social insurance to hitherto uncovered groups. On the basis of experience gained with these activities, the social security partners could then also be trained and helped to formulate their own policies and activities with regard to social security for informal sector workers.

One novel feature of these pilot projects would be to experiment with so-called area-based social insurance schemes, which aim at full coverage within an area and are mainly run by the (local) government in collaboration with a wide variety of possible social security partnerships. In comparison with sector- or occupation-based schemes, area-based schemes have the advantage that administration costs are low, and that local participation and control can be included in the design of the project. In addition, most importantly, coverage could be extended to other areas relatively quickly, because governments would be able to replicate the schemes on the same conditions.

References

Bailey, C. 1994. *Extension of social security to small establishments and the non-wage earning population* (Geneva, ISSA), ISSA African Series No.14.

Bennett, S.; Creese, A.; Monasch, R. 1998. *Health insurance schemes for people outside formal sector employment* (Geneva, WHO), ARA Paper No. 16.

Dror, D.M.; Jacquier, C. 1999. "Micro-insurance: Extending health insurance to the excluded", in *International Social Security Review* (Geneva, ISSA), Vol. 52, No. 1, pp. 71–97.

Eswara Prasad, K.V. 1998. "Health insurance for tribals: ACCORD's experience in Gudalur, Tamil Nadu", in van Ginneken (ed.), 1998.

van Ginneken, W. 1995. "Employment promotion and the social safety net", in Griffin, K. (ed.) *Poverty and the transition to a market economy in Mongolia* (New York, St. Martin's Press).

—. 1996. *Social security for the informal sector: Issues, options and tasks ahead* (Geneva, ILO), Working Paper for the Interdepartmental Project on the Urban Informal Sector.

—. (ed.) 1997. *Social security for the informal sector: Investigating the feasibility of pilot projects in Benin, India, El Salvador and Tanzania* (Geneva, ILO), Social Security Department Discussion Paper No.5.

—. (ed.) 1998. *Social security for all Indians* (New Delhi, Oxford University Press).

—. 1999. "Social security for the informal sector: A new challenge for the developing countries", in *International Social Security Review* (Geneva, ISSA), Vol. 52, No. 1, pp. 49–69.

Guhan, S. 1994. "Social security options for developing countries", in *International Labour Review* (Geneva, ILO), Vol. 133, No. 1, pp. 35–53.

Gupta, R.C. 1994. *NGO experiences in social security* (New Delhi, Friedrich Ebert Foundation).

IILS. 1996. *Social exclusion and anti-poverty strategies. Research project on the patterns and causes of social exclusion and the design of policies to promote integration: A synthesis of findings* (Geneva, IILS).

ILO. 1993. *Social insurance and social protection*, Report of the Director-General (Part I), International Labour Conference, 80th Session (Geneva).

—. 1994. *Informal sector statistics: Coverage and methodologies* (Geneva, Interdepartmental Project on the Urban Informal Sector), unpublished document.

—. 1995. *The coverage and financing of social protection: Tensions and main issues*, Report of the Director-General (Part II), Fifth European Regional Conference (Geneva).

—. 1997. *La réforme et l'extension de la protection sociale: Nouveaux besoins*, Report of the Second Meeting on "Les conséquences de la dévaluation du Franc CFA sur les pays africains de la zone franc", Yaoundé, 23–25 April 1997 (Abidjan, ILO Regional Office for Africa).

—. Forthcoming. *Social security pensions: Reform and development* (Geneva).

ILO-SAAT. 1996. *Social protection for the unorganized sector in India*, report prepared for the UNDP (New Delhi).

ISSA. 1992. "Report of the ISSA Regional Meeting for Asia and the Pacific on cost-containment measures applied under social security health-care schemes", in *Social Security Documentation: Asian and Pacific Series* (New Delhi), No. 15.

Jenkins, M. 1993. "Extending social protection to the entire population: Problems and issues", in *International Social Security Review* (Geneva, ISSA), Vol. 46, No. 2, pp. 3–20.

Kane, P. 1997. "Reform of pension schemes: The perspective of the informal sector" (Geneva, ILO Social Security Department), mimeograph.

Mesa-Lago, C. 1994. *Changing social security in Latin America: Towards alleviating the social costs of economic reform* (Boulder, Colorado and London, Lynne Rienner Publishers).

Midgley, J. 1984a. "Social assistance: An alternative form of social protection in developing countries", in *International Social Security Review* (Geneva, ISSA), Vol. 37, No. 3, pp. 247–264.

—. 1984b. *Social security, inequality and the Third World* (Chichester, John Wiley).

—. 1994. "Social security policy in developing countries: Integrating state and traditional systems", in *Focaal* (Nijmegen, Stichting Focaal), Vol. 22–23, pp. 219–229.

—.; Tracy, M.B. 1996. *Challenges to social security: An international exploration* (Westport, Connecticut, Auburn House).

—.; Sherraden, M. 1996. *Alternatives to social security. An international inquiry* (Westport, Connecticut, Auburn House).

Park, T-W. 1992. "Cost-containment measures in the provision of hospital care under social security health-care schemes", in ISSA, 1992.

Paukert, F. 1968. "Social security and income distribution: A comparative study", in *International Labour Review* (Geneva), Vol. 98, No. 5, pp. 425–450.

Sankaran, T.S. 1998. "Social assistance: Evidence and policy issues", in van Ginneken (ed.), 1998.

Shaw, R.P.; Griffin, C.C. 1995. *Financing health care in sub-Saharan Africa through user fees and insurance* (Washington, DC, World Bank).

Singh, H. 1994. "ISSA studies on extension of social security to unprotected groups in Asia and the Pacific", in Sankaran, T.S.; Subrahmanya, R.K.A.; Wadhawan, S.K. (eds.) 1994. *Social security in developing countries* (New Delhi, Har-Ahnand Publications).

Social Security Administration (SSA). 1997. *Social Security Programs throughout the World – 1997* (Washington, DC, US Government Printing Office).

UNDP. 1998. *Human Development Report 1998* (Oxford, Oxford University Press).

World Bank. 1998. *World Development Report 1998/99* (Oxford, Oxford University Press).

BASIC SOCIAL SECURITY IN INDIA

2

by Shashi Jain, Administrative Member of the Board of Revenue of Madhya Pradesh

The concept of social security has evolved considerably over the years. In a broad sense, it has now come to mean ensuring social support for a dignified life, the constituents of such a life necessarily including a viable source of income or employment, and access to opportunities or means of acquiring basic capabilities. Construed in a somewhat narrower sense, it implies protection against employment injury, death and disability; survivors' benefits; health care and maternity benefit; and old-age security. The quality of protection and the level and extent of social benefits that are or can be made available by any society or government to its people would, of course, depend on the country's level of development, its resources and priorities. Given the variability of the concept and its constituent parts, there is, however, universal acceptance that provision of a minimum level of protection, as locally determined, for all its people must be one of the principal goals of any country.

In order to achieve the above goals, different approaches have been adopted to reach various groups of people. In India three principal mechanisms have been used:

(i)   legislation and statutory schemes have extended various social security benefits primarily to workers from the organized sector;

(ii)   social assistance is extended through targeted programmes (including social insurance) for vulnerable and disadvantaged sections; and

(iii) self-financing mechanisms have been established by different agencies and groups.

For each of these mechanisms, the extent of protection and their impact and success are briefly examined, so as to identify the gaps and the possibilities for enhanced coverage and improved social security protection. Finally, an attempt is made to identify the features of specially designed self-financed social insurance programmes that are area-based.

1. Status of human development

Among the countries of the world, India has a low position, 135th in 173 nations ranked against the Human Development Index (HDI), a composite measure of three basic components of human development, namely, longevity, knowledge and standard of living. Various disaggregated studies of human development have shown that there is also a great deal of disparity between states and population groups within India.

India has a higher proportion of people in absolute poverty (40 per cent) than the average level among all developing countries (31 per cent). India's expenditure on social security benefits as a percentage of GDP is assessed as substantially less (0.5 per cent compared to an average of 2.7 per cent for developing countries). Public expenditure on health in India is, on the other hand, much higher (6 per cent as against 4.2 per cent) while on education it is only marginally less (3.5 per cent against 3.9 per cent average expenditure in all developing countries). Comparatively, India also averaged a 7 per cent lower workforce participation rate (at 38 per cent) and fewer women in its labour force (6 per cent less at 29 per cent) according to the UNDP (1994).

Realistic estimation of the prevalence of poverty in India has been an area of vital concern for the Planning Commission. The poverty line is drawn up taking into account the minimum per capita expenditure and income required to fulfil the barest consumption needs. Such estimations have now been prepared at national and state level using state-specific poverty lines; they are based on the quinquennial consumer expenditure surveys of the National Sample Survey Organization. Estimates indicating the number and percentage of people below the poverty line are now available covering a period of 20 years from 1973 to 1993, as shown in table 2.1.

Although there has been a persistent decline in the overall poverty ratios over the past two decades (by 19 percentage points), over 320 million persons were still estimated to be below the poverty line in India in 1993–94. The rural areas hold most of the poor, the incidence of poverty being higher by 5 per cent as compared to that in the urban settlements. While the overall poverty ratio still remains at a high 36 per cent, a positive feature has been a somewhat greater reduction in rural poverty, resulting in a narrowing of the gap between urban and rural poverties. In fact, a contrary trend is also noticeable, with a number of major states having higher levels of urban poverty vis-à-vis the rural areas. These include Madhya Pradesh, Gujarat, Karnataka, Rajasthan and Tamil Nadu.

There has been a great deal of variation in the pace of development in different states and its impact on the extent of poverty. Almost all the states (with the exception of Himachal Pradesh and the union territories of Andaman and Nicobar plus Dadra and Nagar Haveli) have shown declining trends in the spread

Table 2.1 Population below the poverty line, India, 1973/74–1993/94

	Millions	Per cent of total population	Per cent of rural population	Per cent of urban population
1973–74	321.3	54.8	56.4	49.0
1977–78	328.8	51.3	53.1	45.2
1983	322.9	44.5	45.6	40.8
1987–88	307.0	38.9	39.0	38.2
1993–94	320.3	35.9	37.3	32.3

Source: *Report of the Expert Group on Estimation of the Population and Number of Poor (Modified)* (Planning Commission, 1993).

of poverty; the decline has been spectacular in the states of Kerala, Gujarat, Punjab and Goa. On the other hand, there are states like Bihar, Orissa, Madhya Pradesh and Uttar Pradesh which continue to remain in the highest bracket.

In a survey of the NCAER in 1994, the states of Punjab and Haryana had the highest per capita incomes in rural India while, on the other hand, Orissa (least), West Bengal, Bihar and Madhya Pradesh had very low income levels.

It has been found that agriculture and allied activities contribute 55 per cent of the total rural household incomes, their share decreasing with the rise in the overall development of the village. The more advanced villages receive comparatively higher incomes from petty trades, salaried and professional services and wage labour in the non-agriculture sectors. A positive correlation has also been observed between village development and adult literacy levels, on the one hand, and household incomes on the other. The lowest income levels in the employment categories are those of landless wage-earners, and among the social groups the scheduled castes – followed by the scheduled tribes – have the lowest levels, as indicated in the HDI Survey conducted by the National Council for Applied Economic Research (NCAER) in 1996 in 16 states (NCAER, 1996).

The position with reference to the other important development indicators – namely, literacy and health status – also need to be considered. With an 8.5 per cent increase having been achieved in the 1980s, India registered an overall literacy rate of 52 per cent in the 1991 Census, while among the rural population it was less than 45 per cent. The wide variation between states ranged from around 39 per cent literacy in Bihar and Rajasthan to 90 per cent in Kerala. The upward trend appears to have accelerated at the beginning of the 1990s; indeed, the HDI Survey in 16 states revealed an increase by 9 percentage points in rural literacy, assessed at 54 per cent (NCAER, 1996). The gender disparity, however, is still significant and is the main factor adversely affecting the overall status. In view of these variations, the states with higher literacy levels tend to have lower gender disparity ratios and vice versa. The achievement of the southern states in the area of literacy is generally quite distinct from those of the northern region, and a similar contrast in gender disparities is also clearly identifiable.

In the Alma-Ata declaration (1978), India had accepted the goal of "Health for All by the Year 2000" (normally referred to as the HFA goals), and a great deal of planned expenditure has since been budgeted to achieve that goal. Although there have been significant achievements with reference to certain basic health indices in some states, a wide gap remains to be bridged for the country as a whole. The performance of Kerala has been as notable in the area of health as it has been in respect of education. On the whole, the position in southern states is again comparatively better than those situated in the central region. The HFA goals in regard to the Crude Death Rate (CDR) and the Infant Mortality Rate (IMR) have been roughly attained in about half the states. Table 2.2 gives the all-India status as well as the position in some of the states vis-à-vis the HFA goals.

Although the production of food grains has been quite adequate for the country's requirement, nutritional deprivation has been noticeable in many areas. India has one of the highest proportions of malnourished children. It has been observed that higher levels of incomes have not necessarily meant better nutritional standards. For instance, in the case of Andhra Pradesh a sizeable proportion of the population has been lacking sufficient calories for a healthy and active life. The diet of the majority, although improving in terms of the protective food intake, is still very much deficient since the total diet is mainly based on food grains. Also, while income poverty has been declining, the reduction in calorie poverty has not been so significant, because of a shift in the relative expenditure from food to non-food items (NCAER, 1994). This aspect would require special attention when efforts are made to enhance provision of security benefits and services.

2. Statutory social security

The social security entitlements provided to workers through statutory schemes would prima facie appear to be a protection that is placed on the soundest footing. Hence it is extremely important to examine the possibilities for bringing larger sections of the workforce into their fold. Most of the laws are central laws applicable to all states, generally with provision for extension to additional categories of workers and employments by the states. The numerous legislative provisions fall into two categories: (a) those that are enforced through dedicated administrative units, and (b) others which are self-enforcing, with the requirement

Table 2.2 Some basic health status indicators, India, 1993

	Crude birth rate (per 1 000)	Crude death rate (per 1 000)	Infant mortality rate (per 1 000)	Life expectancy rate (years)
India	28.7	9.3	74	58.7
Andhra Pradesh	24.3	8.6	64	60.2
Gujarat	28.0	8.2	58	59.5
Kerala	17.4	6.0	13	71.3
Orissa	27.2	12.2	110	55.4
Goals under "Health for all by the Year 2000"	21.0	9.0	60.0	—

Source: Sample Registration System Estimates 1993.

of the aggrieved approaching the courts or other competent authorities in cases of denial of benefits. The two major enactments in the first category are the Employees' State Insurance Act 1948 and the Employees' Provident Fund (& Miscellaneous Provisions) Act 1952. There are also the laws constituting the different welfare funds which have an administrative network for delivery of benefits mainly targeted to unorganized workers. However, despite being statutory they provide a much weaker basis for enforcement of individual security rights. The second category, self-enforcing laws, mainly comprises the Workmen's Compensation Act 1923, the Maternity Benefit Act 1961, and the Payment of Gratuity Act 1972. While the EPF and the ESI schemes are financed through the joint contributions of the employers and the employees, for most of the others the liability rests on the employers.

2.1 The ESI Scheme

This is a composite insurance scheme to provide health care and cash benefits in the case of sickness, maternity and death or disability due to employment injury. It covers employees of factories and other establishments having a minimum of ten workers who draw wages up to a ceiling. The scheme is applicable, according to a phased programme, to notified areas having a concentration of at least 1,000 coverable employees. The composite package of benefits is quite substantial and is generally at par with levels required under the ILO's Social Security (Minimum Standards) Convention, 1952 (No.102), its non-ratification by India being mainly on account of the coverage under the ESI Scheme (ESIS) not being extensive enough. It includes full and comprehensive health care for insured workers and their families; payment of the full average wage for 12 weeks during maternity; compensatory insurance assuring payment of a monthly pension at the rate of up to 70 per cent of the wages in cases of death as well as permanent and temporary disabilities caused by injuries sustained during the course of employment; and payment of funeral expenses. The employers and the employees contribute 4.75 per cent and 1.75 per cent of wages respectively (the rates of 4 per cent and 1.5 per cent have been enhanced with effect from 1 January 1997).

The ESI Scheme is operative in most states and union territories, and is implemented through various centres (622 in total). The extensive coverage of the scheme includes 6.79 million employees working in around 170,000 factories and establishments. Along with family members of the employees, the benefits of the scheme are available to almost 30 million persons. In percentage terms the ESIS reaches 2.2 per cent of India's workers and 3.5 per cent of the overall population. The highest numbers of insured persons are in the states of Maharashtra, West Bengal and Uttar Pradesh (around a million each).

The comprehensive medical care, which is a distinguishing feature of this scheme, is provided through the respective state governments (unlike the cash benefits which are administered directly by the ESI Corporation). The service system operates through the scheme's own hospitals and dispensaries, as well as through reservation of beds in other hospitals. The cost of medical services to the extent of one-eighth is shared by the state governments, the balance being reimbursed to them by the Corporation. Although a ceiling of Rs. 410 per insured person per year is operative for the purpose of sharing the seven-eighths cost by the Corporation, there is indeed no ceiling on the actual expenditure on a patient's treatment.

While as a composite insurance the ESIS has been appreciated in its conception, limitations and difficulties have been experienced in its implementation. The level and quality of medical care has not been found to be satisfactory in many areas. The dual administrative control (of the state Government and the Corporation) has added to the problems of administering health services, which is by itself a daunting task. The dissatisfaction is greater in areas where good infrastructure is lacking, and in establishments having well-managed health care systems for its senior employees who earn wages above the ceiling and who are not compelled to join the ESIS. On the other hand, the scheme has been recognized as extremely useful where alternative facilities do not exist, and where the centres are staffed by sincere and competent professionals. The ESI Scheme has also been appreciated by non-regular employees, such as casual and contract workers, whom employers normally like to exclude from any protection.

The expansion of the scheme to newer areas is rather slow, mainly due to the requirement of setting up infrastructure for health services. In India only around 150,000 additional employees are brought into its fold every year, while the scheme's extension to another million or so employees in the unimplemented areas according to a phased programme remains to be done. Moreover, since the scheme is mainly applicable to the organized sector, its extension has limited possibilities in real terms. The common difficulties of extending formal sector schemes to unorganized workers are considered later. However, even the recommendations of an internal Committee on Perspective Planning (1972) to reduce the threshold for coverage to establishments with 5 employees was not accepted by the Corporation, because it felt that the first priority should be given to qualitative improvement of services.

2.2 Employees' Provident Fund (and Miscellaneous Provisions) Act 1952

The benefits under this Act originally included a contributory provident fund, a family pension and a deposit-linked insurance. Through an Amendment of the Act in 1995, a comprehensive pension scheme has been added which gives retirement pension benefits to the employee and his or her family, thus enlarging the scope of survival benefits (in case of death during service) already available through the erstwhile Family Pension Scheme (since 1972). The scope of the Act covers factories and establishments employing 20 or more in scheduled industries, 177 of which have been notified so far by the central Government. The wage ceiling operable for deciding the eligibility is Rs. 5,000 per month. Under the EPF Scheme, the contribution of the employees is a minimum of 8.33 per cent of the wages (in fact 10 per cent in most cases), deductible at source and deposited into the Fund by the employer. The matching contribution required to be deposited in favour of the employee by the employer is now deposited in the new Pension Fund. Set up at an all-India level the EP Fund, inclusive of the employers' contribution, today stands at a significant amount of Rs. 400,000 million.

Apart from the terminal disbursals, the EPF permits withdrawals for purposes of life insurance policies, house building, medical treatment, marriage, higher education, etc. The family pension payable under the old scheme ranges from Rs. 250 to Rs. 1,050 per month. Further, to encourage savings and give benefit to the family in case of death during service, an amount equivalent to the average balance in the EPF of the deceased – subject to a maximum of Rs. 25,000 – is paid under the Employees' Deposit Linked Insurance Scheme. With the addition of sound and substantial old-age security through a superannuation pension under the new Pension Scheme 1995 (effective from 16 November 1995) the statute's efficacy in terms of providing a lifelong social insurance benefit has increased. While the minimum service for eligibility is 10 years, pensionable service of 33 years entitles a member to a pension estimated to be around 50 per cent of the last wages.

The all-India coverage under the EPF (& MP) Act is roughly 20 million employees in about 264,000 establishments. In terms of the overall working population, 6.4 per cent come within its purview. Among the different employment sectors in the National Industrial Classification, the most substantial share in overall coverage is of the manufacturing industries (over 51 per cent); next is mining and quarrying (over 20 per cent); agricultural and allied fields only represent 5.7 per cent. The unorganized sector as a whole accounts for 10.4 per cent of all EPF subscribers, the majority of them being *beedi* workers, and yet 70 per cent of them (out of a total of 4.25 million) are still not included. There is a large concentration of covered establishments and subscribers, as under the ESI Scheme, in the three states of Maharashtra, Tamil Nadu and West Bengal, which account for 42 per cent of the total membership. These states, along with Gujarat, Andhra Pradesh, Uttar Pradesh and Karnataka, comprise almost 70 per cent of subscribers in the country.

The EPF scheme also permits voluntary coverage which has been taken up by over 16,000 establishments in India. With the addition of the comprehensive pension benefit, extension of voluntary coverage to a much larger number appears likely.

Benefits similar to those under the EPF Act are also available to workers in coal mines and the Assam tea plantations under special enactments (the Coal Mines Provident Fund Act 1948 and the Assam Tea Plantations Provident Fund Act 1955). The number of employees thus covered is around 1.25 million.

2.3 Workmen's compensation, gratuity and maternity benefits

The employees of factories, mines, plantations, railways and other scheduled employments are covered under the Workmen's Compensation Act 1923. The Act seeks to provide compensation to workmen or their survivors in case of injuries and occupational diseases sustained during the course of employment and resulting in disablement or death. The compensation amounts are a factor of the wage and age indices, which, after the enhancement in 1995, are a minimum of Rs. 50,000 and may extend to around Rs. 200,000. The scheduled employments also include certain hazardous agricultural and forestry operations after the recent amendment.

The Payment of Gratuity Act 1972 is applicable to various establishments having a minimum of 10 employees, and provides for gratuity payments at the end of service. To be eligible for gratuity the employees should have a minimum continuous service of 5 years. Since the 1994 amendment, the wage ceiling has been completely removed as an eligibility condition for gratuity. With the benefit of 15 days of wages for every year of service, the gratuity amount can now reach Rs. 100,000. The entitlement for seasonal employees is at a rate of 7 days for each season.

The Maternity Benefit Act 1961 mainly provides for maternity protection before and after childbirth, through payment of wages for up to 12 weeks during absence on account of maternity, and certain other benefits. Women employees of factories, mines and other commercial establishments are covered under this Act. The take-up of claims under this Act has been estimated at only 0.5 per cent nationwide. This compares unfavourably with maternity claims at the national level under some other Acts – 2.5 per cent under the ESI Scheme, 12 per cent under the Plantation Labour Act and 8 per cent under the Mines Act. Although the Maternity Benefit Act has been extended to shops and establishments since 1989, it is not known how many women have benefited from this extension. Maternity benefits are generally available to *beedi* workers through their common welfare fund.

There is no organization administering the benefits under the above three Acts. These laws being self-enforcing, the employers themselves are liable to pay the benefits to eligible employees. Hence, compilation of data regarding the actual beneficiaries has severe limitations. Although required to provide information, statistical returns are hardly ever forthcoming from the numerous establishments covered. The courts and other competent authorities deal only with specific cases of violation coming to their notice.

For ensuring the provision of maternity benefit, the method of employers' liability has been considered unsuitable by a number of expert bodies such as the National Labour Commission, the Economic Administrative Reforms Commission and the National Commission on Self-Employed Women. One option would be to set up a central fund. Another would be to link the employer's liability to contributions for a composite social security package including maternity benefit, as in the case of ESIS (Ganapathi, 1994). Some state governments, including the states of Gujarat and Andhra Pradesh, have introduced special schemes for extending maternity benefit to landless agricultural workers. The Gujarat State scheme has since been replaced by the National Maternity Benefit Scheme, which appears to be less advantageous for some – the subject is briefly considered in section 3, on social assistance.

2.4 Extending statutory social protection

About 19.5 million government and public sector employees are also covered by statutory social protection; together with the 21 million private sector employees having comprehensive cover under the EPF and other funds, they represent only 13 per cent of all Indian workers. The coverage under the other major social security scheme (the ESIS) and legislation largely overlaps with the scope of provident funds.

In principle, these major social security laws do not distinguish between the organized and unorganized sectors and are therefore applicable to casual and contract workers in the covered establishments as well as to home-based contract and agency workers in industries like *beedi*-making, construction works, carpet manufacturing, *khadi* (homespun cloth) and village industries, etc. However, very few informal sector workers are in practice covered under these statutory schemes. The courts have made important judicial pronouncements in favour of their coverability, but there are many difficulties in establishing employer-employee relationships and in operating an effective system for the collection of contributions. The enforcement is further weakened by the complex procedures followed by these industries, the absence of unrebuttable evidence, and a lack of awareness and unity among the informal sector workers themselves.

Social protection extended through the above legislation is also subject to other limitations. Apart from the operational shortcomings and the practical difficulties mentioned earlier, the statutes explicitly exclude groups of workers such as

- those working outside the scheduled industries and establishments;
- those in smaller enterprises;
- those drawing salaries beyond the wage ceilings; and,
- the very substantial category of the self-employed (comprising 54 per cent of the workforce) who are not eligible under current regulations.

Despite the above limitations, coverage of a substantial number of *beedi* workers, who are mostly home-based, has been possible under the EPF Act in some states, notably in Andhra Pradesh (covering around 425,000 workers, i.e. a substantial figure, about 95 per cent of the total of 450,000 who have been issued identity cards). The crucial factor here has been the issuing of the identity cards. This indicates that a procedural mechanism can assume a significant role in making formal sector benefits accessible to categories of informal sector workers. The constitution of a welfare fund for the *beedi* workers, and the efforts of certain key intermediary agencies, the so-called "nodal agencies", have had an important impact. The example of Andhra Pradesh has also encouraged other states to seek coverage for their *beedi* workers.

Various statutory modifications also provide a possibility for extension of the scope of these laws. One such modification would be the elimination of the existing stipulations concerning the wage ceiling and the minimum number of workers required for coverage. In addition, subject to the eligibility conditions being fulfilled, the laws could be made applicable generally to all types of employment rather than only to those included in the schedules; however, contrary to the current practice, the laws should specify the various exemptions. Although an employee – once covered – continues to be a subscriber to the EPF scheme even when the worker starts drawing higher wages, there is no reason why it should not in the first instance be applicable to the higher salary group, nor why the wage ceiling should not be removed altogether under the EPF and ESI Acts, as has been done for other social security laws. The minimum number of 20 employees is rather high as a condition for applicability. Its reduction to 10 has been seriously considered at various times, although in the case of the EPF this idea has not been accepted lately, on account of the EPF's preoccupations with computerization and with the new Pension Scheme. Both developments, however, should facilitate extension of the scheme to smaller units – computerization will provide an easier system for maintenance of accounts and statements of claims, and the Pension Scheme will make the package of benefits more attractive.

Moreover, since the Pension Fund is financed mainly out of the employers' own contributions, it should be possible to have viable arrangements for its use by the self-employed. Contributions to the Pension Fund could be made through a suitable agency, so that the pension benefits could also become available to the self-employed. There is also an increasing trend for voluntary coverage under the EPF Act. In this case, benefits could be provided under a special arrangement, as part of an integrated package for those who can afford to set aside small sums on a regular basis, but do not do so for lack of a viable arrangement. The self-organization groups, the cooperatives and the voluntary agencies could take an initiative in this area.

For the informal sector, linkages should also be possible through the specially constituted welfare funds and group insurance schemes. This would seem particularly promising for (mainly women) workers in the household industries sector, especially in the major urban centres, where they account for more than 50 per cent of employment.

2.5 Welfare funds and group insurance schemes

In order to give certain welfare and social protection benefits to specified categories of unorganized labour, statutory welfare funds have been constituted for workers employed in *beedi*, film and mining industries. Five such welfare funds have been set up by the Government of India as central funds administered through the Ministry of Labour. The funds are constituted from the cess (earmarked tax) monies collected from employers and manufacturers in the industries concerned. Through special schemes, the funds provide various facilities for the workers, including: financial assistance for housing through subsidies and low interest loans, medical care through special dispensaries, hospitals and reservation of beds in general hospitals, and special grants for specific treatments. As the schemes operate outside the framework of specific employer-employee relationships, the employees are not in fact required to make any contribution, and the cess levies paid by the employers are not linked to identified individual employees. The delivery of welfare services is also, thus, effected without linkage to individual employment relationships. The estimated labour force in these employments is over 4.4 million in the country, all of whom are prima facie entitled to receive benefits under the welfare funds. It is significant that *beedi* workers (4.25 million) – who constitute the majority of such workers – are concentrated in a dozen states, the most prominent among them being Madhya Pradesh, Andhra Pradesh, Tamil Nadu, West Bengal and Uttar Pradesh.

In 1993 a group insurance scheme was introduced for *beedi* workers. The workers themselves are not required to pay any premium; premiums are centrally paid from their welfare fund and, in case of death, the Life Insurance Company (LIC) pays the assured amount of Rs. 3,000 to the family, a much higher amount being payable for accidental death and disability (Rs. 25,000). The experience with this scheme at the national level has not been very satisfactory but, in comparative terms, claims made by the *beedi* workers of Andhra Pradesh (around 2,000 in 1994–95) account for about 50 per cent of the total claims.

Under the five central funds, 650,000 workers are prima facie covered in Andhra Pradesh, the majority of them being *beedi* workers. Andhra Pradesh is one of the notable and often-quoted examples for undertaking successful housing projects for *beedi* workers. Even so, only 18,000 houses in all have been or are being built under the welfare fund schemes, which is a small number when compared to the total number of *beedi* workers. In addition, the take-up from the welfare funds in terms of scholarships for the children and other facilities has also been better in Andhra Pradesh as compared to most other states. These achievements have mainly been the result of the Beedi Workers' Welfare Fund. As noted earlier, once the system of identity cards being issued to such workers became operational, it facilitated their coverage under the EPF scheme, a prominently formal sector affair. In 1998, 425,000 (mostly home-based) *beedi* rollers in Andhra Pradesh out of the 450,000 having identity cards under the welfare fund have individual PF accounts, and would now be entitled to the superannuation pension as well. The overall coverage of *beedi* workers under the EPF is now around 1.3 million in India as a whole, which is 30 per cent of the 4.25 million such workers who have identity cards.

Recently, a new welfare fund law for construction workers has been enacted. While the law is for India as a whole, the welfare funds are expected to be set up and operated by the central and state governments, with the latter taking most of the action. This central legislation was inspired by the example of Kerala, which already has such a law; most of the other state governments have yet to consider the matter.

2.6 State legislation and action

Various states have taken initiatives to constitute welfare funds, the efforts made by Kerala, Gujarat and Maharashtra having been significant. Extension of social security – including insurance, health care and certain welfare benefits – has been organized on a contributory basis for those working in agriculture, construction, *coir* (coconut fibre), cashew and other industries, through setting up welfare funds separately for each employment sector. In Kerala, 35 such welfare funds are operating. Apart from mixing up different types of benefits, the coexistence of these numerous funds all over the state is now being seen as administratively expensive, and it is felt that an integrated fund should now be preferred. Maharashtra is also implementing laws to extend similar benefits to certain categories of unorganized workers, such as headload workers in urban areas.

Apart from welfare funds, many states have introduced schemes to provide support to workers in different types of employment, but since they do not have a statutory base, they are considered as social assistance measures and hence dealt with in the next section. However, some states have enacted specific laws. Gujarat has introduced the Gujarat Shops and Establishments Employees' Life Insurance Act 1980, which provides for schemes assuring benefits of up to Rs. 2,500 for workers with six months' continuous service, the insurance premium being equally shared by employers and employees. The Act requires that the schemes be formulated by the local bodies. The subject seems not to have been actively pursued by the Gujarat State Government, and the extent of compliance appears to be unknown. By the current standards, the sum assured has become insignificant and is in sharp contrast with the amounts now stipulated as life insurance cover for rural workers under the new state scheme (Rs. 20,000 maximum for accidental deaths). In a state which has an urban population of 35 per cent, it is clear that social security for urban workers is a much neglected area.

The Andhra Pradesh Labour Welfare Fund Act of 1987, set up on the basis of small annual contributions from workers and employers, as well as a matching grant from the Andhra Pradesh State Government, covered more than 1 million workers by 1998, mainly in factories, shops and establishments (having even one employee), motor transport undertakings and the societies. The Board grants emergency aid in cases of workers' accidental death while on duty, provides merit scholarships to children for middle and higher education, and encourages recreational activities through its welfare centres.

Although statutorily constituted, the availability and level of benefits under the welfare funds *per se* is quite modest, and the entire orientation of the schemes is towards general welfare rather than establishing individual rights and entitlements. The absence of a substantial field agency and of a coordinating mechanism, together with a lack of awareness on the part of the beneficiaries themselves, contribute to a rather weak implementation of these schemes. The schemes do not necessarily provide a platform for bringing together all workers, as there is no direct participation of employees.

3. Social assistance

In the context of developing countries, it has now been recognized that the formal model alone cannot be relied upon and the concept of social security has to reach beyond social insurance to include social assistance. While the impact of economic growth on poverty reduction is well established and is indeed inherent in the process of growth itself, it is also beyond doubt that such a process does not equally benefit all sections of society. In fact, disadvantaged groups are often unable to take advantage of growth opportunities; hence the need for special policies and programmes aimed at benefitting certain specific areas and groups. In this section two programmes will be reviewed: the National Social Assistance Programme and the (subsidized) group insurance schemes for vulnerable groups.

3.1 The National Social Assistance Programme

Different states have introduced a number of social assistance programmes aimed at averting or alleviating helplessness and destitution due to poverty. They are broadly similar, although there are some variations in conditions regarding coverage, eligibility and benefits. Welfare measures for this purpose have generally included a grant of monthly pensions to various categories of destitutes, i.e. those without subsistence income or family support among the aged, widows and the disabled. Starting with Andhra Pradesh and Kerala in 1960, all states have been granting monthly pensions to the aged (above 60 years) since 1983 or earlier, subject to the conditions of income being below the stipulated levels and to having the "niradhar" or "without support" status (i.e. not having a son above 21 years of age). The rates have varied between Rs. 50 and Rs. 120 per month; however, since 1995, pensioners above 65 years can receive Rs. 75 per month from the central Government under the new National Social Assistance Programme (NSAP). In many states, widows are also entitled to a pension; in Gujarat, an additional amount per child is payable for up to two children, but the pension is admissible only for one year, during which time widows are expected to follow skill training for self-employment. The physically disabled, apart from receiving free education, lodging and boarding facilities in state-run institutions, are also eligible for the monthly pension if above the age of 45 years. In Gujarat as well as Andhra Pradesh, landless agricultural workers above the age of 60 years are also disbursed monthly pensions under conditions as stipulated for the aged. The amounts of pension differ according to category of recipient.

Apart from the fact that the amount of pension is considered too low to ensure the minimum subsistence level, the scheme has also been criticized for prescribing normative eligibility conditions such as not having an adult son. In view of the objective of assisting the most disadvantaged categories, it has been recommended that this condition be removed, and that the assistance be provided instead to low-income group families who are willing to have their elderly parents stay with them. As compared to some other states, administration of the scheme has been generally found to be quite efficient in Gujarat. According to the field surveys under a recent study, the pension schemes are quite well known even in the tribal areas, and pension claims are sanctioned in three months as against one year in some other states. Regular transmission of pensions is made through postal money orders. In Andhra Pradesh, on the other hand, the quarterly disbursement of pensions is not made regularly, and payments are made through two separate agencies responsible for the state and the central government components of the pension. In addition, the number of beneficiaries is restricted by state budgetary limitations and central guidelines, so that benefits have been low and many deserving persons have been left out (Sankaran, 1998).

Some states, notably Gujarat, Kerala, Karnataka, Andhra Pradesh and Maharashtra, have schemes for extending maternity benefits to women workers in different sectors. Since 1986, a maternity benefit scheme for landless agricultural women labourers has been in operation in Gujarat. Amounts equivalent to notified minimum wages for six and four weeks respectively for the first and second deliveries are paid to the pregnant women, apart from medical care available at the Primary Health Centres. About 100,000 women per year obtain this benefit. After the introduction of the National Maternity Benefit Scheme (NMBS), the state scheme has been discontinued since March 1996. Under the NMBS, women in all households below the poverty line are eligible for maternity benefits, not merely female agricultural labourers. As a result, the numerical ceiling prescribed under NSAP is much larger (388,200). The NMBS now entitles women to a cash amount of Rs. 300, whereas earlier the state scheme provided for higher amounts (Rs. 630 and Rs. 420 for the first and second deliveries). In the operation of the national scheme, certain other problems have come to the surface. Even though the NMBS now covers all women in families below the poverty line, it excludes women farm labourers above the prescribed poverty level who were previously within the purview of the state scheme. The NMBS also stipulates a minimum age of 19 years, but it has been felt that younger mothers who are more at risk should not be excluded. Thus, it appears that the matter requires to be critically considered and the scheme modified. Maternity assistance to women agricultural labourers has also been extended by the Government of Andhra Pradesh since 1991. The assistance amount – limited to two pregnancies – is Rs. 900, payable in four instalments. Assistance is being granted to over 100,000 women per year.

The new NSAP which came into effect on 15 August 1995 introduced the national policy for social assistance benefits to poor households, as a composite programme of three schemes to cover the contingencies of old age, maternity and death of the breadwinner. Reference has already been made to two of these – the National Old Age Pension Scheme, under which a monthly pension of Rs. 75 is provided for destitutes above the age of 65 years, and the National Maternity Benefit Scheme, which entitles women (above 19 years) from families below the poverty line to cash assistance of Rs. 300 each for the first two live births. The third benefit provides insurance coverage against the death of the primary breadwinner (between 18 and 65 years old). Under this National Family Benefit Scheme, the surviving members are paid Rs. 5,000 or Rs. 10,000 in cases of death due to respectively natural and accidental causes. While the schemes are to be implemented through the state governments, which in turn involve the local governments, 100 per cent central government assistance is made available to the states under prescribed norms. It is expected that with the additional central funds, the states will be able to provide enhanced social security levels for those in need.

3.2 Group insurance schemes

Many states have also taken the initiative to introduce (and subsidize) a number of group insurance schemes (GIS) for various categories of workers. A few characteristics of such schemes in Gujarat are given in table 2.3.

At the national level, the benefits of social insurance have also been available to different categories of vulnerable groups under the various GISs subsidized with the Social Security Fund under the Life Insurance Corporation. Prominent among these are the Landless Agricultural Labourers Group Insurance (LALGI); the IRDP scheme; and the GIS for the weaker sections, extended to 23 different occupations. The amounts for which the insurance cover is extended vary from Rs. 1,000 to Rs. 10,000, generally the accidental deaths being assured for twice the amount of natural deaths. The premia are paid mostly by the state governments and the Social Security Fund; only in occupational GIS is part of the premium borne by the beneficiary. Although advantageous as an initial step, these schemes generally suffer from various deficiencies. The sum assured – especially in the case of natural death – is rather low; and very few deaths qualify as natural deaths – only six to seven out of every 1,000. Hence, most families get either no support

Table 2.3 Group insurance schemes under implementation, Gujarat State, 1995–96

Category of workers	Sum assured	Number of beneficiaries	Amount disbursed (in Rs. million)
Landless agricultural labourers	State scheme: (i) Rs. 1 000 (natural death) } (ii) Rs. 2 000 (accidental death)	21 427	21.8
	Central scheme: Rs. 2 000	14 046	22.8
Rural workers (all classes)	(i) Rs. 3 000 (natural death) } (ii) Rs. 6 000 (accidental death)*	431	1.2
Salt workers	Same as above	877	1.8
All rural workers**	i) Rs. 20 000 (accidental death and permanent disability) } (ii) Rs. 10 000 (for partial disability)	covering 7 million unorganized rural workers	

* From October 1995, Rs. 25,000 for accidental death and total disability and Rs. 12,500 for partial disability.
** New scheme introduced in January 1996.
Source: Government of Gujarat.

or very little. Since the losses of the surviving families are similar irrespective of the cause of death, differentiation in the sum assured does not stand to reason. On the contrary, in cases of prolonged illnesses leading to death the family is required to bear substantial additional costs for medical treatment. Moreover, the take-up of the schemes is too low partly because they are not widely known, and partly because there is no liability of premium payment by the beneficiary. However, numerous new schemes have been introduced in recent years which are aimed at assisting the poor and the low-income families, in which the rates of premium are kept at very low and affordable levels. These include:

- the Rural Group Life Insurance Scheme introduced on 15 August 1995, in which insurance is available between ages 20 to 60 years for an assured amount of Rs. 5,000, the premium being around Rs. 60 per annum;
- the Savings and Pension Scheme;
- the Janata Personal Accident and the Gramin Personal Accident policies;
- the Jan Arogya Policy introduced on 15 August 1996, which gives a health insurance cover for hospitalization to the extent of Rs. 5,000 for a premium of around Rs. 70 per annum.

These are in line with and in pursuance of the recommendations of the Committee on Reforms in the Insurance Sector (Government of India, 1994). The Committee had taken note of the vast potential for insurance business in the rural areas, and had recommended looking for ways to spread non-traditional insurance business. The Committee also recommended devising special cover for self-employed women, and pension schemes for informal sector workers in various employments (especially professionals, traders and agriculturists). For this purpose, it suggested active association, assistance and even intermediation of *panchayats*, cooperatives and carefully selected voluntary agencies, particularly in the areas of insurance education and communication. In addition, cooperative institutions at the national and state level should be allowed to be in the general insurance business when they satisfy certain prescribed conditions. The recently established group insurance schemes show the trend towards expansion of social insurance cover to new areas. Thus, especially for the unorganized sector, the climate is very favourable for extending the scope of self-financed group insurance with superior benefits.

4. Self-financed social insurance

Self-financed social insurance schemes represent yet another way in which the social security needs of individuals are met through a community or group effort. The mechanism used is one of providing mutual support through pooling of resources on the principles of insurance, help being extended to those in need within the overall framework of certain basic regulatory conditions. This, in a sense, is the most basic of all social security systems, having its genesis in requirements that are common to all members of a society and their own immediate collective response in fulfilling them. In this system, it is the group itself that decides about the size and the source of contributions that group members are meant to make. The collection and management of contributions as well as the disbursement of benefits are again matters for the group to consider and arrange.

There is a wide variety of self-financed social insurance schemes, ranging from the totally informal and unwritten systems within a small group to the more formal ones catering to the needs of larger numbers and based on more complex arrangements. In addition, the initiative may originate from within the group or be motivated by non-governmental and voluntary agencies. In India there is a wide variety of ventures promoted and successfully experimented with, in the areas of credit, health care, education, employment and overall development. For the poor and lower-income groups, the need for money exists universally and continuously, almost by definition. Hence, it is not surprising that most self-help groups operate around credit requirements. These, in turn, are integrally related to contingencies such as death, disability and disease, old age, unemployment and destitution, the very areas with which social security schemes are concerned.

4.1 Examples of NGO schemes

While the significance of these self-help efforts is quite evident, in order to understand and appreciate the strengths as well as the limitations of these self-financing mechanisms it is worthwhile to examine some of the efforts made by non-governmental organizations.

The *Self-Employed Women's Association (SEWA)* is a registered trade union working mainly with women in the unorganized sector and, since 1972, has focused on employment- and income-related issues. Realizing that crises concerning health, death, natural calamities and the like lead poor families into downward poverty spirals, SEWA established a women's bank which became the central point for many of its programmes. An integrated social security package has been offered to its members on payment of Rs. 60 per year. Protection is available to 12,000 women who have joined this scheme, covering illness, widowhood, maternity, accident, fire, communal riots, floods and so on. The scheme is run by the SEWA bank in collaboration with insurance agencies. The risks covered include sickness (up to Rs. 1,000), natural or accidental death or disablement of the woman member or husband (for varying amounts up to Rs. 10,000), a maternity benefit (of Rs. 300), and loss of working tools, house and property (up to Rs. 5,000). In 1996, 1,529 claimants could receive claims amounting to a total of Rs. 1.58 million as life insurance, work security and maternity benefits. The social security package and the medical insurance were found by SEWA to have received a very positive response. The organization felt that its members were willing to pay for need-based social security services, and that the quality of service was more important than its being given free of charge. In the case of health insurance, dissatisfaction was experienced on account of non-coverage of family members, and the exclusion of a number of illnesses and of domiciliary treatments. While the insurance amount of Rs. 1,000 was found to be adequate in about 50 per cent of cases, there were difficulties with completing claims procedures, even though SEWA shares the responsibility for documentation (Chatterjee and Vyas, 1997).

The *Action for Community Organization, Rehabilitation and Development (ACCORD)* has been working for over a decade among the tribals of Gudalur in Tamil Nadu State. The tribals were facing acute problems on account of alienation of land and exploitative working conditions. Hence ACCORD built its comprehensive tribal development programme based on a campaign for land rights. The strategy involved organizing the tribals into small groups at hamlet level *(sangams)* with Adivasi Munnetra Sangam (AMS), a federative body at the top. While lobbying for a rethink on tribal development at the ground level, development activities relating to employment generation, education, plantation, health, credit, etc. were implemented through the *sangams*. The main emphasis was on participation and collective action. The major programmes of AMS included a credit fund to meet emergency consumption needs and indebtedness, set up on a 1 rupee per week contribution by members, with a matching share from ACCORD; a variation of this was the revival of a traditional savings scheme by some women's sangams; where a handful of rice was contributed daily to the pool by each family. Other programmes related to veterinary assistance and training as barefoot veterinarians, vocational skills and a health programme. In view of lack of medical facilities in the area, the extension of these through the self-help groups has been a significant achievement for ACCORD.

The health programme was conceived and carried out by community health specialists who trained health workers, particularly women, to identify health-related problems, to monitor antenatal and immunization programmes, and to disseminate health information. A hospital was also set up in 1990, with the aim of being eventually staffed by the tribals (from ACCORD's own funds and donations). Linking up with an insurance company, a composite social insurance package was drawn up on a premium of Rs. 60 per month. For a family of five, it covers the risk of damage to their hut and belongings (up to Rs. 1,500), death and permanent disability of the head of family (Rs. 3,000), and all illnesses requiring hospitalization (Rs. 1,500). The scheme has received an encouraging response from the tribals, but its sustainability seems to be confronted with a number of issues. Although payments are promptly made where the group is active, regular contributions and renewals of the insurance have been posing a problem. To ensure the collection of premiums, one approach could be to link the insurance programmes to the credit fund, a linkage that has been successfully used by some other agencies (Eswara Prasad, 1998).

The *Cooperative Development Foundation (CDF)*, generally known as Samakhya, is an institute which aims at strengthening cooperatives and is mainly working with thrift and credit groups. The CDF groups are mostly in Andhra

Pradesh, particularly in Warangal and Karimnagar Districts. However, it has also formed a federation of 14 thrift and cooperative regional associations in Tamil Nadu, Karnataka and Kerala. For social security, a death relief fund has been constituted by the CDF covering about 25,000 members. Each member deposits an initial Rs. 100 and can make further deposits in multiples of Rs. 50. The scheme covers the risk of death (natural or accidental, up to the age of 60 years), the assured amount being a multiple of the deposit ranging between 5 and 20 times, depending on the age of the member. The maximum admissible amount is Rs. 20,000. Besides life insurance, the other benefit under the scheme is security for the thrift cooperatives loans, which gives total debt relief for the surviving family and the guarantors. On reaching the age of 60 years, or on withdrawing from the scheme, the deposit amount is returned with a 2 per cent bonus. Extension of the scheme to other contingencies like illnesses is also under consideration (Gupta, 1994).

The *Association for Sarva Seva Farms (ASSEFA)*, based in Tamil Nadu and Andhra Pradesh, is working in five other states as well. The organization works by encouraging the formation of people's associations and running various development programmes through them. In Hyderabad, ASSEFA has started its own insurance scheme for payment of compensation on the death of the insured, against a contribution of Rs. 10 per family per year. In a pilot project in Madurai area, about 1,200 families are being covered for an amount of Rs. 3,000, payable in case of death, whether natural, accidental or suicidal. But in the first year itself, the death claims amounted to Rs. 15,000 against the total premium of Rs. 12,000. Obviously the scheme needs to be put on a sound footing, with a more professional management on the basis of actuarial calculations. The organization is now considering linking up their scheme with one of the various life insurance policies now available through the insurance companies, often at a reduced premium especially for the rural areas.

ASSEFA is also running a comprehensive scheme for preventive and curative health services, including referral services, for about 4,000 families at different centres, initially funded under the Plan International Programme, and managed by a cluster-level committee having representation from the villages. The families are required to pay a premium of Rs. 50 per year and can avail themselves of various services from the centres which are run by ASSEFA's own staff. Tie-up arrangements for referral services are made with government and non-government hospitals in Madurai. While the hospitals provide free beds, meals and nursing, the balance of costs, mainly of medicines, is shared between ASSEFA (two-thirds) and the beneficiary (one-third). Although the operational deficits in running the schemes have been declining, there is a need for income-generation activities to be taken up by each cluster committee in order to support expenses in the health care scheme (Gupta, 1994).

The *Society for Promotion of Area Resource Centres (SPARC)*, which started its activities among slum dwellers and women pavement dwellers in Bombay, has now spread to 14 cities in India. Realizing that access to services was the key problem, SPARC retained the just distribution of urban resources as its major goal. This it seeks to achieve through (a) making local governments responsible and accountable to the people, and (b) organizing and empowering the people to demand the services rather than receive them as doles. The women are formed into groups known as "Mahila Milans", and collective leadership is promoted. It is running a successful crisis credit scheme in which women are organized into saving groups. Small amounts (Rs. 1 to 5) are saved daily and given to collectors who, in turn, deposit the total amount at a central meeting place. From this composite credit fund, members can conveniently draw small amounts without procedural difficulties. Repayments are also normally made in time. SPARC has taken up an insurance policy with a professional company. A premium of Rs. 30 is payable by each member against which these risks are covered – hospitalization (normally Rs. 1,000), accidental death and disability cover for self and for husband (Rs. 25,000), for partial disability (Rs. 12,500), and loss of home, household goods and tools (Rs. 3,000) (Krishnamurthy,1998).

4.2 Assessing the NGO schemes

All these initiatives show that there are many ways to organize social insurance through self-financing mechanisms. The strengths of the participative approach have also been established very clearly; the members of the groups have a crucial role to play in the identification of critical needs, the collection of contributions as well as in the delivery of benefits. However, some professional help is required in the overall design of the scheme, especially when benefits are substantial and sustained over a long period. In many of these experiments the voluntary agencies have depended on outside financial help. Although efforts have also been undertaken to make them self-sustaining and self-managed after withdrawal of technical assistance, including the professional supervision of the NGO itself, this area will need further attention. While outside financial support may be required initially, it is fundamental that the financing of the benefits themselves is independent of such support.

Although the objectives, approaches and processes of voluntary self-financed activities are multifarious, there are certain common characteristics. The most striking of these are participation and self-management by the beneficiaries themselves. In the schemes the clarity of objectives can generally combine with suitability of measures and an easy accessibility of the benefits. Moreover, the operational overheads are minimal, the monitoring is close and, since the group is so familiar with the circumstances of individual beneficiaries, the chances of misutilization or leakages are practically eliminated. The extent of availability of local resources and the support of professional agencies differs with organizations, many of them in addition being able to obtain outside assistance in the form of institutional credit, government subsidies and, at times, foreign funding as well (Gupta, 1994). Apart from the social assistance programmes of the Government mentioned earlier, the Rashtriya Mahila Kosh (RMK), a National Women's Fund set up in 1993, seeks to provide credit as an instrument of socio-economic change through provision of funding and social development services for women. The credit facilities are being made available for a wide range of objectives that include consumption, as well as social and contingency needs. While encouraging innovative methodologies, RMK mainly supports participatory approaches in the organization of women's groups, for effective utilization of credit resources leading to self-reliance. Within the first two years of its existence (by March 1995) the RMK had reached thousands of women through collaborating with 118 NGOs in its Credit Limit, Self-Help Group Development and Promotional schemes.

Until recently, availability of institutional credit to the poor was extremely limited, since they were considered as "non-viable high-risk clients" by the banks. The experiments made through the mediation of voluntary agencies and certain other factors, however, encouraged the National Bank for Agriculture and Rural Development (NABARD) in 1992 to launch a nationwide pilot project that envisaged linking up 500 self-help groups (SHGs) with commercial banks and later with regional and cooperative banks as well. Collectively, these banks have now built up a countrywide network of more than 150,000 retail credit outlets for the formal financial sector. The project started with the broad objective of evolving supplementary credit strategies by combining the strengths of the formal and informal credit systems and encouraging banking activity among the poor. With the emphasis on savings, the linkage project focused on self-reliance in management and group dynamism. It is not the poor alone who have been found to benefit from the project: it has been realized that the banks also gain substantially through reduced transaction costs, a larger mobilization of small savings and an assured timely recovery leading to a greater recycling of funds. By September 1996, around 6,000 SHGs were estimated to have been linked with banks, covering approximately 120,000 families who have received more than Rs. 60 million worth of loans. A working group constituted by the Reserve Bank of India (RBI) has recommended expansion of the linkage programme, which has been found to be cost-effective, transparent and flexible in its approach and, thus, expected to solve the twin problems faced by the banks in rural credit, namely, recovery of loans and high transaction costs. In 1996, the

RBI issued guidelines to all commercial banks to accelerate the SHG linkage programme and to treat it as a business opportunity and part of their corporate strategy. The quick impact studies have brought out encouraging features of the programme. Apart from a significant reduction in transaction costs for both the banks and the borrowers and nearly 100 per cent repayment performance, a shift towards production activities from the credit resources has been found. The most outstanding impact of the linkage has been observed to be the empowerment of the poor, particularly women (Aggarwal, 1996).

4.3 The case for self-financed health insurance

As noted in Chapter 1 and section 4.1, health insurance is the first social insurance priority for workers in the unorganized sector. In fact, the impact of illnesses on families, especially poorer ones, is very burdensome. When it is the worker or an earning member who suffers the sickness, then it is not only the direct cost of treatment which needs to be borne but also – and even more so – the loss of income, especially in situations where there is no social security back-up. The burden of treatment is thus distinguishable from its cost as it depends on a variety of factors like the nature and duration of illness, the income level of the family, availability of external support from an employer or insurance, loss of income, and so on. The relative burden of treatment, defined as the ratio of treatment cost to the annual per capita consumption expenditure, is higher for those with low incomes in the rural sector. For treatment at the government hospitals in rural areas, it varies from below 30 per cent in Kerala, Tamil Nadu and West Bengal, to 100–230 per cent in Bihar, Assam, Rajasthan, Harayana and Uttar Pradesh. The rural patients, except in Kerala, pay more for health care and bear a higher burden, the distribution of facilities being generally sparse. In contrast, the burden for the urban poor is comparatively lower both in the public and private hospitals. The cost and burden of treatment through private providers is very much higher. It is also evident that treatment costs are higher where the public infrastructure is least developed, either for in-patient or out-patient care. Competition from the government hospitals has been observed as having an important bearing on the determination of private hospital charges (Krishnan, 1995).

Despite concerted efforts, there is a high level of morbidity and a relatively high incidence of communicable diseases associated with low levels of sanitation, poor quality of drinking water and malnutrition (NCAER, 1996). The morbidity prevalence rate for India has been worked out as 1,476 per thousand population, the rate for major morbidity being 4,578 per hundred thousand population. The direct costs (which include expenditure on fees and medicines) incurred on treatment of illnesses have been assessed at Rs. 121 and Rs. 49 per person per year respectively for short duration and for major episodes. This amounts to an annual expenditure of Rs. 170 per person or Rs. 969 per household. Expenditure incurred for treating a major morbidity has been worked out at Rs. 1,071 per sick person. But the direct costs represent only about 75 per cent of the total reported costs, which include travel, board and lodging expenses. The indirect expenses are relatively high in Andhra Pradesh, Gujarat and Madhya Pradesh, and relatively low in Punjab. The burden of providing health care falls more heavily on the vulnerable population groups, especially those with low income levels. Households having an income of less than Rs. 20,000 per annum spend an average of 8.3 per cent on health care. This brings out clearly the need for public provision of health services for poorer families, as well as the desirability and feasibility of a well-organized health insurance that can be financed out of the expenditures already incurred by families.

The poor in both urban and rural areas seeking private medical care, as well as the rural poor receiving treatment from government facilities, are bound to incur (sometimes large) debts. The position of the urban poor, who have access to government care, is quite comfortable in contrast. Hence, a two-pronged action is called for: (i) to enhance the spread of public infrastructure, more especially in the rural areas, and, (ii) to consider more appropriate channelling of at least a part of the private expenditure made on health services. This could be done through an appropriately designed health insurance system.

As noted in section 2.1, health insurance at present is available only under the ESI Scheme (confined mainly to formal sector workers) and to government and public sector employees. Under different schemes introduced by the insurance companies, health cover is made available to individuals and groups on payment of premiums. Group health insurance policies have been mainly taken by the larger companies for their employees. However, the mediclaim policy has been found to be generally rather costly and the packages also not so attractive. The Committee on Reforms in the Insurance Sector had briefly noted the dissatisfaction with these policies on account of too many exclusions leading to rejection of claims, as well as inadequacy of financial arrangements with the providers. The insurance companies themselves have felt the need for greater expertise to operate health insurance policies, which is a non-traditional sector for insurance business. In view of its large potential the Committee recommended "a wholesale revamp of these policies" and exhorted the insurance industries to "urgently address the issue".

Some changes have since been brought about in the health insurance packages and, on 15 August 1996, a Jan Arogya Bima Policy was introduced which provides reimbursement of hospitalization and domiciliary hospitalization expenses for illness or injury to the extent of Rs. 5,000. Besides professional fees, the following are also reimbursable: hospital charges for boarding, nursing, room rental, diagnostics, drugs and certain pre- and post-hospitalization expenses. Indoor treatment must take place in hospitals and nursing homes which are either registered or comply with minimum conditions regarding staff and facilities stipulated. Annual premiums range between Rs. 70 (up to 45 years of age) and Rs. 140 (up to 70 years), with certain discounts offered for family insurance. Although there are certain restrictive conditions regarding satisfactory health status at the time of taking the policy, the initial response to the new scheme has been encouraging. Obviously, there is great scope for improving the benefit packages, with suitable cost reductions through substantial group discounts (to the extent of over 66 per cent) for larger informal sector groups under a special integrated social security scheme.

5. Options for the future

It is evident that there is now a favourable climate for extending social security coverage to the majority of workers in the self-employed and informal sector categories. Progressive efforts have been made to extend protection against life's contingencies to the entire population in some form or other. In addition, there has been a quantitative expansion in the scope of social security mechanisms and a qualitative improvement in their benefits.

Prominent among the statutory initiatives are amendments in the laws removing wage ceilings as a condition for applicability; extension of coverage to larger groups of employees; higher benefit amounts (in the Workmen's Compensation Act and the Payment of Gratuity Act); coverage of some non-formal sectors including certain home-based workers (notably *beedi* rollers in Andhra Pradesh) under the Employees' Provident Fund Act, and a new comprehensive pension scheme under the same Act; the setting up of newer welfare funds and central legislation for construction workers.

In the sphere of *social assistance*, mention should be made of the National Social Assistance Programme, introduced by the central Government and providing minimal social security benefits for the aged and destitutes. Finally, new and better group insurance policies are being introduced, especially aimed at the lower income groups, in life insurance and non-life areas as well as for health insurance.

Various non-governmental agencies are also organizing local groups to ensure their socio-economic upliftment and access to public services. There has been rapid growth in *self-financing measures* and approaches through the instrument of self-help groups. The recognition of the valuable role and the immense possibilities for use of these mechanisms by the formal banking sector is indeed a significant phenomenon.

All this amply establishes the existence of a commitment beyond the level of a mere concern and willingness for expansion of social insurance. It is equally clear that, while each of the three main mechanisms hold possibilities for extension of coverage and improvement, there is still a need to work out a viable mechanism for extending substantial benefits to all people on a sustained basis. The informal sector workers can apparently be effectively reached only through local and participative groups. Financial participation through contributions is also an essential requirement for any meaningful social security system. Hence, it would appear that for cost-effective universal coverage, area-based social security schemes that are contributory and largely self-financing could provide a useful new mechanism.

In order to universalize access to social protection for the self-employed and workers in the unorganized and informal sectors, an appropriately designed scheme would need to take into account certain inherent characteristics of the unorganized labour force. Besides the absence of a clear and continuing employer-employee relationship, they include seasonal work and underemployment, marginal and peripheral jobs, at times involving migration, dispersed workplaces which are mostly home-based, low levels of earnings and hardly any unionization. While the need for a secure contributory base is evident for any scheme to be financially viable, the establishment of a workable collection mechanism continues to be a challenge. Since the collection of contributions through deduction at source from wage payments made by employers is either not available (in the case of self-employment), or not easy (in indirect and informal employment), a pragmatic and workable arrangement has necessarily to be found and implemented. A similar arrangement would be essential for organizing a worthwhile delivery of benefits. Schemes built around individual employment areas and rooted in the employer-employee relationship are unsuitable. Sectoral welfare funds, besides leaving out many undefined informal sector jobs, are not as cost-effective because they deal with so many different benefits. Thus, a reasonable alternative seems to be to design schemes on an area basis that would move away from the vertically organized employment spheres, towards a person-centred approach with the aim of covering all workers within a compact geographical area. The following are some of the conditions that an area-based social security scheme for the unorganized sector would have to fulfil:

- Its scope and applicability must extend to all categories of workers including home-based, self-employed and women workers, irrespective of the duration of any specific work.
- The scheme must be economically viable and self-financing, being worked out on the basis of adequate identified sources of funds, including compulsory contributions from the workers and agencies carrying out economic activities.
- The insurance benefits and the extension of coverage should be self-evident to, and considered advantageous by, the contributors and beneficiaries of the scheme.

- A certain amount of flexibility must be built in, beyond prescribed minimum levels, in order to cater for local needs and priorities.
- It must be easy and cheap to administer and enforce the scheme, involving decentralization down to the local level.
- The delivery of benefits and services must be worked out with reference to the convenience of the covered members.

Pilot projects in carefully selected areas would need to be carried out to test and develop a scheme, permitting modifications in the package of benefits as well as experimenting with procedures. Apart from special schemes, better social protection can also be achieved through two other channels – first through extending formal sector schemes, and secondly through ensuring better access to the social assistance programmes of the Government. Besides the qualitative improvement and expansion of such schemes and programmes in general through legal and other means, the area-based pilot projects would provide further opportunities to improve the outreach of social assistance and formal social insurance programmes. Areas can be selected where the present availability of such protection is insubstantial, where workers have the capacity as well as willingness to contribute towards insurance, health services and other security benefits, and where some organizational and group base also exists. The choice and level of social security benefits will have to be worked out under the project, in consultation with the beneficiaries, their representative organizations such as cooperatives, voluntary agencies, insurance companies as well as local and state administration. Some of the priority areas requiring support and protection are health care, insurance against death and disability, old-age pension, availability of credit for productive enterprises and education of children. To be realistic, it may be better to begin with benefits that are seen as the most crucial and the very minimum, including perhaps a system of health insurance and life security. Other benefits can be considered for addition after the scheme establishes itself and its various mechanisms are worked out. It has been observed that although insurance companies prefer to limit health insurance to major illnesses and hospitalized treatments, the beneficiaries themselves favour a more comprehensive package that would include primary health care as well. Since the day-to-day requirements are seen as more immediate and real, it would be desirable to devise a system that can take care of primary and even preventive health needs. This would further necessitate a decentralized delivery system which can ensure locational access to the insured workers and their families. Apart from assigning doctors for identified geographical areas, the health insurance scheme would require tie-up arrangements with hospitals (public and private). A certain degree of managerial control by the local groups would also be necessary for an effective and satisfactory service. The organization of medical assistance in terms of professional service and financial arrangements could take different forms with reference to the primary, secondary and referral services. The premium collected would have to be pooled for the entire project area in order to provide a broader base for offsetting the higher expenditure levels in complicated and chronic cases. However, there could be provision for allocation or retention of a portion of the fund at intermediate levels, to defray certain types of expenses. The public and private infrastructure could both be considered for utilization as providers, but the extent and manner of use would need to be worked out.

Since most current group insurance schemes are unable to give adequate security *in cases of death and disability*, it would be desirable to extend coverage for these contingencies. The level of benefits may be graded according to different economic strata and priorities in rural and urban areas. Insurance schemes covering large groups offer significant discounts – extending to over 66 per cent for groups of more than 50,000 in some cases – which could be availed of. Past experience has shown that simplicity and convenience of procedures will be essential, as well as a degree of flexibility. The role and association of certain nodal agencies (that is, agencies that have a pivotal or key position) will be crucial at all stages, from elaborating the scheme to delivering services and organizing its supervision. It would thus be possible to formulate viable schemes, keeping in mind the normative requirements mentioned earlier. State governments have generally shown a great deal of commitment, and would be willing to make a financial contribution, but other sectors and sources could also be identified.

As it is complicated to collect contributions from, and disburse benefits to, informal sector workers, the process of designing and developing a scheme would involve a number of activities, such as background studies; extensive and intensive consultations; workshops and training; monitoring and evaluation; and efforts towards replication. An initial study would be needed to gauge the extent to which people are already covered by formal social insurance systems, social assistance programmes and self-financing initiatives.

Once the pilot projects succeed within a certain district, there would be much scope for replication. The district framework is likely to ensure the continuance and sustainability of the scheme, and also facilitate its replicability, because the administrative framework at the district level is broadly similar throughout the country. The need for such schemes all over the country is quite evident. Central as well as state governments have been increasingly concerned and committed towards programmes for social protection. When a framework has been established for large-scale coverage, especially of the self-employed and informal sector workers, many local variations could then be considered and developed. The important point is to develop a practical model that would give confidence and hold promise for extension and replication.

References

Aggarwal, G.K. 1996. *Linkage banking in India – An overview*, unpublished paper presented at a National Seminar on Linkage Banking – NGOs and Intermediaries in Micro-Finance – the Indian experience, organized by NABARD, Hyderabad, Oct. 1996.

Chatterjee, M.; Vyas, J. 1997. *Organising insurance for women workers: The SEWA experience* (Ahmedabad, SEWA).

Employees' Provident Fund Organization. 1996. *42nd Annual Report 1994–95* (New Delhi).

Employees' State Insurance Corporation. 1996. *Annual Report 1994–95* (New Delhi).

Eswara Prasad, K.V. 1998. "ACCORD's health insurance for tribals (Gudalur, Tamil Nadu)", in van Ginneken, W. (ed.), *Social security for all Indians* (New Delhi, Oxford University Press).

Ganapathi, A. L. 1994. "Social security for women – maternity benefits", in Subrahmanya, R.K.A. (ed.), *Social security for women* (New Delhi, Friedrich Ebert Foundation, in collaboration with the Social Security Association of India and the National Commission for Women).

Government of Gujarat, Directorate of Economics and Statistics. 1994. *Basic Statistics, Gujarat and India, 1994* (Ahmedabad).

Government of India, Ministry of Finance. 1994. *Report of the Committee on Reforms in the Insurance Sector* (New Delhi).

Government of India, Ministry of Labour. 1995 and 1996. *Annual Reports 1994–95, 1995–96* (New Delhi).

Government of India, Ministry of Rural Areas and Employment. 1996. *Annual Report 1995–96* (New Delhi).

Guhan, S. 1994. "Social security options for developing countries", in *International Labour Review*, Vol.133, No. 1 (Geneva).

Gupta, R.C. 1994. *Experiments in social security measures in NGOs*, in Subrahmanya, R.K.A. (ed.), *Social security for women* (New Delhi, Friedrich Ebert Foundation, in collaboration with the Social Security Association of India and the National Commission for Women).

Hirway, Indira. 1994. *Towards employment guarantee in India: Indian and international experiences in rural public works programmes* (New Delhi and Thousand Oaks, California, Sage Publications).

Krishnamurthy, L. 1998. "SPARC's crisis credit scheme for poor women in Bombay", in van Ginneken, W. (ed.), *Social security for all Indians* (New Delhi, Oxford University Press).

Krishnan, T.N. 1995. *Access to health and burden of treatment in India – Inter-state comparison,* paper presented at the International Workshop on Health Insurance in India, Bangalore, Sept. 1995.

National Council for Applied Economic Research (NCAER). 1994. *Human development profile of Andhra Pradesh*, 1994 (New Delhi).

—. 1995. *Human development profile of Gujarat*, 1995 (New Delhi).

—. 1996. *Human development profile of India: Inter-state and inter-group differentials* (New Delhi).

National Sample Survey Organization. 1989. *42nd Round* (July 1986 – June 1987) No. 364 (New Delhi).

Planning Commission. 1993. *Report of the Expert Group on Estimation of Proportion and Number of Poor (Modified)* (New Delhi), July.

Planning Commission, Programme Evaluation Organization. 1993. *Evaluation report on JRY – A quick study 1991–92* (New Delhi).

—. 1995. *Evaluation report on revamped PDS – 1995* (New Delhi).

Sankaran, T.S. 1998. "Social assistance: Evidence and policy issues", in van Ginneken, W. (ed.), *Social security for all Indians* (New Delhi, Oxford University Press).

United Nations Development Programme (UNDP). 1994. *Human Development Report 1994* (New Delhi).

World Health Organization (WHO). 1978. "Declaration of Alma-Ata", in *Primary Health Care: Report of the International Conference on Primary Health Care, Alma-Ata, USSR, 6–12 September 1978* (Geneva).

—. 1981. *Global Strategy for Health for All by the Year 2000* (Geneva).

EXTENDING THE COVERAGE OF SOCIAL SECURITY PROTECTION IN CHINA 3

Xiaoyi Hu, Director-General, Social Insurance Management Bureau, Ministry of Labour and Social Security, China,
Renhua Cai, former Director-General, Law and Regulations Department,Ministry of Public Health, China, and
Xu Zhai, Official, Ministry of Civil Affairs, China

China's economy is mainly based on agriculture; thus at the end of 1995, out of a population of 1.2 billion, only 30 per cent lived in urban areas. In the same year, about 625 million people were in employment, of whom more than 50 per cent worked in primary industries, and somewhat less than 25 per cent in secondary and tertiary industries. Less than 30 per cent of the workforce lived in urban areas and more than 70 per cent in rural areas. As shown in table 3.1, the percentage of people employed in urban areas increased from about 26 per cent in 1986 to almost 28 per cent in 1995.

Like most other developing countries, China faces two major challenges – employment creation and poverty alleviation. As a complement to employment promotion and poverty alleviation policies, the social security system plays an extremely important role in protecting the basic interests of people (Hu, 1997), in mitigating social contradictions, promoting social justice and maintaining social stability. It also greatly helps to promote economic development and social progress.

In the 18 years since the beginning of the reform and the open-door policy, people's living standards and quality of life have improved enormously. At the same time, with further reform of the economic system and readjustment of the economic structure, income disparities among the population have widened. In addition to those already living in absolute poverty, others exist in relative poverty, and new members of the absolute poor have emerged. It is the unavoidable responsibility of the Government to provide basic social protection for poor and vulnerable population groups. The Government should formulate policies, promote legislation, set up specialized institutions and mobilize social forces to help establish and improve the social security system.

This chapter will first look at the extension of health insurance in urban and rural areas. It will then evaluate how the social assistance benefits can be

Table 3.1 Total number of employees, and percentage located in urban areas, China, 1986–95

Year	Total (millions)	Urban (percentages)
1986	512.8	25.9
1987	527.8	26.1
1988	543.3	26.3
1989	553.3	26.0
1990	567.4	26.0
1991	583.6	26.2
1992	594.3	26.3
1993	602.2	26.5
1994	614.7	27.4
1995	623.9	27.8

Source: *China Statistical Year Book 1996* (State Statistical Bureau, 1996).

improved and extended, before focusing on pension insurance. Finally, the chapter will examine the factors that constrain the extension of social security coverage and provide various recommendations to improve the situation.

1. Social health insurance

Since the founding of new China, a nationwide network of medical care, prevention and health promotion has been established – at the county, township and village levels in rural areas and at the provincial, city and district or subdistrict levels in urban areas. The three-level network consists of medical institutions that are publicly owned, some of which are state-owned units financed by different government levels or directly run by industrial and mining establishments, while others are collective units financed with subsidies from local governments. According to the year-end statistics from 1995, China had more than 190,000 medical institutions and 5.4 million health professionals.

With regard to prevention and health promotion, China has been able to eliminate many infectious and parasitic diseases, such as smallpox in 1961, and schistosomiasis (bilharzia). Filariasis was eliminated in 1994. No polio virus has been discovered since 1995. Planned immunization for children has taken place, and more than 85 per cent of rural townships have carried out vaccine inoculation. The incidence of four infectious childhood diseases including measles is now more than 90 per cent lower than it was before the planned immunization. Remarkable achievements have also been made in the health status of women and children. The mortality rate of infants dropped from 200 per thousand before the founding of new China to 31.4 per thousand in 1995, and the mortality rate of women in pregnancy and childbirth dropped from 1,500 per 100,000 to 61.9 per 100,000.

Public hospitals are the backbone of China's curative health programme. The Government supports the public hospitals with a system of "transitional budget subsidies" which amounted to 6.5 billion yuan (about US$0.8 billion) in 1995. In addition, public hospitals also receive compensation from medical service charges. Thanks to constant government subsidies, public hospitals can provide all urban residents with basic medical services at prices lower than the costs. Patients with low income and limited financial capacity can also get basic medical protection.

The social health insurance protection system is very different for residents in urban areas compared to those in rural areas because of the great variation in basic conditions of the dual economy.

1.1 Health insurance for urban employees

The health protection scheme for urban employees consists, first of all, of a free medical care scheme for civil servants and employees in other public institutions, such as those working in science and technology, education, culture and public health, as well as college and university students and disabled ex-servicemen. It covered around 32.5 million[1] people at the end of 1995 and its cost totalled less than 14 billion yuan. The Government paid more than 11 billion yuan, accounting for 81 per cent of the total. Employees themselves usually do not have to pay for medical services. The free medical care scheme could be considered as a "government insurance".

The second system is the workers' health insurance scheme, established in 1951 and intended for employees and their dependants in state-owned enterprises and some collective enterprises. It covers around 114 million people. Medical care is basically free (half payment for dependants). Medical care costs totalled around 46.6 billion yuan in 1995. Medical care costs of active employees are charged to the welfare fund in their enterprises. The workers' health insurance scheme is in the nature of an "employer-based insurance" and is not highly socialized.

In more than 40 years, the two schemes have played a significant role in protecting people's health, promoting economic growth and maintaining social stability. With further economic and social development, however, their

---

[1] This figure only includes insured employees. However, the children and spouse without employment of an insured employee can obtain reimbursement of half their medical costs.

drawbacks have started to show. Most prominent among these are the lack of a rational and stable mechanism to fund medical care costs, and of an effective mechanism to restrain both the provider and the consumer of medical services. In spite of the "transitional budget subsidies" offered by the Government, public hospitals can no longer obtain enough compensation by themselves to provide medical services at below cost price. Patients can hardly afford the rapidly increasing medical care costs because public hospitals often make excessive use of costly medical equipment and prescribe expensive medicines, in order to survive and develop their services. On the other hand, people are accustomed to the provision of free medical care and they lack cost-awareness, leading to a great waste of medical services and medicines. The total cost of free medical care and workers' health insurance rose from 2.4 billion yuan in 1978 to 55.8 billion yuan in 1994, representing an average annual growth rate of 20.8 per cent. These fast-increasing costs could be borne by some high-performing enterprises, but not by the rest, thereby leading to a lack of basic medical protection in some enterprises and inadequate coverage elsewhere.

In 1993, the "Decision of the Plenary Conference of the Communist Party on Certain Issues concerning the Establishment of the Social Market Economy System" (State Commission for Restructuring the Economic System, 1995) proposed two basic reforms for health insurance schemes for employees:

(i)   The premium is to be shared by employing units and employees, and
(ii) Social pooling of an enterprise medical care fund is to be combined with individual medical care accounts.

At the beginning of 1994, the State Council selected two medium-sized cities in Southern China – Zhenjiang, Jiangsu Province and Jiujiang, Jiangxi Province – to test the scheme. Under the new scheme, the premium is related to the total pay-roll. The contribution rate for employing units is determined as follows. After deducting unreasonable expenses and allowing for factors such as change of disease categories and fluctuation of prices, the average of the actual medical care cost in the previous three years is converted into a percentage of the annual total wage bill. This percentage was 8.4 in 1993 and 1994 and 8.3 in 1995, so it was decided to fix the contribution rate for enterprises and institutions at around 10 per cent of overall wages. At the same time, to enhance participation and cost-awareness among employees, they were required to contribute 1 per cent of their annual total wage, and this percentage will gradually increase with rising wages in the future.

The health insurance fund is divided into two portions. Around half of the contribution made by employing units and the full amount of the contribution made by employees are put in the individual medical care account. The other half of the contribution made by the employing unit is used as the medical care fund for social pooling. The amount in each individual account is earmarked for payment of the worker's and dependants' medical care costs. Both the principal and interest are owned and used by the employees themselves. The amount in the individual account can be carried over to the next year or inherited by legal heirs, but cannot be withdrawn in cash or used for other purposes. The medical care fund for social pooling is managed and regulated centrally by a specialized management institution.

Payment of medical care costs (for consultation or hospitalization) is in three portions. The first is from the individual account, for the reimbursable cost. The second portion is self-payment by employees. If the amount in the individual account is not enough to cover costs, employees themselves have to pay the balance in cash. The third portion is co-payment. If the annual total medical care cost exceeds the amount in the individual account plus 5 per cent of the annual total wage of employees, the balance is paid mainly by the social pooling fund and partially by employees themselves in cash. The greater the total cost, the higher the proportion paid by the social pooling fund and the lower the proportion paid by employees themselves in cash. A maximum amount (also called the ceiling) of medical care cost (say, five times the annual total wage of employees) is set for payment by the social pooling fund. Medical care costs above that ceiling will be paid by a supplementary medical insurance fund or through other channels.

The experimental medical insurance scheme for employees combines "horizontal" mutual help by social pooling (mutual aid insurance) with "vertical" accumulation by individual account (self-insurance), and integrates motivation through individual accounts with restraint by three-portion payment. It can both satisfy the need for basic medical care and contain the rapid growth of costs. After more than two years' experimentation in Zhenjiang and Jiujiang, the scheme was operating well and more than 90 per cent of the enterprises in both cities were participating. The assessment made of the reform shows that basic medical protection for employees in these two cities has been considerably improved. In Zhenjiang, the two-weekly rate of consultation increased from 69.7 per cent in 1994 before the reform to, respectively, 75.4 and 83.5 per cent in 1995 and 1966, after the reform. Some employees should have been hospitalized but were actually not, because of "financial difficulties". However, this factor – accounting for 26.5 per cent in 1994 – dropped to, respectively, 13.7 per cent and 14.3 per cent in 1995 and in 1996. In Zhenjiang, 92 per cent of enterprises were satisfied with the new scheme, saying that it can really provide basic health care protection for employees. In Jiujiang, 71.3 per cent of employees were satisfied or fairly satisfied. Middle school and primary school teachers, employees in enterprises suffering losses and retired employees were especially happy with the new scheme.

The new health insurance scheme has heightened awareness of both the provider and the consumer of medical services. Hospitals have standardized their technical behaviour in diagnosis and treatment, formulated a list of basic medicines, defined the scope of basic medical care and adopted a method of "average quota" in the settlement of medical care costs. They have also started to implement the three-portion payment and made a moderate increase in the self-payment rate. The rapid growth of medical care costs has therefore been brought under control. The per capita medical care cost in administrative agencies and institutions in Jiujiang in 1996 rose by 11.6 per cent between 1994 and 1996, considerably less than the growth rate of 20 per cent in the national per capita free medical care cost. In Zhenjiang, costs rose 21 per cent between 1994 and 1996, considerably less than the average annual growth rate of 33.4 per cent between 1990 and 1994, while the average prescription value went down from 68.9 yuan in 1995 to 59.7 yuan in 1996, a fall of 15 per cent, and the average annual hospitalization cost of each in-patient fell from 3,118 yuan in 1995 to 2,758 yuan in 1996, a decline of 13 per cent.

In order to test the new health insurance concept further, the State Council decided in May 1996 to extend the experiment to 57 more cities.

1.2 Health protection for rural residents

The main form of health protection scheme for rural residents is the system of cooperatively provided medical care which first came into being before the liberation of China (1949). It was gradually developed further in the days of agricultural cooperatives after the founding of new China. In 1955, two townships (Zhaohe Township, Zhengyang County, Henan, and Mishan Township, Gaoping County, Shanxi) took the lead and set up a system of cooperatively provided medical care jointly funded by farmers and the collective economy. In February 1960, the Central Party Committee transmitted a report submitted by the Ministry of Public Health, confirming the importance of the cooperative medical care system. In December 1968, Chairman Mao gave instructions to disseminate the experience in cooperative medical care gained by Leyuan Commune (in Changyang County, Hubei). In 1976, around 90 per cent of production brigades (equivalent to villages) started cooperative medical care. In the early 1980s, a thorough-going revolution was launched in the rural economic system, resulting in the disintegration of people's communes. After the implementation of the output-linked household responsibility system, the collective economy made much smaller contributions to cooperative medical care, so that the system began to suffer from financial difficulties and poor management. In the mid- and late 1980s, only 5 per cent of the village-level administrations still provided cooperative medical care. In the early 1990s, new experiments were made on various types of cooperative medical care, on the basis of historical experience. The system now covers around 10 per cent of the village-level administrations, which means that most rural residents have to pay medical care costs themselves and do not have much basic medical protection. In poor areas, there are numerous instances of farmers becoming poor or returning to poverty because of sickness. According to a survey in poor counties, 72.6 per cent of sick farmers do not go to the doctor because they are in financial difficulties, 89.2 per cent of them are not hospitalized because they cannot afford medical care cost, and 5.5 per cent of households sell off family properties because they have to pay medical care costs for sick family members. It is therefore imperative to explore effective ways to enable poor farmers to have basic medical protection as soon as possible.

The "Decision of the Central Party Committee and the State Council on the Reform and Development of Public Health" issued in January 1997 (Ministry of Public Health) points out that "cooperative medical care should be organized by the Government and put under government leadership. The principle of local people running cooperative medical care and the State subsidizing it, as well as the principle of voluntary participation, should be observed. Funds should come mainly from rural residents, the collective economy should provide subsidies, and the Government should offer appropriate support. The type of cooperation, contribution rate and reimbursement rate should be defined in line with local conditions to gradually improve medical care protection." On the type of cooperation, there is choice as to whether medical services and medicines should be paid by the insurance or by self-payment. With regard to the reimbursement mechanism, there is a choice between reimbursement for minor and/or major (and costly) diseases. Reimbursement at a certain rate for medical care costs for common diseases and "minor diseases" can promote early disease treatment. This type of mechanism has an extensive coverage but a poor ability to withstand risks. Reimbursement for medical care costs for major diseases has a risk-sharing effect and can prevent rural residents from becoming poor because of sickness.

Finally, there are three main options with regard to the funding and management of cooperative medical care systems:

(i)   A system established and managed by villages. The fund is raised, regulated and managed by village-level administrations. This kind of system does not have a strong pooling mechanism and therefore has little ability to withstand risks.

(ii) A system established by villages but managed by townships. The fund is raised, regulated and managed centrally by townships or towns, and thus has an extended scope of mutual help.

(iii) A system established by townships but managed by counties. This sort of system has a strong pooling mechanism and can withstand risks very well.

China is characterized by vast rural areas and extremely uneven economic and social development. Therefore, in the dissemination of cooperative medical care, practical measures must be taken that fit in with local conditions.

In relatively developed areas, the total contribution rate could be 2–3 per cent of annual per capita net income, with that of the farmers at 1.5–2.5 per cent. In the rural areas of South Jiangsu, for instance, the cooperative medical care system is mostly of the "risk type", i.e. only medical care costs for major diseases are reimbursed. This scheme is run by local people and subsidized by the State, while the fund is raised jointly by the county, the township and the village. Each villager contributes an average of 10–20 yuan a year. The village public welfare fund provides a subsidy equivalent to an average annual per capita amount of 1.5–2 yuan. In addition, the township or county government contributes an average annual per capita amount of 0.5–1 yuan. Some township and village enterprises also make contributions to the social pooling fund. Medical care costs below 500 yuan a year are paid by rural residents themselves. If the amount is between 500 yuan and 6,000 yuan, 50 to 60 per cent will be paid (or reimbursed) by the social pooling fund of the township or town. If the amount exceeds 6,000 yuan (around five times the average annual per capita net income), additional subsidies will be provided by the social pooling fund of the county or city.

In underdeveloped areas, both contribution and reimbursement usually start from a low rate, according to local conditions. In Kaifeng county, Henan, for instance, the fund is financed with an average per capita amount of 2–6 yuan a year. A moderately tight control on the reimbursement rate is exercised to maintain a balance between income and expenditure, as well as to allow sustainable functioning of the cooperative medical care system. The level of medical protection will gradually be raised with the development of the economy and increases in farmers' incomes.

1.3 Some policy issues

Since the 1980s, the total costs of public health have been increasing fast in China, simultaneously with the sustained rapid growth of the national economy. In the period from 1980 to 1994, public health expenditure increased at an annual rate of 20.2 per cent, well above the corresponding GDP growth rate. However, within total health expenditure a significant change has taken place. The government contribution fell from 36.4 per cent to 20.6 per cent between 1980 and 1994, while the contribution by the community (mainly enterprises) fell from 40.4 per cent in 1980 to 37.4 per cent in 1994. On the other hand, the individual residents' share rose from 23.3 per cent in 1980 to 31.3 per cent in 1990 and again to 42 per cent in 1994. All this shows that China has passed beyond the stage of a planned economy, but that residents, especially the majority of farmers who are not yet covered by the social health insurance scheme, carry an increasingly heavy burden of medical care. Government at all levels is requested to assume its financial responsibility in developing medical and health undertakings, in improving the social health insurance scheme and in increasing its contribution to public health. Efforts are being made to increase public health expenditure to 57 per cent of GDP by the end of the twentieth century, with the government contribution accounting for no less than 25 per cent of total health expenditure. The function of "transfer payment" in the central Government and provincial governments should be fully employed to concentrate financial strength on the supply of medical services in early revolutionary areas, minority areas, border areas and poor areas. The three-level network of medical care, prevention and health promotion should be improved. Start-up funds should be provided for the cooperative medical care system in poor rural areas to satisfy the basic medical care needs of farmers and to contribute to a fair distribution of health protection throughout the country.

The health insurance scheme for urban employees is funded by the Government or directly by state-owned enterprises, whereas the cooperative rural medical care system is mainly funded by farmers themselves. Both are managed by the Government, which has the advantages of centralized leadership and macro control, but which can also give rise to such drawbacks as inflexibility, rigidity and inefficiency. Thus, while it is necessary to further develop and improve compulsory social health insurance, various forms of supplementary medical insurance should also be encouraged.

The All-China Federation of Trade Unions is engaged in mutual aid insurance among employees, an effort which has been successful and appreciated by its members. Commercial insurance companies such as China People's Insurance Group are expanding their insurance business for costly diseases, surgical operations, special nursing as well as for primary and middle school students. These types of insurance should be regarded as a supplement to social basic health insurance and need to be accompanied by policy support and guidance. However, a cautious attitude should be taken in opening the commercial insurance market to foreign companies.

2. Social assistance

Social assistance refers to an allowance financed by the State and the community to protect the basic livelihood of poor population groups, and is divided between urban and rural social assistance.

2.1 Social assistance in urban areas

Since the 1950s social protection has become increasingly independent of employing units, especially enterprises. Enterprises turned themselves into economic entities with management autonomy and assuming sole responsibility for profits and losses. With the gradual introduction of the market economy, enterprises began to fulfil a different function towards social protection. Enterprises and employees now share the responsibility for contributing to social insurance schemes, such as pensions, medical care, unemployment and employment injury. For example, after paying minimum wages to employees, enterprises are no longer committed to solving the financial difficulties of their employees' families: this has now become the job of the Government's social assistance departments.

In this new situation, the traditional urban social assistance system has the following shortcomings and drawbacks:

(i)   The scope of application is narrow and the coverage is limited. In the planned economy system, social assistance was mainly intended for population groups who were unable to work and were in financial difficulties. In the market economy system, people capable of working can also become poor. Contradictions between supply and demand of social assistance will therefore be sharper. According to the statistics from the State Statistical Bureau, in 1994 there were 13 million poor people in urban areas but only 3 million received social assistance.

(ii)   The social assistance payments are too low to protect the basic livelihood of target groups. The average annual per capita rate of regular social assistance in 1994 was 585 yuan for the orphaned, old, sick, disabled and infants and 421 yuan for households in financial difficulties. It was one-seventh of the urban average annual per capita income (3,000 yuan) and also well below the urban poverty line (the per capita income being 1,440 yuan according to the State Statistical Bureau).

(iii) The social assistance fund is insufficiently funded. This is the reason for the low level of social assistance rates. Unlike prices, the social assistance fund's resources have not risen. On the contrary, with the expansion of coverage and target groups, the social assistance fund has become all the more insufficient.

It is therefore imperative to reform the old social assistance system in order to maintain social stability and promote economic development. In June 1993, Shanghai, China's biggest city, took the lead and formulated the "minimum livelihood protection scheme for urban residents" (Ministry of Civil Affairs, 1995a). In 1994, the Tenth National Working Conference on Civil Affairs proposed to disseminate the scheme to all big cities. In 1997, the State Council issued a circular to demand the establishment of the minimum livelihood protection scheme in urban areas throughout China by the end of 1999.

Under the minimum livelihood protection scheme for urban residents, poor people in urban households whose average per capita income is lower than the minimum livelihood protection line can obtain top-up subsidies from the Government. The scheme operates in the following ways:

(1) *Target groups.* Based on causes of poverty and types of poor people, the following are covered by the minimum livelihood protection scheme:

- people who have no regular income, are unable to work and have no legal provider;
- retired households that have an average per capita income lower than local minimum living standards;
- people who are not re-employed after long-term unemployment and whose households have an average per capita income lower than local minimum living standards;
- people whose households have an average per capita income lower than local minimum living standards because of other reasons.

(2) *Rate.* The amount of minimum livelihood protection is determined by minimum living expenses, with consideration being given to price indexes and local financial affordability; thus rates are allowed to vary between different areas. To encourage employment, the amount should be lower than the local unemployment benefit rate, the basic living standards and the minimum wage rate. The rate should be low in the initial years and can increase in future in line with the economic development and price rise indexes. At a suitable time each year, local governments should announce the minimum livelihood protection line for the year. Current rates vary between 120 and 280 yuan per month.

(3) *Fund.* It is the local government's duty to organize the finance for minimum livelihood protection. The resources can be raised by city or district governments, or jointly by city or district governments and employing units (including their higher economic responsible departments). If employing units have no such capacity and cannot make full contributions to the fund, the balance should be made up by local governments. From a long-term point of view, social assistance is a local government task, but donations and activities towards poverty alleviation and helping "employees in financial difficulties" provided by the community should also be encouraged.

(4) *Form.* Social assistance, regular or temporary, is usually provided in cash, and sometimes also in a combined form – in cash and in kind.

(5) *Management.* The scheme of minimum livelihood protection is the responsibility of the civil affairs departments of local governments. Civil

affairs departments of city and district governments, neighbourhood committees and autonomous units of residents (residents' committees) are jointly responsible for the overall management of the scheme, from investigation and registration to payment of social assistance.

From 1993 when the first scheme was established in Shanghai to October 1996, 129 cities (including municipalities directly under the central Government, cities with independent planning, provincial capitals, cities at the prefectural level and cities at the county level) established such schemes, and in total they employed 664,000 public servants.

2.2 Social assistance in rural areas

This refers to protection provided by the Government and the collective economy to the basic livelihood of the rural elderly, disabled and infants who have no legal providers, are unfit to work and have no income sources, as well as poor people who are in financial difficulties because of sickness, disaster or unfitness for work. The allowance can be in the form of providing goods or giving support to production.

Social assistance in rural areas is an important component and the last defence line of rural social protection. Many people in rural areas are well below the poverty line, so social assistance is a challenging task which can play a significant role in maintaining social stability and promoting sustained and sound economic and social development.

Over the past 40 to 50 years, China has relied on the collective economy and the masses, on mutual aid and self-help through production, and on the provision of necessary assistance by the State. Work on social assistance has been improved and expanded with the integration of the State, the collective economy and farmers themselves. Therefore, the characteristics of a Chinese rural social assistance system would be as follows:

(1) Dissemination of the method of regular social assistance allowances. For many years, the main type of social assistance in rural areas has been the temporary allowance, which is an optional system, and the assistance fund is often used for other purposes. The inflation resulting from reform and opening up has seriously affected the basic livelihood of poor people in rural areas. To ensure a correct use of the assistance fund and to enhance protection of the basic livelihood of poor people, some areas have started to provide regular social assistance payments to target groups; and they have achieved gratifying results. According to statistics, the amount of regular social

assistance and compassionate allowance provided by the State and the collective economy in rural areas reached over 800 million yuan in 1994. More than 3 million poor people received regular social assistance allowances and subsidies.

(2) Experimentation with the minimum livelihood protection line scheme. Rural areas with suitable conditions have started to experiment with this scheme – some rural areas in Guangdong, Guangxi, Shandong, Shanxi and Shanghai had established such schemes by the end of 1995. Intended target groups are villagers whose households have an average per capita income lower than the minimum livelihood protection line. Assistance allowance is provided by a combination of cash and goods. The rate of minimum livelihood protection is determined by governments at the county or township (town) government level, that also manages the social assistance fund. Target groups first submit an application to the villagers' committee who – after an initial examination – submit the application to the civil affairs department in the township (town) government for examination and approval. The civil affairs department of the county government keep a record.

3. Extending pension insurance

3.1 Pension insurance for the urban sector

In the early 1950s China issued the "Regulations of the People's Republic of China on Labour Insurance" and established a unified pension insurance scheme. The scheme defined uniform contribution rates, eligibility criteria, rates of pension benefits and a unified management system across the nation. Owing to the political and economic events in the late 1960s, responsibility for pension insurance was devolved to enterprises, but uniform rates were still followed nationwide. In the mid-1980s, social pooling of pension funds was introduced and "enterprise insurance" was converted into "social insurance". As the pooling took place mainly at the county level, the scheme became less and less transparent. Local areas defined their own rates of pension benefits by increasing contribution rates and subsidies. These rates changed so much with the passage of time that there was no unified yardstick to measure the level of pension benefits in China. Even in areas practising social pooling, contribution rates were vastly different, so that pension funds could hardly be regulated. There were clashes between province and city as well as between city and county; in addition, there were sustained conflicts between management mode systems organized along industrial and geographical lines. All these problems with the past pension system made its reform inevitable.

In the 1990s, the State Council issued the "Decision on Reform of the Pension Insurance Scheme for Enterprise Employees" (Decree No. 33, 1991) and the "Circular Concerning Further Reform of the Pension Insurance Scheme for Enterprise Employees" (Decree No. 6, 1995) (see Han and Shi, 1995). A series of unified principles and standards for reform of the pension insurance scheme are stipulated in these two documents. The most important ones provide that:

(i)   the basic pension insurance scheme should cover all enterprise employees and self-employed workers in urban areas;

(ii)   the insurance contribution premium should be shared by the State, the enterprise and individuals in a rational way;

(iii)   a multi-tier pension insurance system should be implemented, with a compulsory basic pension insurance protecting only the basic needs of retirees, and a voluntary, enterprise-level depository pension insurance for individuals, covering supplementary needs;

(iv)   social pooling should be combined with individual accounts, so that the combined system will reflect the principles of government responsibility, social mutual aid and basic protection, but would also provide pension benefits that are more closely related to the contributions of individual workers.

In July 1997, the State Council issued a document "Decision on the Establishment of a Unified Pension Insurance System for Enterprise Staff and Employees" and decided to unify pension schemes in the whole country by the end of 1998. The new unified scheme follows a dual-structured basic pattern. An individual account will be established at 11 per cent of the employee's wage income, to which the employee will eventually contribute 8 per cent of his or her own wage income, and another 3 per cent will come from the enterprise's contribution. The enterprise will contribute at a progressively decreasing rate on a pay-as-you-go basis, but initially not more than 20 per cent of the total payroll of the enterprise. Pensioners could be entitled to pension benefits after 15 years of accumulated contributions. Pension benefits are divided into two portions: the first will be a flat-rate basic pension that – depending on a minimum number of years of contribution – is equal to 20 per cent of the average wage income of employees. The second portion will be individual account pension benefits, and a monthly payment will be made based on the accumulated amount in the individual account divided by 120.

Plans for extension

It is stated in the "Regulations on Workers' Insurance" issued in 1951 that such insurance applies to "all public and private enterprises". In practice, however, it mainly covers employees in state-owned and collective enterprises, and few employees in non-public enterprises were covered by or participated in workers' insurance. Table 3.2 shows the situation in pension insurance in 1995.

In state-owned enterprises, the large majority of active and retired employees are covered by labour pension insurance, while most remaining employees are covered by an enterprise retirement payment plan. In urban collective enterprises, the coverage by labour pension insurance is much lower, particularly among active employees. Most remaining employees are covered by retirement payment plans managed by small-sized collective enterprises.

Urban self-employed workers, active employees in foreign-funded companies and other types of enterprises total 29.4 million, while retired employees total 720,000. Only 2.4 million active employees and 250,000 retired employees have contributed to the workers' pension insurance scheme. Those who have not contributed to the scheme have no retirement protection.

According to the Labour Law of China and the spirit of international labour Conventions, it is of momentous significance to secure the basic rights of employees and maintain social stability through extending the coverage of the pension scheme. Especially in China, extending coverage to all kinds of enterprises in cities and towns and to their employees would alleviate the burden of state-owned enterprises.

Since state-owned and urban collective enterprises have been basically covered, the focus of extending the coverage of the workers' pension scheme should be on the foreign investment enterprises, private enterprises, some township and village enterprises (TVEs) with stable labour relations, the self-employed and rural migrant workers to urban areas. Of course, since these types of enterprises have a relatively young workforce, they have a fairly light pension burden and a little awareness of the need for social insurance. Thus, the plan of extending the pension scheme's coverage should proceed step by step, level by level, from easy to difficult. In China, the first priority should be to cover foreign investment enterprises, private enterprises and their employees (including rural migrant workers), and then to cover the self-employed.

Foreign and private enterprises should join the pension scheme on the same conditions as the state-owned enterprises. But considering their favourable age-structure and light old-age burden, they may pay slightly lower contribution rates at the beginning, and progressively move towards the unified rate of the state-owned enterprises.

For the rural-to-urban migrant workers, a lump-sum payment would be the appropriate form of pension benefit. In a standard pension insurance scheme, employees who have reached the statutory retirement age and completed the required contributory years are entitled to periodical (monthly) pension benefits, while employees who have met only one of the two conditions are entitled to a lump-sum payment. These benefits cannot be withdrawn in advance, and insurance premiums already contributed cannot be returned. Farmers who have jobs in urban

Table 3.2   Workers' pension insurance coverage, by type of urban enterprise, China, 1995

Type of enterprise	Active employees		Retired employees	
	Number (thousands)	Coverage (per cent)	Number (thousands)	Coverage (per cent)
State-owned	76 000	93.4	22 300	83.9
Urban collective	30 000	45.7	5 700	75.4
Others	29 400	8.2	720	34.7

Source: Based on data from *China Labour Statistical Yearbook 1996* (Ministry of Labour, 1996).

areas are very mobile and their employment is unstable. If standard pension insurance rules were applied to them, both employing units and employees would consider that they were unfairly subsidizing "city dwellers", while the farmers would not be entitled to any real benefits. For this reason, sectors such as coal mining and construction and areas like Shenzhen and other coastal cities employing large numbers of rural workers have begun to adopt a flexible measure which differs from the standard pension insurance scheme. Rural workers leaving the enterprise or the city are paid a lump sum equal to between 60 and 70 per cent of the total insurance premium contributed by the farmers and the employers. For farm workers who find jobs in another city, the insurance premium is transferred there. For farm workers who return to rural areas, the insurance premium is transferred to the insurance management organizations operating in that particular area, if they exist.

The *first* measure for self-employed workers in urban areas has been to use the local average wage as the basis for determining their contribution. These workers usually consist of own-account workers in household enterprises and in small partnership enterprises. It is stipulated in the "Plan for Coverage of Basic Pension Insurance" issued by the Ministry of Labour in 1995 that the local average wage of employees can be taken as the base number for contributions for the self-employed in urban areas. This technical measure has saved a great deal of work for social insurance management organizations in checking and determining the income of the self-employed, and simplified the procedure for them to participate in social insurance.

A *second* measure should be to adopt a policy of low contribution rates and pension benefits. According to the new unified pension scheme, basic pension benefits will be equal to 50 to 60 per cent of the wage income of employees, and the total contribution rate (for both employing units and employees) will be 17 to 18 per cent of the total payroll. At present, basic pension benefits for enterprise retirees are between 70 and 80 per cent of the wage income of employees. It needs a transitional period of several decades to reduce pension benefits to the lower target level. Since there are already 30 million retired enterprise employees, there is a need for extra contributions on top of the 17 to 18 per cent of total payroll, resulting in a total contribution rate of about 24 to 25 per cent.

A *third* measure could be to allow different contribution rates and pension benefits for the self-employed. It is stipulated in the "Plan for Coverage of Basic Pension Insurance" that the contribution rate for the self-employed "should not be higher" than the sum of the rate for employing units and the rate for employees in enterprises, which implies that it could be lower. Measures allowing for the difference have been taken in some cities. Starting from the day when the self-employed participate in pension insurance, an individual account equal to 11 per cent of the employee's own wage will be established according to the provisions of the new scheme. When the 6 to 7 per cent for paying basic pension benefits is added, the total rate will be 17 to 18 per cent. Pension benefits will also be adapted according to the level of the contributions paid.

3.2 Pension insurance in rural areas

Apart from the cooperative medical care system, the social pension insurance scheme is another important component of the social security system in rural areas. At present, the social pension insurance scheme in rural areas is organized by the Government, with voluntary participation from farmers. Farmers themselves are the main source of contributions to the insurance premium, in addition to subsidies from the collective economy. The State offers policy support. A mechanism of accumulation based on self-contribution and mutual aid is established to protect the basic livelihood of farmers when they grow old.

In 1991 China started to establish the social pension insurance scheme gradually in rural areas. With the implementation of the output-linked household responsibility system in rural areas after 1978, constant readjustments were made to the production structure, production became more specialized, socialized and geared to the market, and farmers were faced with higher risks in their production activities. Moreover, the family planning policy in rural areas weakened the function of family protection. The traditional protection system based on the collective economy no longer suited the needs in economic and social development in rural areas. As a result of rural economic development, farmers in many areas became rich, and most farmers had enough food and clothing. The growth rate of agriculture after the 1980s was maintained at 4.1 per cent, while the growth rate of the average per capita income of farmers stayed at 4.5 per cent. A sound environment and necessary conditions were created in rural areas for conducting social pension insurance based on self-accumulation. In May 1991, the central Government summed up the experience gained by rural grass-roots initiatives in social protection, formulated the "Basic Scheme for Social Pension Insurance in Rural Areas" and started massive testing. Great progress was made in the five subsequent years. By the end of 1995, 1,600 counties in 28 provinces, autonomous regions and municipalities had launched the movement, more than 60 million rural residents participated in the insurance, and a fund of over 6 billion yuan had been accumulated. Governments of 200 counties (cities or districts) formulated the "Methods for Social Pension Insurance in Rural Areas" (Ministry of Civil Affairs, 1995b) and started to establish a management system linking up governments at the provincial, city, county, township and village levels. Operating and management procedures have been standardized, the insurance fund has increased its value as required, and the scheme has shown a great potential for development.

Rural pension insurance mainly operates in the following ways:

(1) Social pension insurance in rural areas is intended for farmers with no registered urban residence. Farmers themselves contribute most of the insurance premiums, in addition to subsidies from the collective economy, while the State provides policy support. This principle underlies rural social pension insurance. In the relationship among farmers, the collective economy and the State, the contribution made by farmers accounts for more than half of the total amount. Villages or township and village enterprises of participating farmers and employees provide some subsidies according to their financial capacity, and the proportion of subsidies should not be more than 50 per cent. Policy support from the State mainly includes pre-tax payment of insurance premiums in township and village enterprises whose employees have participated in pension insurance, and tax exemption on the value added gained from operation of the insurance fund.

(2) Individual accounts are used in rural pension insurance to achieve accumulation. The contributions made by farmers themselves and subsidies provided by the collective economy are put into the individual accounts. The rate of pension benefits is determined by the accumulated total amount in each individual's account and by the relevant regulations.

(3) The insurance fund is now both regulated and managed at the county level; it will be regulated at the county level but managed at different levels in future. The system of overall responsibility by government leaders in charge is established. The fund supervisory committee – composed of relevant government departments and representatives of insured farmers and communities – supervises and monitors the operation of the insurance fund to ensure the maintenance and increase of its value. The State has stipulated

that the rural social pension insurance fund should increase at 12 per cent per year. The reform process in the financial, taxation, banking and investment systems is still under way in China. Since the financial market is not yet fully developed, and to avoid investment risks, the rural pension insurance fund is mainly used to buy state bonds, make bank deposits, or maintain or increase asset values through banking institutions, but only for the transition period. Prolonged use of this method would not help spread risks and develop diversified investment structures. Efforts are being made to find a solution, the general concept being to invest the assets of the insurance fund in the market, carrying out careful management of the investment to attain the target of spreading risks, developing rational investment structures and reaping maximum value increase.

(4) Management of rural social pension insurance is carried out by a top-down chain of government agencies. Central Government established the Rural Social Insurance Department in the Ministry of Civil Affairs to provide guidance in administrative affairs, and the Rural Social Pension Insurance Management and Service Centre (a separate institution) to advise on insurance fund management. Provinces (autonomous regions and municipalities), prefectures (cities at the prefectural level) and counties (cities at the county level and districts) have also set up such units in their departments (bureaux) of civil affairs. Units at the county level deal with the day-to-day business of insurance fund management as well as value maintenance and increase. Pension insurance stations have been set up in townships and towns to collect insurance premiums and pay pension benefits. Work is being undertaken to conduct management through a computer network. When rural residents move to other regions, their individual accounts will be transferred with them.

Employment injury insurance for TVEs

Employment injuries and occupational diseases are the biggest labour risks for employees in township and village enterprises, as the incidence of industrial accidents in TVEs is much higher than in urban enterprises. This is closely related to factors such as backward technologies and processes, poor labour protection, lack of experience among managers and lack of formal training among workers. Thus, the implementation of a compulsory employment injury scheme for employees in TVEs should be a high priority. In August 1996, the Ministry of Labour issued "Methods for Trial Implementation of Employment Injury Insurance for Employees in Enterprises" (Ministry of Labour, 1997), which stipulates that the employment injury scheme should be implemented in all enterprises, including TVEs. This means that TVEs can no longer "settle the matter privately" by paying injured or sick employees a certain amount of compensation, let alone sign contracts with employees that include a provision according to which workers themselves should be fully responsible for injuries and deaths. Full employment injury insurance contributions are made by employing units at an average of 1 per cent of the total payroll. In sectors with higher incidence of employment injuries and occupational diseases – such as the mining, chemical and construction industries – the rate is higher. The rate is readjusted each year within a maximum range of 40 per cent, according to the occurrence of employment injury cases. Payments from employment injury insurance include employment injury benefit, medical care cost, disability benefit and survivor benefit.

Most employees in township and village enterprises are farmers. Their pension insurance and medical insurance schemes are different from the schemes for urban enterprises. The pension insurance scheme is based on voluntary participation, and its fund mainly consists of individual deposits. Their medical insurance scheme is part of the cooperative medical care system being implemented in rural areas (see section 2).

4. Conclusions

In this concluding section, we shall concentrate on measures to extend the coverage of social security protection in China, examining the main obstacles to extension policies, reviewing opportunities to extend coverage to non-public enterprises, and emphasizing the importance of coordination as well as the roles of trade unions and NGOs.

4.1 Main obstacles

According to the Ninth Five-Year Plan for National Economic and Social Development (1996–2000), it is an important task to establish a multi-tiered social security system consisting of social insurance schemes, social assistance pro- grammes and social welfare that is compatible with China's national conditions. The analysis carried out in this chapter shows that – based on practice and inter- national experience – China has already established the basic framework for a social security system, which needs further development and improvement (Hu, 1997).

This chapter has also shown that extending the coverage of social security and providing basic social protection for all represents a huge, complicated and difficult task. Various governments and the international community have become increasingly concerned about the poverty problem besetting developing countries. They have given all kinds of support to efforts to alleviate poverty. As the factors causing poverty are many-sided, measures and methods of poverty alleviation should also represent a variety of actions. However, if poverty still exists after every possible poverty-alleviation measure has been taken, governments should provide poor people with basic social protection through the social security system. It is one of the functions governments should perform to protect people's basic rights to work and subsistence. According to this view, the social security system is the last line of defence in the field of poverty alleviation and also an indicator of social civilization and development.

Poor awareness of social insurance. China has long been operating under a planned economy system, within which – at least before the 1980s – there was virtually no place for non-public enterprises in urban areas. Since the implementation of the reform and the opening-up policy, the number of employees in non-public enterprises and the informal sector has increased rapidly. As these changes have taken place in the course of 10 to 15 years, these sectors are all characterized by a relatively young workforce. Because of this, most young employees do not realize that they should make preparations for protecting their basic livelihood in case they become unfit for work. Even if a few employees do realize, they usually protect themselves through saving, and they remain unaware that they can protect their basic livelihood in old age through social pension insurance. Their relative youth also means that they are not often ill and they feel in no hurry to participate in health insurance. When employment injuries or occupational diseases occur in township and village enterprises (TVEs), neither owners nor workers are familiar with the concept of insurance; instead, they use the method of "settling the matter privately" by paying the injured or sick workers a certain amount of compensation.

Unstable employment. In the course of industrialization and urbanization, large numbers of Chinese farmers have found jobs in urban areas. The number of former farm workers who are employees in the formal sector alone has reached 30 million. They are concentrated in mining, construction, electronics and light industry, especially in coastal areas and major cities. However, very few of them have worked in a particular city for more than 10 years, and most of them have labour contracts for a duration of 3 to 5 years. Upon termination of labour contracts, they return to rural areas or go and find jobs in other cities. Unstable employment complicates the operation of social insurance schemes, such as pensions, that are based on long-term insurance contributions.

Income fluctuation and diversification. The income of the urban self-employed fluctuates greatly. Owing to factors such as the macroeconomic environment, seasonal variations and individual investment decisions, they can sometimes enjoy high incomes, while at other times they may lose part of their capital and investments. One part of their income derives from assets while the other part may originate from labour income, and it is hard to distinguish between the two. Their income is partly used for consumption and partly for new investment, and again the proportion of each can vary greatly. Thus, it is difficult to establish the monthly labour income of the urban self-employed that can serve as a base for collecting insurance premiums.

High contribution rate. The formal sector contribution rate for the pension insurance fund is more than 20 per cent of the total payroll. The reason behind this high contribution rate is the rapid change in the ratio between active and retired employees[2] in recent years. Around 30 active employees financed one retired employee in 1978, but this ratio fell to 4.5:1 in 1995 (see table 3.3). In enterprises covered by the pension insurance system, the ratio between active and retired employees is as low as 3.9:1.

As noted earlier, the relatively young urban self-employed would consider that a contribution of 20 per cent of the total payroll was far too high a price for entitlement to pension benefits they would receive several decades later. They would rather save individually in order to protect their basic livelihood in old age. However, such a protection mechanism is far from reliable. If their savings are inadequate and they become poor in old age, the Government will still have to give them assistance.

High management cost. There are 43,000 staff in social insurance organizations (unemployment insurance organizations not included) in China. They manage schemes for pension, medical, employment injury and maternity insurance covering 110 million active and retired employees in more than 800,000 employing units in formal sectors. On average, each professional has to collect insurance premiums in nearly 20 employing units. In informal sectors, employees in private enterprises and the urban self-employed amount to 20.5 million. Although the total amount is only one-fifth of the amount in formal sectors, they are scattered in nearly 9 million employing units, mostly with fewer than five employees per unit. Ensuring the coverage of so many scattered employees by the social security scheme will vastly increase the workload of social insurance organizations.

4.2 Extending coverage to non-public enterprises

Non-public enterprises, which are mainly foreign-funded or private enterprises, are not very keen to participate in social insurance. They are worried about possible labour cost increases and lower profits. Some local government officials also fear that compulsory participation in social insurance would

---

[2] Here active employees include employees in state-owned enterprises, collective urban enterprises and other forms of ownership of economic units such as foreign investment enterprises, shareholding enterprises and joint management enterprises in urban areas.

Table 3.3 Ratio of active employees to each retired employee, China, 1979–95

1979	16.7	1985	7.5	1991	6.0
1980	12.8	1986	6.9	1992	5.7
1981	11.5	1987	6.7	1993	5.4
1982	10.1	1988	6.4	1994	5.1
1983	8.9	1989	6.2	1995	4.8
1984	8.0	1990	6.1		

Source: *China Labour Statistical Yearbook 1995* (Ministry of Labour, 1995).

worsen the investment climate, with the result that they often yield to pressure from non-public enterprises. The following measures should be taken to deal with the problem.

(i) *Take the law as the legal basis.* It is stipulated in Article 2 of the Labour Law (Ministry of Labour, 1997) that the law applies to all enterprises and employees within the boundaries of the People's Republic of China, while social insurance (mentioned in Chapter IX of the law) has the same scope of application. This is the legal basis for compulsory implementation of pension insurance. Payment of the pension insurance premium is a social obligation that all categories of enterprises should perform, and it does not represent an additional financial burden. The wages of employees in non-public enterprises are relatively high, thus enterprises that are really worried about labour cost increases might reduce the wage costs of employees and use the balance on social insurance premiums. The investment climate will be improved by the implementation of a legal system with equal rights and obligations for all categories of enterprises and by efforts to ensure the functioning of a unified labour market by local governments.

(ii) *Raise the employees' awareness of their social protection rights.* Employees in non-public enterprises know little about their right to social protection, and efforts should be made to raise their awareness. After introducing individual accounts in pension insurance, employees would lose their right to social protection or receive lower pension benefits if enterprises contribute nothing or relatively smaller insurance premiums for pensions. This should be made known to employees so that they can urge enterprises to participate in pension insurance soon and make timely and full contributions of insurance premiums.

(iii) *Adopt flexible policy measures.* Compared with public enterprises, employees in non-public enterprises are relatively young. Contributions to the pension insurance fund at more than 20 per cent of the total payroll would indeed be a heavy financial burden for them. As most employees in non-public enterprises will be entitled to pension benefits only after several decades, the contribution rate can be determined by the target replacement rate of around 60 per cent. For example, the total rate could be somewhere around 17 per cent, in which the rate for employees would be 3 per cent and the rate for enterprises around 14 per cent. The rate for employees can then gradually increase to 8 per cent, with a corresponding decrease in the contribution rate for enterprises. In this way, non-public enterprises will have the financial capacity to make the contribution. The difference between the contribution rates will not be permanent, so that the rate for non-public enterprises will finally be the same as for public enterprises. Non-public enterprises may have to increase their contribution rate, but it is more likely that public enterprises will be able to reduce their contribution rates in line with their decreasing pension benefits.

4.3 The importance of coordination

The Chinese Government should strengthen leadership and coordination in social security work, define division of work between various departments, and promote and improve social security legislation. Relevant central government departments should be responsible for managing the social security system as a whole, for formulating implementation plans and measures, as well as for guiding and supervising social security work in local areas. Local governments should formulate social security development programmes and action plans in line with the overall policies and local conditions, and must mobilize human, material and financial resources to carry out relevant plans and attain desired objectives.

In China, the Government's social security policies and plans are mainly formulated by the Ministry of Labour and Social Security and the Ministry of Civil Affairs. The Ministry of Labour and Social Security is in charge of preparing social insurance policies and plans for all active employees in urban areas, as well as all retired employees and unemployed people who were once employees in enterprises. It is also responsible for developing social insurance policies and plans for civil servants in administrative agencies and employees in institutions. The Ministry of Civil Affairs is in charge of social security including social relief in rural areas, as well as social welfare for urban residents. In formulating social security policies and plans, other related ministries and commissions of the State Council such as the State Planning Commission, the State Commission for Restructuring the Economic System, the Ministry of Finance and the Ministry of Public Health also play an important role. Moreover, non-governmental organizations such as the All-China Federation of Trade Unions and the China National Women's Federation also participate in the work.

In cities and towns, social insurance for all workers except civil servants is managed by the labour administration departments. Special agencies (departments, divisions and sections) in the labour administration departments have the task of formulating regulations and polices related to social insurance and supervising their implementation. (Owing to its peculiar features, unemployment insurance is usually the responsibility of the employment agencies in labour administration departments.) Moreover, local governments have usually set up social insurance management bureaux, social insurance fund management bureaux or similar institutions to take care of the collection and management of insurance premiums as well as the payment of insurance benefits. The level of activity and efficiency of the labour insurance administrative system is a key factor for extending the coverage of the social insurance schemes.

In rural areas, civil affairs departments at all levels are responsible for social security, including social insurance and social assistance.

The most basic and most effective organizations to take charge of the management of schemes for the self-employed are industry and commerce administrations or taxation departments. In many cities, social insurance organizations ask such institutions to collect social insurance premiums at the same time as industrial and commercial charges or taxes. This practice has both raised the efficiency and reduced the cost of insurance premium collection.

4.4 The role of trade unions and NGOs

Extending the coverage of social insurance is a very difficult task, which should be taken on not only by governments but also by trade unions and NGOs.

Trade unions have already done much work in this area. For example, Mutual Assistance Supplementary Insurance for Employees is a type of insurance launched by local organizations of the All-China Federation of Trade Unions. It provides material help through special organizations, beyond statutory social insurance benefits, for employees who encounter special financial difficulties because of old age, sickness, death, injury or disability. By the end of 1993, more than 40,000 trade union bodies established various forms of supplementary insurance, covering more than 12 million employees. Some of them are trade union organizations in enterprises and industrial sectors while others are at the provincial, city or county level. In addition, the fund for the "Relief-sending Project" intended for "employees in financial difficulties" in some enterprises with poor economic performance has been established by 21 trade union organizations at the provincial level, more than 200 at the city level and more than 1,000 at the district or county level. The total amount of the fund has reached more than 1 billion yuan. The project is becoming a regular, institutionalized and socialized practice.

In the improvement of the social security system and in the alleviation of poverty, employers' organizations are also playing an indispensable role. In the final analysis, poverty alleviation depends on the overall development of the economy and the rapid growth of productive forces in all trades and professions. It also depends on the constant improvement of the social security system through a concerted effort of the social partners.

Non-governmental organizations are also playing an important role in poverty alleviation. The China National Women's Federation is the biggest non-governmental organization in China. For many years, the Federation has contributed greatly to safeguarding the rights and interests of women and children, promoting the employment and occupational development of women workers, protecting women in maternity and helping women to shake off poverty.

References

Han Liangcheng; Shi Mingcai. 1995. *Practical manual on China's social security reform* [in Chinese]. (Beijing, China Metrology Publishing House).

Hu, A. 1997. "Reforming China's social security system: Facts and perspectives", in *International Social Security Review* (Geneva, International Social Security Association), Vol. 50, No. 3, pp.45–65.

Ministry of Civil Affairs. 1995a. *Exploring and establishing a scheme for a minimum livelihood protection line in urban areas* (Beijing).

Ministry of Civil Affairs, Rural Social Insurance Department. 1995b. *Reports on basic schemes of social pension insurance in rural areas* (Beijing).

Ministry of Labour. 1995. *China Labour Statistical Yearbook 1995* (Beijing, China Statistical Publishing House).

—. 1996. *China Labour Statistical Yearbook 1996* (Beijing, China Statistical Publishing House).

Ministry of Labour, Law and Policy Department. 1997. *Compilation of relevant regulations of the Labour Law* (Beijing, China Statistical Publishing House).

Ministry of Public Health, 1997. *Building socialist health enterprises with Chinese characteristics* (Beijing, People's Health Publishing).

State Commission for Restructuring the Economic System. 1995. *Reform of the social security system* (Beijing, China Reform Publishing House).

State Statistical Bureau. 1996. *China Statistical Yearbook 1996* (Beijing, China Statistical Publishing House).

EXTENSION OF FORMAL SOCIAL SECURITY SCHEMES IN THE UNITED REPUBLIC OF TANZANIA

4

Peter Kamuzora, Lecturer, Institute of Development Studies, University of Dar es Salaam

The country's statutory social security schemes have mainly targeted wage workers in the formal sectors – both private and public – leaving the majority of workers without social security coverage. Can these statutory schemes extend their activities to cover more workers in the formal sectors as well as workers in agriculture and the informal sector? What are the obstacles to the extension of formal social security schemes, and how can these be overcome?

This chapter focuses on the National Social Security Fund (NSSF), known until 1998 as the National Provident Fund (NPF), the largest formal social security scheme in the country. Two main sources of information are the basis for the analysis contained in this chapter.

The first is the Dar es Salaam Informal Sector Survey conducted in 1995 within the context of the ILO's Interdepartmental Project on the Urban Informal Sector (United Republic of Tanzania, Planning Commission and Ministry of Labour, 1995). The second source is a survey carried out in 1997 among managers and workers of four formal sector companies, which was conducted especially for this study, the aim of which was to gather information on the National Provident Fund. The size of enterprises and nature of activities were taken into account when the selection of companies was made, drawing from both the industrial and services sectors and from small, medium and relatively large enterprises. The selected enterprises are Tanzania Distilleries Limited (TDL), Tanganyika Textiles Industries (TTI), IPP Media, and Tanzania-Zambia Railway Authority (TZR). All of them are based in Dar es Salaam, the capital and the largest city in the United Republic of Tanzania. Tanzanian employment figures for 1995 show that 707,646 workers were employed in the formal sector. Out of these, 122,343 employees were employed in Dar es Salaam, representing almost one-fifth of the capital's total employment. The private sector in Dar es Salaam, which was the target of this survey, employs 68,068 persons. A sample for this survey was drawn from Dar es Salaam's private sector employees. Owing to resource and time constraints, only 103 workers participated in this survey.

A questionnaire with semi-structured and open-ended questions was used to interview the workers (Appendix 1). In addition, eight managers from the companies studied and four key informants from organizations involved in the designing and implementing social security schemes (Appendix 2) were interviewed using interview schedules.

This chapter is divided into five sections. The first reviews the existing statutory and private social security arrangements; the second examines the social protection needs of Tanzanian workers; section 3 discusses obstacles to the extension of formal social security schemes; section 4 looks at possibilities for reform of statutory social security schemes; and section 5 provides conclusions.

1. Existing social security arrangements

There are two types of social security protection systems in the country – the formal statutory social security schemes and the privately organized schemes. One of the remarkable features of these systems is their limitation in terms of coverage. Hence the objective of protecting all socially vulnerable groups in Tanzanian society has yet to be achieved, but this is not unique in the African context. In most African countries, about 90 per cent of the population are not covered by any formal social security scheme, while in the developed countries this percentage is about 20 per cent (Jenkins, 1993).

1.1 The statutory social security schemes

Before 1964, the only formal social security scheme was the non-contributory pension scheme for senior civil servants. In 1964 a new scheme, the National Provident Fund, was established as a department within the Ministry of Labour, in 1975 it was transformed into a parastatal, and now it has become the NSSF. Several other social security schemes were established in later years covering different categories of workers.

There are now five social security institutions – the National Social Security Fund (NSSF) mainly covers the private sector as well as workers in central Government and the parastatal sector who do not come under the Government or Parastatal Pension Schemes; the Parastatal Pension Fund (PPF), established in 1978, protects all parastatal sector employees; the Local Authorities Provident Fund (LAPF), includes all local government employees; the Government Fund, comprising the Pensions Department and the Government Employees' Provident Fund (GEPF), covers different categories of central government employees; and the National Insurance Corporation (NIC), a state insurance organization, manages occupational pension and provident schemes organized by individual companies.

The NPF is the largest formal scheme, providing insurance to all private sector employees and non-pensionable workers in the parastatals and the civil service. In June 1996, formal sector employment was estimated at 906,500 workers, and the NPF alone covered slightly over 60 per cent of them. The importance of the NPF in terms of insured persons is brought out by the survey carried out for this study. As the NPF is a compulsory scheme, all respondents (i.e. 100 per cent) were NPF members and were registered into the scheme by their employers. However, 906,500 workers, or only 3 per cent of the Tanzanian population are covered directly, indicating the relatively low status of social security protection and its narrow coverage. The large majority of the 2.4 million inhabitants of Dar es Salaam depend on the informal or agricultural sectors and are therefore not covered by any formal social security scheme.

1.2 Private social security arrangements

Since the precolonial period the Tanzanian population has depended on traditional social systems to meet their social security needs (Baker, 1988). However, with socio-economic change, the traditional social security systems have gradually been replaced (Bossert, 1988) by private social security arrangements. The latter are mainly mutual aid schemes or collective arrangements set up by people to provide social protection for themselves (Madihi, 1995). However, it must be borne in mind that these different kinds of arrangements are not exclusively for the informal sector labour force, but are also extended to people not necessarily participating in informal sector activities.

The 1995 Dar es Salaam Informal Sector Survey distinguishes three categories of informal social security schemes, the first of which is commonly known as "UPATU" – which simply means a "rotating savings and credit group." Under this arrangement, group members regularly pay a fixed sum and, after a certain period, the fund total is given to one member, and then the sequence is repeated for each member, in turn. There are many rotating savings and credit groups, mainly found among urban communities. Their organizational structures are rudimentary and founded on mutual understanding among the group members. The head of the group is usually elected, to ensure that contributions are collected and that the planned rotation of the lump sum is implemented.

The second category represent groups that are organized along cooperative principles. The country has 906 Savings and Credit Cooperatives (SACCOs): 440 cooperatives for formal sector workers and 466 for the informal sector. Under this arrangement, members make contributions to the cooperative's fund, which provides loans that may be used for meeting children's education and health care. Under a different type of cooperative agreement, group members pay a fixed sum into a common fund that is used for contingencies. For example, the group fund may be used to finance part of the expenses incurred in a variety of social ceremonies, particularly marriages and funerals. In some instances, members may be asked to make contributions to such ceremonies in kind, for example food or labour. In order to generate more money for the group, part of the fund is sometimes invested in a business venture. Unlike UPATUs, groups in this category have a constitution and clear organizational structures, with an elected chairperson, secretary and treasurer to manage the scheme.

The third category is that of social protection schemes established by NGOs, self-help organizations or producers' co-operatives. These are formally organized with elaborate structures and leaderships.

Coverage of the workforce by private social security arrangements is not that much higher than that by statutory social security schemes (see table 4.1). The vast majority of the respondents (84.6 per cent) were not covered by any of the abovementioned private social security schemes.

1.3 Nature of social security benefits

Both the formal and the private social security schemes offer two categories of benefits – main and subsidiary benefits. The main benefits category includes old age, invalidity and survivorship, whereas the subsidiary benefits category consists of withdrawal, maternity, marriage and emigration. Some schemes deal with one category only, but others offer benefits from both. The main benefits are mostly offered by pension-based schemes. The NPF, which was the largest Tanzanian social security institution, offered both categories of benefits. Employers usually offer employment injury benefits under the Workmen's Compensation Ordinance and medical care benefits under the Employment Ordinance and other state regulations.

Some informal sector operators insure themselves with private sector companies. As shown by table 4.2, there is a considerable variety of benefits available to informal sector workers, but the rate of coverage is very low. The majority of the respondents (high percentages) indicated that they were not covered. The old-age pension is the most popular benefit, mentioned by nearly half the respondents.

Private social security arrangements provide a wide range of benefits. Out of 222,915 operators who took part in the 1995 Dar es Salaam informal sector survey, 34,284 participated in such arrangements. One-sixth of respondents were covered by the medical care-sickness/injury benefit while five-sixths indicated

Table 4.1 Coverage of the workforce by private social security arrangements, Dar es Salaam, 1995 (percentages)

Scheme	Coverage
Rotating savings and credit groups (UPATU)	13.2
Savings and credit cooperatives (SACCO)	0.8
NGO protection	1.4
None	84.6

Source: 1995 Dar es Salaam Informal Sector Survey data.

Table 4.2 Coverage of informal sector operators by private sector insurance benefits, Dar es Salaam, 1995 (percentages)

Scheme	Covered	Not covered
Medicare-sickness/injury	24.5	75.5
Medicare-maternity	3.7	96.3
Sickness/injury	19.5	80.5
Invalidity	5.8	94.2
Old-age pension	44.5	55.5
Funeral costs	15.2	84.8
Survivors' benefit	2.5	97.5
Maternity benefit	8.7	91.2
Education for family members	5.2	94.8
House insurance	8.3	91.7
Car insurance	10.8	89.2
Third party liability	26.5	73.5
Other	1.1	98.9

Source: 1995 Dar es Salaam Informal Sector Survey data.

that they were not (see table 4.3). Similar proportions were mentioned for the medicare-maternity benefit. Relatively high coverage percentages (more than 20 per cent) were reported by funeral costs, house insurance and survivors' benefits.

However, the benefits provided have serious defects. These defects are reflected in two important respects. First, the benefits are narrow in scope – the social security schemes are not comprehensive enough to address the wide range of social protection needs of the population. Secondly, by their nature, the benefits lack a

Table 4.3 Coverage of informal sector operators by private social security
arrangements, Dar es Salaam, 1995 (percentages)

Type of benefit	Covered	Not covered
Medicare-sickness/injury	15.4	84.6
Medicare-maternity	14.9	85.1
Sickness/injury	11.2	88.8
Invalidity	10.4	89.6
Old-age pension	14.2	85.7
Funeral costs	35.9	64.1
Survivors' benefit	20.5	79.4
Maternity benefit	6.5	93.5
Education for family members	18	82
House insurance	32.9	67.1
Car insurance	12.1	87.9

Source: 1995 Dar es Salaam Informal Sector Survey data.

mechanism for promotion of effective social security protection. The majority of
the statutory schemes in the United Republic of Tanzania have been provident
funds (i.e. NPF, LAPF, GEPF) based on compulsory individual saving. As a means
of providing protection against contingencies such as old age, disability and death,
provident funds are inherently deficient. This is due to the fact that provident funds
do not provide adequately for retirement. The benefit system is based on a lump-
sum payment rather than on periodic benefits. This payment bears little or no
relation to need, and inflation is likely to erode its value, leaving members without
adequate resources throughout the retirement period.

Moreover, since workers have various needs which may not be taken care of
by any social security provision, the lump-sum payment is likely to be spent on
current needs instead of saving it for the intended contingency. Many workers
use savings from the provident fund for current needs such as housing, purchase
of equipment or education (Fultz, 1996). This point is well demonstrated by the
expenditure patterns of the NPF where, under the withdrawal benefit
arrangement, a large proportion of the provident fund was withdrawn by workers
to meet their current needs. During the 1994/95 period, T.sh. 1,442 million
(accounting for 74 per cent of expenditures on small benefits) were withdrawn
from the NPF (ILO, 1996).

In addition, in the case of contingencies such as employment injury and
maternity, Tanzanian social security schemes use the single employer liability

technique. This approach is outdated, its weakness being that an individual employer is exclusively liable for providing the required protection, with no risk sharing, as under social insurance arrangements. This may become a heavy burden for some employers, and creates a situation whereby such employers may evade their responsibilities and leave workers without protection.

1.4 Sources of contribution

Operations of all social security schemes, formal and private, are based on the principle that their members will pay a prescribed contribution to the scheme. That is why groups with regular incomes are targeted by most schemes. Contributions are obtained from both employees and employers in Tanzanian formal social security schemes, and are usually prescribed by legislation. In private schemes, members are obliged to make contributions to the scheme in order for it to operate. Depending on the nature of the schemes, contributions could be in the form of cash or in kind (food, labour).

However, there are problems associated with contributions for social security which weaken the whole idea of social security provision in the Tanzanian context. The main problem relates to the wage levels upon which contributions for formal schemes are based. Wage levels in the United Republic are so low that social security deductions adversely affect workers' incomes. The deductions reduce the amount of resources at the workers' disposal to support themselves and their families. In fact, one of the reasons for the delay in implementing the newly designed health insurance scheme by the Ministry of Health is the currently low wage levels. This factor makes the scheme unviable and practically unfeasible to implement. The Ministry of Health is hoping that the present civil service reform will raise wage levels, arguing that pay rises are the precondition for the scheme to take off.

2. The social protection needs of workers

In the survey of the four Dar es Salaam formal sector enterprises, the majority of respondents indicated that social security provision should be given high priority on the government's social development agenda. Respondents were required to indicate the social security benefits they needed most. The most needed benefit is medical care, which was mentioned by a third of the respondents (see table 4.4), while the next priority is education for children, which was mentioned by around one-sixth. Subsidies for families with children, and employment injury benefits were mentioned by, respectively, 12.2 and 10.6 per cent of the respondents.

Table 4.4   Social protection needs of workers in four companies, Dar es Salaam, 1997

Most needed benefit (mentioned as 1st, 2nd or 3rd priority)	Company									
	Tanzania Distilleries Ltd. (TDL)		Tanganyika Textiles Industries (TTI)		IPP Media		Tanzania-Zambia Railway (TZR)		Total	
	Resp.	%	Resp.	%	Resp.	%	Resp.	%	Resp.	%
Medical care	26	35.6	9	27.3	23	31.1	20	20.6	78	28.6
Education for children	12	16.4	4	12.1	11	14.9	15	15.5	42	15.2
Subsidies for children	6	8.2	4	12.1	12	16.2	12	12.4	34	12.3
Employment injury	10	13.7	1	3.0	8	10.8	14	14.4	33	11.9
Unemployment	8	10.9	1	3.0	6	8.1	12	12.4	27	9.7
Survivorship	2	2.7	1	3.0	8	10.8	13	13.4	24	8.7
Invalidity	5	6.8	0	0.0	5	6.8	11	11.3	21	7.6
Maternity	4	5.4	0	0.0	1	1.4	0	0.0	5	1.8
Old age	0	0.0	5	15.2	0	0.0	0	0.0	5	1.8
Housing	0	0.0	5	15.2	0	0.0	0	0.0	5	1.8
Funeral	0	0.0	2	6.0	0	0.0	0	0.0	2	0.7
Loan	0	0.0	1	3.0	0	0.0	0	0.0	1	0.4

Resp. = number of respondents
Source: Field data.

In the 1995 survey, informal sector operators were asked whether they would be interested to join social protection schemes, which was indeed the case for the majority of them (see table 4.5). The proportion showing an interest in joining such schemes ranges from half those working in the transport sector to over nine-tenths of those in the finance, insurance and real estate sector.

Informal sector operators who participated in social protection schemes and those who were interested in joining such schemes were then asked to rank the three social security benefits they would need most. The medicare-sickness/injury benefit came out as a clear priority among the benefits desired by informal sector operators; it was ranked number one by three-fifths of respondents (see table 4.6). Old-age pension was second on the general priority list, with a quarter giving it the first ranking for the second priority. Education for family members was mentioned by 38.0 per cent of the respondents as priority number three. This pattern of priorities is roughly the same for respondents of different age, sex and economic activity. Moreover, there does not seem to be much difference either between the priorities of formal and informal sector workers. In both cases medical care featured as priority benefit number one, with education for children as priority number two.

Table 4.5 Percentage of informal sector operators interested in joining social protection schemes, Dar es Salaam, 1995

Sector	Interested	Not interested
Agriculture and livestock	73.4	26.5
Mining and quarrying	56.3	43.7
Manufacturing	59.8	40.1
Construction	62.9	37.1
Trade, restaurant and hotel	58.0	42.0
Transport	52.0	48.0
Finance, insurance and real estate	92.7	7.3
Commerce and personal services	61.4	38.6

Source: 1995 Dar es Salaam Informal Sector Survey data.

3. Obstacles to extension of formal social security schemes

It has always been assumed that with economic development the majority of the labour force would end up in formal sector employment. But experience in many developing and also developed countries has shown the contrary. The trend is that more and more workers are found outside the formal sectors in less secure employment such as self-employment, domestic work and casual employment. As a result, they are inadequately covered by the existing social security provisions.

In principle, social security can be provided to workers outside formal sectors through three major means: self-financed social insurance schemes, social assistance, and the extension and reform of formal social security schemes (van Ginneken, 1996). This section will concentrate on the third means, to investigate whether and how formal social security schemes can be reformed and extended so as to cover more formal sector workers, and to begin coverage of informal sector workers and their dependants. The focus of this section is on obstacles identified at the time of writing to the extension of the NPF, the largest social security scheme in the country, some of which have been resolved subsequently in establishing the NSSF.

3.1 Policy and legal obstacles to extension

At the policy and legal levels certain constraints needed to be overcome at the highest level of policymaking within the Government. At the policy level for example, there was no clear vision as to how the NPF could be further extended,

Table 4.6 Desired benefits for informal sector operators, Dar es Salaam, 1995

Type of desired benefit	Priority 1		Priority 2		Priority 3	
	Per cent	Rank	Per cent	Rank	Per cent	Rank
Medicare-sickness/injury	62.4	1	8.4	5	0.3	8
Medicare-maternity	6.3	3	0.1	10	0.1	10
Sick/injury benefits	5.6	5	15.0	3	2.0	7
Invalidity benefits	5.7	4	12.3	4	4.5	6
Old-age pension	9.3	2	26.7	1	12.0	4
Funeral costs	3.7	7	24.0	2	23.8	2
Survivors' benefits	0.7	9	7.6	6	12.8	3
Maternity benefits	0.1	10	2.3	8	6.2	5
Education for family	1.6	8	3.3	7	38.0	1
Do not know	4.6	6	0.3	9	0.3	9

Source: 1995 Dar es Salaam Informal Sector Survey data.

as demonstrated when in December 1996 the Government announced its decision to convert the NPF into a comprehensive social security scheme. In the opening speech by the Minister for Labour and Youth, and in the round-table paper presented by the Director-General of NPF, it was explicitly stated that the proposed new social security scheme will "widen coverage to include other sectors, particularly the informal economic sector and the agricultural sector." This should have been good news for informal sector workers. But both statements also echoed the concern that this policy objective would be difficult to achieve.

At the practical level the NPF scheme was funded by both employers' and employees' contributions – a procedure that cannot be operationalized for informal sector workers. Thus, the issue at stake is not that informal sector workers should not pay contributions; it is the nature of informal sector workers' incomes and the modalities of paying contributions that need to be considered at policy level. No firm decision had been made on this issue at the time of writing. A policy clarification has therefore yet to be made on how the objective of extending coverage to the informal sector can be achieved.

Legal obstacles still also limit the extension of formal social security schemes coverage. About three-quarters of 165 countries with social security programmes have legal provisions which exclude many workers from the purview of social security provision (Bailey and van Ginneken, 1998). In the United Republic of Tanzania, the self-employed, casual wage workers, seasonal workers and domestic workers, who form the large majority of employees, are not legally entitled to any social security arrangements.

3.2 Unreliability of informal sector income: A constraint to extension

Most categories of informal sector workers have *unreliable sources of income*, as is clearly demonstrated in three aspects. First, most informal sector employment is unpredictable and irregular. Casual and seasonal wage employment, for example, depends on the availability of jobs in specific periods. When there is no work, employment is immediately terminated, hence incomes lost. Irregularity of informal sector employment makes it unreliable as a source of income. Secondly, the findings of the 1995 Dar es Salaam Informal Sector Survey indicate that supplementary income opportunities from which contributions could be made for financing social security provision are not dependable. Table 4.7 provides data on such opportunities, and it shows that the large majority of respondents have very few supplementary income opportunities. To take on a job as an apprentice is one of the worst alternatives – such work is often not remunerated, because apprentices are supposed to receive training on the job.

Thirdly, the sources of funding upon which informal sector workers depend to deal with contingencies are basically unsound. Information was collected within the 1995 Dar es Salaam informal sector survey on how informal sector operators would finance long-term sickness and large medical expenses. Table 4.8 shows that for large medical expenses, four-fifths of the respondents mentioned that they would raise money to meet those costs through their own family savings and assistance from relatives. The same is true for the financing of long-term sickness; 97.8 and 56.8 per cent of the respondents would raise funds through family support or assistance and own savings, respectively. A relatively small number of respondents, 7.2 per cent in the case of large medical expenses and 13.6 for long-term sickness cost, indicated that they would not be able to raise such funding. So, for major contingencies, the majority of informal sector workers rely on their own savings and on social assistance, particularly from relatives. It is highly questionable whether either source of funding for social security is reliable. With regard to family savings, there may be many other competing demands. As for social assistance, its importance or effectiveness depends on the courtesy and ability of relatives to contribute something out of their pockets.

The respondents were also requested to indicate what kind of provisions they had made for old age. Around two-fifths of the respondents had acquired land as a form of security for old age, whereas 30.8 per cent of the respondents had made savings for old age. Land may not be a reliable means to sustain an elderly person

Table 4.7 Supplementary income opportunities for categories of informal sector
workers, Dar es Salaam, 1995 (percentages)

Supplementary income opportunities	Categories of informal sector workers					
	Paid employment			Apprentice		Total
	Permanent	Temporary	Casual	Paid	Unpaid	
Wage job (private sector)	3.0	1.4	4.4	4.6	0.0	2.7
Wage job (government)	1.4	0.0	0.0	0.0	0.0	0.3
Wage job (domestic)	0.7	0.0	4.3	0.0	0.0	1.0
Self-employment (non-agriculture)	9.3	1.4	11.5	10.8	0.0	6.6
Self-employment (agriculture)	0.6	0.0	3.9	58.1	0.0	0.9
Household member support	20.1	34.8	36.9	0.0	10.8	32.1
Rent/savings	4.5	0.0	1.0	0.0	0.0	1.1
Social assistance	0.6	0.0	0.0	0.0	29.7	6.1
Remittance/alimony	0.0	1.2	0.0	0.0	0.0	0.1

Source: 1995 Dar es Salaam Informal Sector Survey data.

unless some funding is made available to turn it into a productive investment for future
income generation. We have already seen the limitation of own savings as a source
of social security funding. One-fifth of respondents had a house for rent as a provision
for old age, which may be a reliable source of income particularly when the flow of
rent is not interrupted. As two-thirds of respondents had made land or savings provisions for old age, it is safe to conclude that the majority of informal sector operators
had not made reliable provisions to take care of the old-age contingency.

It is, therefore, important to recognize that the income base for informal sector
workers is shaky and unreliable, and this must be taken into account when social
protection schemes are designed for them. However, not all categories of informal
sector workers are trapped in this situation. As noted later, statutory social security
schemes could be extended to informal sector employees with regular incomes.

3.3 Organizational obstacles

The *lack of a viable organizational structure* within the informal sector is a major
constraint against extension. Much of the informal sector is not well organized,
for two main reasons. First, the majority of informal sector employees are found

Table 4.8 How informal sector operators would fund large medical expenses and
long-term sickness and how they provide for old age, Dar es Salaam,
1995 (percentages)

Alternative sources of funding	Large medical expenses	Long-term sickness funding	Provision made	Old age
Own family savings	80.5	56.8	Acquisition of land	38.1
Relatives' assistance	79.9	97.8	Savings	30.8
Loan	9.6	—	House for rent	19.3
Unable to finance	7.2	13.6	Children's education	6.9
Funds (UPATU, SACCO)	1.0	0.5	Life insurance	2.1
Sale of property	1.0	4.6	Acquisition of livestock	1.1
Pawn shop/broker	0.6	—	Others	1.7
Cooperative assistance	0.4	—		
Support from charity/NGO	0.4	—		
Social scheme/insurance	0.1	0.3		
Renting of property	—	3.3		
Employment and retire	—	2.6		
Take up other job	—	0.3		
Other	0.4	1.4		

Source: 1995 Dar es Salaam Informal Sector Survey data.

in unregistered business enterprises. Information about the nature of informal
sector enterprises and their trade union status was sought in the Dar es Salaam
Informal Sector Survey of 1995, which indicates that less than 10 per cent of
informal sector enterprises are registered. Unregistered business enterprises are
not legally recognized, and are construed to be unreliable or short-lived. This
makes it very difficult for formal social security schemes to do business with
informal organizations. Secondly, the majority of employees are not unionized.
In some cases workers organize themselves around trade unions which take
responsibility for social protection arrangements for their members. The 1995
survey shows that less than 1 per cent of informal sector employees is unionized.
This means that informal sector employees are not in a position to utilize trade
union organization structures for social security purposes.

3.4 Obstacle of poor mobilization

A fourth obstacle – on the part of NPF staff – was a *lack of initiative to mobilize
more members* to register with the scheme. It appeared that the NPF still had a good

image as a social security institution. In the survey among the four enterprises, the majority of respondents were of the opinion that the NPF was a useful organization. The attitude and perception of respondents towards it was measured by ranking the level of respondents' satisfaction with the NPF scheme. Two-thirds of the 103 respondents said that the NPF was good or satisfactory, while only 4.9 per cent said that NPF was a very good scheme and 27.2 per cent said it was bad. We can conclude that the NPF still maintained a good image. When those who were satisfied with the NPF scheme were asked why they thought so, all of them said it was due to the fact that NPF offered terminal or retirement benefits. Thus the NPF was clearly seen as very useful for security in old age.

However, the NPF had not taken advantage of this strength to recruit more members for the scheme. Little effort had been made by NPF staff to go out and recruit more workers into the scheme. In the survey mentioned above, almost all respondents indicated that they had not been visited by an NPF inspector. Moreover, one of the weaknesses pointed out by the respondents was that – at least in 1997 – the NPF did not have a programme for educating, informing and creating awareness among workers about NPF services. This comment is supported by the findings shown in table 4.9, which reports the main reasons why informal sector operators did not become NPF members.

The table shows that 29.5 per cent of respondents did not know why they were not NPF members. However, it seems the majority of the respondents were ignorant of the NPF scheme. For example, a relatively large number of respondents (21.9 per cent) indicated that they were not entitled to join the scheme, 12.3 per cent were not obliged to and 2.5 per cent mentioned that they had not joined the NPF due to fear of taxation. It is interesting to note from the table that 2.9 per cent of the respondents felt that they had not joined the NPF because NPF officials had not come to register them into the scheme. One of the NPF officials, who was interviewed on this afterwards, commented that there had been lack of adequate personnel to run the scheme. For quite a long time the NPF scheme had been managed by poorly motivated and inexperienced staff with few if any qualifications.

The majority of company managers interviewed observed that many of the NPF's operations were not well known to workers and that the NPF could improve its image by educating and sensitizing workers about its usefulness and the benefits it offered.

4. Three areas for reform

Given the various obstacles identified in the previous section, most of which remain valid for the NSSF, the Government needs to focus on three areas to reform social security systems in the country.

Table 4.9   Main reasons why informal sector workers did not join the NPF scheme,
Dar es Salaam, 1995 (percentages)

Reason	Percentage
Not obliged	12.3
Not entitled	21.9
Officials haven't come	2.9
Too high contributions	12.6
Not attractive	2.0
Fear of taxation	2.5
Covered by relatives	1.1
Covered by other schemes	1.0
No need for protection	4.7
Other	9.3
Do not know	29.5
Not stated	0.2

Source: 1995 Dar es Salaam Informal Sector Survey data.

1. Policy and legal reforms are inevitable to back up the required necessary changes. As noted in the previous section, the Government needs to state clearly which groups or categories of formal and informal sector workers will be covered, and what policy and legal measures would be adopted to ensure that these workers are covered. Such policy clarification would include a statement about how the Government would assist private initiatives aimed at mobilizing and organizing workers for social security protection.

   Related to this is the need for legal reforms. As noted in the previous section, various legal provisions exclude many workers from social security provisions. Labour protection legislation therefore needs to be reviewed in the context of social policy-makers having recognized that all different categories of workers need social protection.

2. Special policies should also be developed for the relatively small numbers of informal sector workers who are well organized and whose incomes of workers are more or less stable. Enterprises belonging to this category need to be identified and NSSF social security provision extended to them. Since the NPF has now been converted into a comprehensive social security scheme, special benefit schemes can be created to deal with such organized groups in the informal sector. In other words, the NSSF should work out exactly how to cover

such groups taking into account their special circumstances. Studies therefore have to be conducted to generate information about the socio-economic characteristics and viability of these groups. A social insurance scheme could be designed for these groups and financed by workers themselves. The NSSF could be involved in designing and running such schemes.

The less-organized groups of the informal sector pose a special problem and cannot be dealt with by the NSSF. A different approach is required to cover such groups. Two options are open for the development of new forms of social security for them. The first, minimum social assistance by the Government (Guhan, 1994), may prove difficult to implement because tax-financed social assistance has been declining, but this option should not be discarded altogether. The Government could look into the possibility of providing assistance using resources that it now spends on social security for the formal sector. For example, the Government could make social security funding for the informal sector available by withdrawing its current support (which is in the form of direct government contributions and tax exemption on workers' and employers' contributions) to the formal sector.

The second option is self-organization of the informal sector itself (Kiwara and Heijnis, 1997). In this respect, informal sector workers should be encouraged and assisted to join or form social organizations such as self-help associations and cooperatives on a local basis. A number of organizations of that nature have been formed in both urban and rural areas. For example, in Dar es Salaam city, self-organized health insurance schemes such as UMASIDA now exist, which are reviewed in Chapter 5. These schemes have an important role to play in Tanzanian social security provision, as they tend to focus on members' needs. Moreover, they are owned by the members themselves, and the cost of running them is likely to be lower than when each member would be expected to devote his/her time to the schemes (Kiwara, 1997). These private or self-help initiatives can be strengthened and popularized through government social policy.

Non-governmental organizations (NGOs) interested in social security should also be encouraged and mobilized by the Government to assist and bolster the initiatives already made to protect informal sector workers. This has happened elsewhere, in certain developing countries. As explained in Chapter 2, NGOs in India have played a major role in mobilizing people for social protection and assisting in the design of social protection schemes.

3. It is vital to reform the operations of the NSSF for it to play a lead role in social security provision in the United Republic of Tanzania. Table 4.10 shows the changes that were recommended for NPF improvement. According to this table, reform was particularly needed in three important areas:

(a) Benefit payment procedures need to be streamlined so as to shorten the period involved in claiming benefits and eliminate excessive bureaucracy in benefits payment procedures. In the past, NPF decision-making was overcentralized, with decisions about benefits payments being made in Dar es Salaam. This created delays of more than 9 months. Now the system is being decentralized so that benefits payment decisions are made by the regional headquarters. Authority to process and pay benefits had already been decentralized to 11 regions at the time of writing. Nevertheless, there remains considerable scope for further reducing the period between the claiming and the paying of benefits.

(b) Record-keeping needs to be improved and statements of account must to be sent to members regularly. The NSSF authorities should maintain a system whereby information about all aspects of the scheme is collected, processed, analysed, well stored and shared with its members. They have already begun to address this problem. When it was recognized that record-keeping was poor, computer facilities were installed in 1991 and the process of updating information about members was initiated. This was implemented in the first phase of computerization of the NPF system. Improvement in record-keeping as well as information collection and processing was planned in the second phase of computerization, in which the operations of the regional directorates were to be computerized as well. The planned improvement became possible after the recruitment of qualified staff, particularly graduates, who could administer the scheme operations. However, accurate record-keeping and information dissemination systems have to be reviewed and strengthened.

(c) NSSF scheme members need to be visited to solve problems related to social security. As noted earlier, respondents from both the formal and informal sectors indicated that NPF officials did not go out to visit workplaces to meet members. Visits would not only create an opportunity to understand and address the problems faced by members, but could also be used as one way of disseminating information about NSSF operations.

5. Conclusion

This chapter has shown that the United Republic of Tanzania needs to develop a comprehensive policy on social protection. A situational analysis of Tanzanian social security systems has indicated a number of limitations. The first is that a relatively small proportion of the population is covered by statutory social security schemes, mainly consisting of formal sector workers. The majority of workers in agriculture and in the informal sector are not covered. The second limitation was that the scope of the schemes did not go beyond terminal benefits,

Table 4.10   Improvements in NPF schemes suggested by formal sector workers,
Dar es Salaam, 1997 (percentages)

Area to be improved	Tanzania Distilleries Ltd	Tanganyika Textiles Industries	IPP Media	Tanzania-Zambia Railway Authority	Total
Shorten benefit payment period	18.2	12.1	25.0	16.3	17.8
Send statements to members	13.4	18.2	15.4	13.3	14.1
Improve record-keeping	10.9	15.2	11.5	11.2	11.5
Raise benefits payment levels	9.8	21.2	9.6	7.1	10.0
Visit members and solve problems	9.8	9.1	15.3	9.2	10.4
Eliminate bureaucracy in benefits payment	15.9	0.0	5.8	5.1	7.8
Advance loans to members	2.4	15.2	0.0	9.2	5.9
Extend benefit coverage	0.0	0.0	0.0	15.3	5.6
Consider inflation in benefit payment	7.3	0.0	3.8	4.1	4.5
Deal with employers not remitting contributions	0.0	6.0	1.9	9.2	4.5
Pay lump sum rather than instalments	4.8	3.0	3.8	1.0	2.9
Decentralize the NPF system	3.7	0.0	1.9	2.0	2.2
Make NPF membership voluntary	2.4	0.0	3.8	1.0	1.9
Let members become NPF shareholders	0.0	0.0	1.9	0.0	0.4
Remove taxation on contributions	1.2	0.0	0.0	0.0	0.4
Total	100.0	100.0	100.0	100.0	100.0

Source: Field data.

but with the establishment of the NSSF, the benefit package will be extended to maternity, work injury and health-care benefits. Fragmentation is another shortcoming of Tanzanian social security systems. Social security provision is administered by a number of institutions which are not coordinated. This makes it difficult to adopt a coherent national policy for social security.

This chapter has also demonstrated that different groups of workers may have different social protection needs. The Government has to reform its social security system further in order to meet this variety of needs. However, a number of obstacles prevent formal social security schemes from extending coverage to different categories of workers. There are, first of all, policy and legal obstacles. Although the Government has begun to reform its social security systems, it is not clear how informal sector workers will be taken on board by social security institutions. Labour protective legislation should also be modified since it excludes certain categories of workers, particularly temporary and casual employees, from social security provision.

The second issue is that sources of income at the disposal of informal sector workers are often unreliable. Statutory social security schemes would usually like to operate with groups that have relatively stable incomes. The third obstacle is that informal sector workers lack a viable organizational structure through which social security can be provided to them. Fourth, there had been a lack of initiative on the part of the NPF (which was the focus of this study) to mobilize more members into the scheme. It appears little has been done so far to disseminate information about the existence and operations of social security schemes such as the NSSF.

Finally, this chapter has attempted to indicate areas for reform, so as to permit social security schemes to extend their services to more workers in the formal sector and to informal sector workers. It has been proposed that reform should focus on policy and legislation for social security. The Government and the NSSF should state clearly which categories of workers are to be covered by social security schemes and how this can be achieved. The policy reform should particularly focus on those categories of workers presently not covered by current schemes. There is also a need to review labour protection laws so that different categories of workers are taken into consideration in social security provision.

It was also proposed that the NSSF should create special benefits for different categories of uncovered workers in the formal sector and organized groups in the informal sector. For unorganized groups from the informal sector, a different approach is needed. Workers in this category should be encouraged to join or form self-help associations or cooperatives. The Government should assist them in this regard, and encourage the development of a social security system which takes into account the social and economic circumstances of these groups. Since self-help organizations and cooperatives exist and a process of mobilizing them for social security has been initiated, the Government should build on this experience and strengthen these organizations. This could be done by providing them with not only financial support but also technical assistance. The Government should mobilize NGOs to come forward and initiate social protection pro- grammes for the informal sector.

The operations of the NSSF scheme need to be reformed as well. Since it has been converted into a comprehensive social security scheme, many of the bottle- necks identified by this study have been addressed. However, this study has put more emphasis on two aspects in relation to reform. These include the establish- ment of an information management system that should gather and disseminate information about NSSF operations, as well as the further decentralization of decision-making to streamline benefits claims and payment systems.

References

Bailey, C.; van Ginneken, W. 1998. *Extending personal coverage of pensions* (Geneva, ILO Social Security Department), mimeograph.

Baker, A. 1988. "Traditional social security as practised in contemporary Tanzania's urban centres", in Benda-Beckmann et al., 1988.

Benda-Beckmann, F.; Benda-Beckmann, K.; Casino, E.; Hirtz, F.; Woodman, G.; Zacher, H. (eds.). 1988. *Between kinship and the State: Social security and law in developing countries* (Dordrecht, Foris Publications).

Bossert, A. 1988. "Formal and informal social security: a case study of Tanzania", in Benda-Beckmann et al., 1988.

Fultz, E. 1996. *Report to the Government on the development of social security in Tanzania: Overview of ILO recommendations*, paper presented at the National Provident Fund Round-Table Consultations on the Development of Social Security in Tanzania, 17–18 December (Arusha).

van Ginneken, W. 1995. *Health protection for the informal sector: Pilot projects for Dar es Salaam,* paper for the ILO INTERDEP Programme Advisory Committee (Dar es Salaam).

van Ginneken, W. 1996. *Social security for the informal sector: Issues, options and tasks ahead* (Geneva, ILO).

Guhan, S. 1994. "Social security options for developing countries", in *International Labour Review* (Geneva, ILO), Vol. 133, No. 1, pp. 35–53.

ILO. 1996. *Tanzania: Report to the Government on the Development of Social Security: Review of policy recommendations* (Geneva, ILO/UNDP/Tanzania/R.15).

Jenkins, M. 1993. "Extending social protection to the entire population: Problems and issues" in *International Social Security Review* (Geneva, ISSA), Vol. 46, No. 2, pp. 3–20.

Kaare, S. 1994. "Social security system in Tanzania: A quest for change" in *The IFM Journal of Finance Management* (Dar es Salaam, Dar es Salaam University Press), Vol. 3, No. 1, pp. 107–121.

Kiwara, A.; Heijnis, F. 1997. "Health insurance for informal sector workers: Feasibility study on Arusha and Mbeya" in van Ginneken, W. (ed.) *Social security for the informal sector: Investigating the feasibility of pilot projects in Benin, India, El Salvador and Tanzania*, Issues in Social Protection Discussion Paper No. 5 (Geneva, ILO).

Kiwara, A. 1997. *UMASIDA Backup Report, June to December 1996* (Dar es Salaam).

Madihi, M. (1995) "Social protection in the informal sector" in United Republic of Tanzania, Planning Commission and Ministry of Labour and Youth Development, 1995.

Mkulo, M. 1996. *The introduction of a comprehensive social security scheme in Tanzania*, paper presented at the National Provident Fund Round-table Consultations on the Development of Social Security in Tanzania, 17–18 December.

United Republic of Tanzania. 1995. *Central Register of Establishments* (Dar es Salaam).

United Republic of Tanzania, Planning Commission and Ministry of Labour. 1993. *Labour Force Survey 1990/91* (Dar es Salaam).

United Republic of Tanzania, Planning Commission and Ministry of Labour and Youth Development. 1995. *Dar es Salaam Informal Sector Survey, 1995,* Vol. 1: Analysis and Tabulations, Report prepared with assistance from ILO/UNDP and SIDA (Dar es Salaam).

Appendix 1: Questionnaire for the 1995 Dar es Salaam Informal Sector Survey

The 1995 Dar es Salaam Informal Sector Survey focused on both statutory and private social protection schemes covering the informal sector workforce. The operators, i.e. the owners of informal sector businesses, were interviewed on various aspects relating to social protection schemes for themselves and their employees. They were specifically asked to respond to the following: (1) whether they were covered by any of the statutory social security schemes; (2) if not covered by statutory schemes, which private social security arrangements they were participating in; (3) which benefits were under private social security arrangements; (4) whether they were interested in joining social protection schemes established by an NGO, self-help organization or cooperative; (5) which benefits they would like to be provided by a social protection scheme, and how much they would be able to pay for such a scheme; (6) how they would raise money if they had to make a large medical expense or pay for a funeral now; (7) whether they had already made provisions for old age after retiring from employment, and which provisions they had made; and (8) what sources of income they would have in case of disability or long-term sickness.

Appendix 2: Questionnaire for formal sector workers

In this survey, workers were asked to respond to the questions about social protection in general and NPF operations in particular. On social protection in general, the questions centred around whether they were covered by any social security scheme; the type of scheme they participated in; what reasons they had if they were not covered by any social security scheme; and the types of social security benefits they needed most.

The questions on the NPF scheme operations were divided into five topics: (1) satisfaction with these operations; (2) regular contact with the NPF through statements of account periodically sent to workers or through visits by NPF staff; (3) merits and shortcomings of the NPF scheme; (4) length of time involved and the kind of problems faced by workers in claiming benefits; and (5) improvement of the NPF scheme and measures required to effect such improvement.

Interview schedule for company managers

The company managers were asked to report on the kinds of problems workers faced under the NPF scheme: whether they thought there were weaknesses in the NPF; the length of time involved in claiming benefits; whether they would continue to participate in the NPF scheme if it was made voluntary; and whether they thought changes were needed to improve NPF benefits.

Interview schedule for designers and implementers of social security schemes

The designers and implementers of social security schemes were asked to comment on the following topics: shortcomings of the existing social security arrangements; how these shortcomings are perceived; the kind of changes being proposed to improve the schemes; and the obstacles likely to be encountered during implementation of the proposed changes.

HEALTH INSURANCE FOR THE INFORMAL SECTOR IN THE UNITED REPUBLIC OF TANZANIA

5

Angwara Denis Kiwara, Director, Institute of Development Studies, Muhimbili University College of Health Sciences, Dar es Salaam

During the 1980s, the Tanzanian economy, and consequently, the Government, went through a very difficult period. As a result, few resources were available for financing the social sector, and the health service was hit hardest. Between 1980 and 1989, health's share of the total budget was reduced from 7 per cent to 3.4 per cent (Meghji, 1996; Kiwara, 1993). These budgetary cuts have led to low quality services and a shortage of drugs and diagnostic equipment. The poorer working environment has had a strong demoralizing effect on workers, while the referral system has practically come to a standstill (Meghji, 1996).

To overcome the increasing shortfalls in finance for the health sector, the Government has introduced cost sharing, and also lifted the ban on private practice in the country (Ministry of Health, 1996a). Private finances have re-established private hospitals, but accessibility is still poor due to the high fees charged. The most affected people are the unemployed and those in the informal sector whose incomes are irregular and marginal. Since these two groups form the country's majority, one of the key measures of the efficiency of the health sector is in terms of the number of people served. There are ongoing attempts to improve accessibility for marginalized groups, in the form of mutual health insurance systems for those outside the formal sector.

This chapter will first examine the key trends in health, poverty and social security coverage, and this is followed by a section on improving access to basic health services. The third section covers the promotion of self-financed health insurance, while the fourth provides some concluding remarks.

1. Poverty, health and social security coverage

At independence in 1961, the country inherited an economic structure that grossly neglected the social welfare of the African population. Within the social

117

sector, the Government introduced the policy of "Mtu ni Afya" (Man is Health), aimed at increasing mass awareness of the importance of health care and at galvanizing community efforts towards the provision of health-care services. As a result of these efforts, rural health centres and district and regional hospitals were constructed, and training institutions for health workers were established. The overall outcome was a marked improvement in the provision of health services. Within 15 years of independence 95 per cent of the population was within 10 kms. of a health-care facility (Maliyamkono and Bagachwa, 1990).

In education the policy of Universal Primary Education (UPE) to promote primary education, and adult education programmes to promote functional literacy throughout the adult population, were introduced. Among the products of these initiatives was the rapid increase in the educational infrastructure and of primary and secondary school graduates. The country was able to achieve a literacy rate of 80 per cent in the late 1970s.

Though the above and other efforts produced positive gains in the eradication of poverty, they were soon eroded by the economic crises of the late 1970s and early 1980s. Today the problem of poverty persists in rural and urban areas, and is getting worse.

1.1 Trends in poverty and health indicators

Poverty in the United Republic of Tanzania is evident in various forms in the daily life of the people, of which the basic level of income is an important measure. Estimates show that the minimum income required to satisfy the basic needs of an adult per month is equivalent to Tanzanian shillings (T.sh.) 46,173 (1996), and that about 70 per cent of the rural population as well as about 50 per cent of the urban population live below the poverty line (Msambichaka et al., 1997). The situation is not likely to change in the near future, because the economy has grown at a dismal 4 per cent per year since the mid 1980s, a rate of growth insufficient to generate adequate income levels for meeting basic needs.

Nutritional intake is another powerful measure of poverty. Studies by the Tanzania Food and Nutrition Centre (1995) have shown that 2,000 calories per day represents the minimum requirement. About 60 per cent of the population has a daily intake of less than 2,000 calories, resulting in a high rate of malnutrition for everyone and, in particular, for children. About 60 per cent of all the under-five children in the country are underweight. Life expectancy at birth is only 52 years, compared to 67 years in other developing countries and 77 years in the developed countries. Infant mortality rate is 92 per 1,000 live births compared to seven in developed countries. The under-five mortality rate is 141, while maternal mortality stands at 200–400 per 100,000 live births, compared to, respectively, nine and six in the developed countries.

A substantial part of the population is illiterate, as continuing budget cuts have seriously eroded the quality of the education system, and a once well-run adult education system has also been weakened. The literacy rate is about 59 per cent among poor people, while the national average stands at 68 per cent. Women have been more adversely affected than men, with illiteracy at 65 per cent compared to 53 per cent for men. This situation reflects a stark contrast with that of the 1970s (Ministry of National Education, 1992).

Poverty is also reflected in the unavailability of basic necessities such as water and health services, with the former, for the majority of Tanzanians, not being within easy reach. Only about 11 per cent of households have water services to their door; about 32 per cent have to walk for up to 15 minutes in order to reach a water source, and the remaining 57 per cent have to spend up to three hours to bring water back home (Msambichaka et al., 1997).

The health sector provides an even clearer reflection of poverty in the country. Current budget levels are down to 50 per cent of their levels in the late 1970s and the early 1980s. The physician/population ratio is 1:24,000 compared to 1:960 in Qatar (Sivard, 1992). All government health-care units are perennially short of drugs and diagnostic equipment. Maintenance of the health sector infrastructure is inadequate.

Lack of a reliable transport infrastructure also shows the extent of poverty in the country, a factor with far-reaching implications on how people travel, on the transportation of goods and services and on the delivery of inputs to rural areas. Lack of storage facilities at household and community level for agricultural output compels farmers to sell their produce early on in the season when prices are usually low. Because of the storage problem, households are unable to store sufficient food for the year and cannot stockpile enough inputs for the coming farming season. Food processing facilities are virtually non-existent in food-producing areas.

The problem of unemployment is also a reflection of poverty, particularly for youth, with unemployment rates as high as 70 to 80 per cent (Kiwara, 1997). This is due to the inability of the economy to stimulate self-employment opportunities for the growing population, but it is also due to the inability of the rural areas to retain young people after their graduation from primary education.

All these factors have contributed to Tanzania's ranking among the ten poorest countries in the world, and consequently, the country's informal sector also as being one of the poorest. The country's capacity to reduce poverty, therefore, is indeed limited. While long-term plans for poverty reduction are underway, basic needs like health care cannot wait.

Table 5.1 Trends in poverty and health indicators, United Republic of Tanzania, 1980–1995

Indicator	1980	1985	1991	1995	Remarks
Per capita income (in US$)	254	308	110	95	Declining
Infant mortality rate (per 1 000)	122	117	115	112	Marginal improvement
Primary school gross enrolment (%)	93	72	63	58	Declining
Access to water supply (%)	47	45	40	37	Declining
Literacy rate (%)	73	68	65	60	Declining
Average calorific intake (daily)	2 244	2 229	2 206	2 100	Declining
Life expectancy at birth (years)	47	50	51	48	Declining

Sources: WHO, 1995, pp. 101–109; UNICEF, 1990, pp. 83–89.

1.2 Coverage by existing social security arrangements

A formalized social security system has not so far been established for the majority of Tanzanians, except for employees in the public and formal private sector. However, since more than 85 per cent of the country's population is in the informal sector or engaged in subsistence agriculture, these groups are not covered by this system. This reality makes it difficult for a formalized social security system – in the western sense – to function. Irregular and low incomes, as well as the lack of an administrative infrastructure, are among the more immediate obstacles to a general social security system, although there are various – formal and informal – social security arrangements in place that will be reviewed briefly below.

Indigenous social security

Indigenous social security has existed in the United Republic of Tanzania for many years, and it "covers" the majority of the population; it is based on cultural norms which encourage mutual protection in family/clan set-ups. This system has ensured that orphans, widows, the elderly, the disabled and those hit by natural calamities such as fire, floods, etc. are supported by the community. Orphans are cared for by relatives, and the elderly remain with their families throughout their lives. Victims of natural calamities are also assisted by their relatives, with help often being in kind or material assistance, with an attempt to minimize the impact of damages sustained.

With the advent of "civilization", however, the typical rural setting has been eroding fast due to urbanization (growth rates of up to 8 per cent per year). The emergence of an urban working population and other social changes have altered age-old cultures and norms substantially. In the past, the elderly were taken care of by their children, but nowadays the children are often away and employed in town. Every year they visit their parents in the rural areas, and those who can afford it hire personnel to take care of elderly parents. In some atypical cases the elderly move to stay with their children in the towns. In general, urban retirees have more problems than the rural elderly.

The lack of formalized social security schemes is becoming more serious as the urban worker population ages. The number of retirees is increasing rapidly in the United Republic of Tanzania, with the average life expectancy after retirement at about five years. Soon after retirement a substantial number of workers suffer hypertension, diabetes, alcoholism or depression (Diyamet, 1996). These diseases are, by and large, precipitated by socio-economic insecurity. Retirees are indeed caught at a crossroads; they don't fit in the informal indigenous social security, nor do they have formalized social protection.

Provident funds for the formal sector

One would expect that retirees covered by provident funds would be better off than the unemployed rural elderly. However, this is not necessarily the case because

(i)   rather than periodic benefits, provident funds provide lump-sum payments which are often spent at once and not used for the envisaged contingencies.

(ii)   payments are not related to needs and are adversely affected by inflation.

Other problems with provident funds are that they are institutionally based, and answerable to a government ministry. The National Social Security Fund (NSSF), for example, is answerable to the Ministry of Labour and Youth Development. It mainly covers the private sector and employees in the central Government and the parastatal sector who are not covered by the government or parastatal pension schemes. Other funds with similar problems are the Parastatal Pensions Fund, the Local Authority Provident Fund, the Pensions Department and the Government Employees' Provident Fund. There are also companies with individual occupational and pension/provident schemes managed by the National Insurance Corporation. As noted earlier, all these schemes exclude 85 per cent of the country's population who are engaged in the informal sector or subsistence agriculture.

Social assistance programmes

In the absence of a comprehensive social security system, social assistance programmes – funded by the Government, donors and non-governmental organizations (NGOs) – have assumed an important role in alleviating social insecurity. The Government tends to become involved only at times of major disaster (floods, epidemics, large-scale fires, drought or refugee influxes). So, these interventions are usually one-time involvements and are responses to an immediate problem. How much help is given is entirely dependent on the financial ability of the Government at times of crisis – and it has a very poor performance record in this area, as floods and fires have caused substantial loss of life and prolonged suffering.

In the area of social welfare, the Ministry of Labour is charged with the responsibility of assisting children from broken marriages, divorcees, street children, the elderly and the mentally handicapped. The social welfare department has an infrastructure in place, but no funds. For the year 1995/96, for example, it received only 15 per cent of its proposed total budget from the Government (Ministry of Labour and Youth, 1997).

The other major players in the social assistance programmes are donors and the NGOs, which include religious bodies. These have ongoing activities, which target certain social needs, concentrate on special groups such as AIDS orphans, the blind, the deaf or children who are mentally retarded. They are often branches of larger international NGOs that are funded from outside the country, and include CARITAS–Tanzania, Red Cross Tanzania, the Islamic Africa Relief Fund, etc. The percentage of the population covered by them is very small.

Mutual social security arrangements

For the past ten years the Government has worked hard to free itself of as many welfare-oriented activities as possible. This has prompted people to establish mutual benefit societies, some of which have taken off successfully, while others have not. The majority of these societies concentrate on critical needs such as health and credit facilities. Good examples of health schemes are UMASIDA and the Igunga Community Fund, which will be reviewed in section 3.

The future of social security schemes

There are substantial gaps in Tanzanian social security coverage, as is the case in most other poor developing countries (Shaw and Griffin, 1995). The majority of the population is unemployed; incomes are irregular and very low, preventing regular contributions to social security systems.

Government policies pursued since independence constitute another reason for the gaps in social security coverage. For the past 30 years the United Republic of Tanzania has attempted to establish a socialist society, with a universal welfare state. The vision of "each receiving according to one's needs" confused a primary need with an unattainable ideal. The State became the universal provider, thereby thwarting any alternative initiatives.

Since the 1980s, the Government has introduced structural reforms so as to become a market economy, but without any comprehensive plan for social security. It was only recently that discussions aiming at the conversion of the National Provident Fund led to the establishment of the comprehensive National Social Security Fund. Delineating the scale of the proposed scheme, Sebastian Kinyondo, the Minister for Labour and Youth Development, said during the first conversion discussions:

"We cannot do everything at once or wholesale. The introduction of the new scheme will be in phases as follows:-

(i)   Pension scheme comprising of old-age, invalidity and survivors' benefits; and funeral grant.
(ii)   Employment injury scheme.
(iii) Health insurance scheme and maternity benefit." (Kinyondo, 1996)

These – as well as previous – plans to convert the NPF into a comprehensive scheme have excluded the informal sector. As regards inclusion of the informal sector in the proposed social security scheme, the Director of the National Provident Fund observed the following (Mkulo, 1996):

"The persons to be covered would be all members of the new scheme and their health insurance will be extended to other categories of employees in the formal sector and possibly the informal sector in organized groups..."

This position represents an encouragement for the informal sector to forge ahead with its own organization of mutual benefit societies, while plans for comprehensive social security schemes are underway.

2.   Declining access to basic health services

The structural adjustment measures in the 1980s and 1990s led to sharply declining public health expenditure and access to basic curative health services. The few development resources available to the Government are mainly spent on preventive and promotive health programmes.

2.1 Declining public health expenditure

The public health sector is mainly financed by the Government through budgetary allocations. The central Government – through the Prime Minister's Office (PMO) – finances regional health services, i.e. regional and district hospitals. The MOH finances special hospitals, consultant hospitals and national programmes. The Ministry of Local Government and Cooperatives (MOL) finances curative and preventive services at the district level other than those provided in hospitals. Local governments usually supplement the above budgets. International donors – the major ones being UNICEF and DANIDA – participate in financing national programmes through the MOH. NGOs also finance some hospitals, health centres, dispensaries and special regional and district programmes. Table 5.2 summarizes the trends in government expenditure for selected years in the pre-reform and post-reform period.

Recurrent expenditure has been on the rise since 1970, when it was 89.5 per cent of the public health budget; by 1980 it reached 90.5 per cent, and in 1992 it reached a record high of 97 per cent when all development projects were frozen.

It should be noted that most development expenditure does not appear in the government budget, as it is mostly donor (aid) financed. This trend is not a viable long-term solution to the development of the sector, because if aid were to stop, a standstill in the sector would unfavourably affect the economy and the government budget. Development projects in the health sector would involve, among other things, the construction of new health facilities (hospitals, dispensaries, rural health centres) and training institutions (nursing schools, training schools for Rural Medical Aids, etc.), the acquisition of new medical equipment, the spread and improvement of preventive services, and an increase in the volume and quality of hospital services. There is evidence of an increased allocation of development resources for preventive services (see table 5.3).

Government efforts to combat disease and improve the health situation of society are being exerted through various programmes. These include the Essential Drugs Programme (EDP), the Expanded Programme on Immunization (EPI), Maternal and Child Health (MCH), the AIDS Control Programme (ACP), the Family Planning Unit (FPU), School Health in Primary Schools (SHPS), the Control of Diarrhoea Diseases (CDD), the Tuberculosis and Leprosy Control Programme, Mental Health, etc. They are designed to make available essential drugs to the rural areas and the informal sector, to immunize children against six killer diseases (measles, tetanus, whooping cough, diphtheria, tuberculosis and polio), to provide basic health education and assistance to mothers and children, to fight malaria and AIDS, and to educate the population on family planning. The purpose of all these programmes is to reduce mortality rates, regulate population growth and curb the prevalence of preventable diseases in communities of all

Table 5.2   Public health expenditure, United Republic of Tanzania, 1970/71–1993/94

Year	Public health expenditure (million T.sh.)	Real public health expenditure (millions of 1970/71 T.sh.)	Health as a % of public expenditure	Public health expenditure per capita	
				Nominal (T.sh.)	Real (1970/71 T.sh.)
1970/71	152	152	6.2	11.5	11.5
.....					
1974/75	426	149	6.1	28.4	19.1
.....					
1978/79	688	274	5.3	40.4	16.1
.....					
1982/83	983	165	5.1	51.1	8.5
.....					
1984/85	1 329	129	4.8	64.8	6.3
.....					
1987/88	3 074	131	4.0	136.0	5.8
1988/89	5 509	416	5.0	238.0	18
1989/90	6 532	393	4.6	272.2	17.2
.....					
1991/92	7 316	393	3.5	299.8	12.8
1992/93	9 764	401	2.8	389.0	15.9
1993/94	11 681	457	2.2	418.2	12.2

Sources: Ministry of Planning, 1980, 1988 and 1994; Ministry of Health 1996b.
...... indicates break in series.

Table 5.3   Allocation of development expenditure, United Republic of Tanzania, 1984/85–1994/95 (percentages)

Facility	1984/85	1986/87	1988/89	1990/91	1992/93	1994/95
Hospitals	34.4	25.8	16.0	15.0	8.0	6.8
Health centres and dispensaries	26.9	23.6	11.0	14.0	9.0	7.2
Preventive services	11.9	31.6	46.0	52.0	56.0	52.0
Training	21.9	10.5	9.0	4.0	3.2	3.4
Other	5.0	8.5	18.0	15.0	12.8	13.6

Sources: Ministry of Finance, Planning and Economic Affairs, 1995 and 1996; Ministry of Health, 1995.

income groups. The ultimate target is to have a healthy nation with a high life expectancy.

A breakdown of recurrent expenditure among the main health sub-sectors indicates that hospital services have received by far the greatest share, down from 82 per cent in 1970/71 to 60 per cent in 1982/83 (Ministry of Health, 1984). While there was a general decline in recurrent expenditure on hospital services, the proportion allocated to health centres was rising – from 4 per cent in 1970/71 to 11 per cent in 1982/83 and 18 per cent in 1991/92 (Ministry of Planning, 1980 and 1992). This is a reflection of the greater emphasis placed by the Government on the development of rural-based health facilities. The same was happening to recurrent expenditure on preventive services. From a 5 per cent share of total recurrent expenditure in 1970/71, this sub-sector received 11 per cent of total recurrent expenditure in 1982/83, and 16 per cent in 1991/92. In line with the objective of self-sufficiency in health manpower, there was also an increase of recurrent expenditure on training.

From the above data we observe that the health sector has faced a continuous decline in health expenditure, and is facing many problems, including lack of equipment and drugs in most facilities, poor conditions of buildings, and staff shortages in some specializations (such as surgeons, paediatricians, gynaecologists, doctors, laboratory technicians, radiographers and physiotherapists). These problems must be solved without further procrastination. These factors have led to a situation where those who were dependent on public health-care services have been receiving less and less care over the years. The poorer segments of the population – particularly those in the informal sector – who are dependent on government health-care services have much reduced accessibility and low quality of care. At this particular time, nothing would be more welcome, politically and economically, than a solution that would restore accessibility and quality care to the average and poorer segments of the Tanzanian population.

2.2 National health policies and strategies

Government efforts to combat disease and improve the health situation of society have been made on the premise that good health is a major socio-economic and personal resource, and that it is an important reflection of a society's quality of life. These efforts have been undertaken over the years under a comprehensive National Health Policy (NHP) designed to provide basic primary health-care services to all Tanzanians. The overall objective of the NHP is to improve health and the general well-being of all Tanzanians and to focus on those most at risk, as well as to encourage the health system to be more responsive to the needs of the people (Meghji, 1996). The specific objectives of the NHP are to:

(i)   reduce infant and maternal morbidity and mortality and increase life expectancy through the provision of adequate and equitable maternal and child health services, promotion of adequate nutrition, control of communicable diseases and treatment of common conditions;

(ii)   ensure that health services are available and accessible to all people, wherever they are in the country, whether in urban or rural areas;

(iii) move towards self sufficiency in manpower by training all the cadres required at all levels from the village to the national level, with a view to attaining high levels of competence and improving the management and administration of the health delivery system;

(iv)   sensitize the community on common preventable health problems, and improve the capabilities at all levels of society to assess and analyse problems and to design appropriate action through genuine community involvement;

(v)   promote awareness in Government and the community at large that health problems can only be adequately addressed and solved through multisectoral cooperation, involving such sectors as education, agriculture, water and sanitation, community development, women's organizations, and NGOs; and

(vi)   create awareness through family health promotion that the responsibility for one's health rests squarely with the able-bodied individual as an integral part of the family.

These objectives were to be attained through a strategy of coordinating the efforts of all concerned in responding to health problems in the country. This strategy was consistent with the Primary Health Care approach adopted in the Alma-Ata Declaration of 1978 (WHO, 1978), for which the MOH developed guidelines for implementation as the means to achieve the social objective of Health for All by the Year 2000 (HFA/2000).

The Government included the health sector plans/targets in its development plans. During the period 1965–80 a plan was designed that gave priority to the rural areas and to the development of preventive services for Maternal and Child Health (MCH). According to the plan, the expansion of hospitals was to match population growth; the bed-to-population ratio was to be kept constant, and a fast construction and staffing of Rural Health Centres (RHCs) and dispensaries was envisaged.

In the 20-Year Development Plan (1981–2000) there was an expanded coverage of the objectives/targets in the health sector – among others, life expectancy was to be raised from 47 years to 60 years by the year 2000, and infant mortality was to decline to 50/1,000 from 137/1,000 (Ministry of Health, 1980).

Further, every village without a dispensary or health centre would have a Village Health Post (VHP). The management of the health services would be left

127

to the individual village, and the role of the Government would be as the supplier of commodities. This would mean involvement of the people in the implementation and management of the health services.

There was also the objective of self-sufficiency in manpower and the need to strengthen the management and supervision of health services at different levels. Seeing the limited resources at the disposal of the Government, it was also intended in the plan that relevant parastatals and ministries should cooperate in order to achieve the targets.

Most targets of the HFA plan and of the three Five-Year Development Plans, however, have not been achieved, with only the increase in the number of dispensaries being above the planned target. The near constant number of RHCs in the face of a growing population resulted in an increase in the ratio of the population per RHC from 73,732:1 in 1980 to 85,774:1 in 1984 (Ministry of Planning, 1986). The same happened to the population per dispensary ratio. This, in summary, shows a lack of achievement of the objective of increasing the number of facilities at the same rate as the population increase. In the area of social indicators such as infant mortality and life expectancy at birth, there has also been little improvement (see table 5.4). There was inefficient distribution of drugs and there were shortages of essential equipment in the facilities, mainly due to insufficient financing.

Following upon the economic difficulties of the 1980s, the Government of the United Republic of Tanzania adopted structural adjustment programmes. Salient features of these programmes were encouragement of the private sector and cutbacks in financing of the social sector – for the health-care sector, this meant a search for alternative sources of funding. The two major alternatives put in place are:

(a) *Restoration of private practice:* After the nationalization of private health-care facilities in 1970, private medical practice for profit was banned in 1977 through the establishment of the Private Hospitals Regulation Act No. 6. In 1991 the importance of private health-care delivery as a source of alternative financing was once again recognized, with the passage of the Private Hospitals Regulation Amendment Act No. 26, allowing private funds back into the health sector. Since 1991 the number of health-care facilities has increased fourfold in Dar es Salaam (Ministry of Health, 1996c).

(b) *Cost-sharing*: Cost-sharing has been introduced at all government care-providing units, above the health centre level.

Private health-care services have been allowed at several levels: individual practice, group practice, NGOs, religious bodies or foreign companies. A Secretariat to regulate private practice, established by the MOH, is not effective. The Secretariat is minimally staffed and equipped, as well as very centralized because it operates

Table 5.4   Performance of the Health for All Plan (1981–2000),
            United Republic of Tanzania, by 1990–96

Main targets (for year 2000)	Achievement (most recent date)
Raise life expectancy from 47 years to 60 years	Life expectancy of 51 years (1995)
Reduce infant mortality rate from 137/1 000 to 50/1 000	Infant mortality rate 112/1 000 (1996)
Decrease service ratios (a) population per dispensary to be 10 000	No significant achievement in most ratios (a) 8 328 people per dispensary (1994)
(b) population per Rural Health Centre (RHC) to be 50 000	(b) 90 942 people per RHC: shortage of 180 RHCs from the target by 1992
(c) decrease population per Rural Medical Aid (RMA)	(c) population per RMA still high (decreased by 42 per cent by 1990)
(d) population per medical doctor	(d) 22 572 people/medical doctor (1995) (still high compared to other less developed countries)
Increase health budget allocation, in particular preventive services, away from curative services	Preventive services take 42 per cent (1990) of health budget as against 20 per cent before 1980
Rural spread of health services	Now more than 80 per cent of population within 5 km of a health service facility; more than 90 per cent within 10 km or less (1989)
Increase availability of equipment, adequate staff, drugs	Still acute shortage of equipment, staff and drugs

Sources: Ministry of Health, 1996c; Ministry of Planning, 1992.

from the Ministry's headquarters in the capital city, Dar es Salaam. Private unit owners have been allowed to arbitrarily set fees, locations and types of practice, with the result that the major towns have had a sudden increase in health-care facilities. Dar es Salaam now has 450 private units, from a previous 70.

Cost-sharing has been introduced at government care-providing units such as the National Referral Hospital, regional hospitals, and district hospitals. It has not been introduced at Rural Health Centres and dispensaries. The current levels of cost-sharing are 500 T.sh. (one US dollar) at the referral hospital for registration as an outpatient case, and 50 per cent of the actual cost of all drugs dispensed. For the general wards at the referral hospitals the cost is 2,300 T.sh. (about five US dollars) and 50 per cent of the actual cost of drugs dispensed. The charges are T.sh. 2,000 (four US dollars) for re-admissions for all hospital stays, plus 50 per cent of the drugs dispensed. In the grade one wards at the referral hospitals, it is T.sh. 3,000 per bed per night plus 50 per cent of the actual cost of the drugs dispensed.

Charges of one to five dollars for a hospital admission may sound like a "fairy tale" by Western standards. However, with normal salaries ranging between 15 and 50 US$ per month, five dollars represents between 10 and 30 per cent of a monthly income.

An assessment of the situation in the mid-1990s (Kiwara, 1997) indicates that there were many more problems than ever in the health sector, despite all the plans mentioned above. First and foremost, there was a substantial loss of skilled work-hours from the general public and the poor in particular. This was a result of many health sector professionals switching to private practice. A large number of doctors had started their own private hospitals or dispensaries; they had either resigned from public service or they were working on a part-time basis. Either way, health sector professionals were spending less time in government health-care facilities. Higher fees being charged kept many needy people away, particularly the informal sector poor who are in most need. These private units have caused an internal brain-drain from the public sector of a large number of nurses, laboratory technicians and all types of support staff.

The majority of health-care facilities have inadequate drugs, diagnostic equipment, and the general infrastructure has no maintenance funds. Many dispensaries, Rural Health Centres, and even District Hospitals, have fallen into disrepair.

Quality of care is another problem that has become evident in the 1990s. With the Private Hospitals Regulation Amendment Act No. 26 of 1991, private dispensaries mushroomed in the country. There is no effective regulatory mechanism to ensure that they adhere to quality standards, and unskilled staff are widely used in most of them. The profit motive may be the incentive, as the less qualified the personnel, the lower the pay they will accept.

In terms of infrastructure, most buildings now used by private practitioners to provide care were designed and located as guest houses, garages, bars, etc.

The health sector as a whole has lost control over local pharmaceutical supplies. Most pharmaceuticals made locally were manufactured in government-owned factories. With structural adjustment programme these plants no longer receive funds from the Government, with the majority ceasing to operate. The main source of domestically produced and imported drugs is now the Medical Stores Department (MSD), which is not owned by the Government.

The introduction of a two-tier system was intended as a means to ensure a free service, but in fact people are paying a high price for service. They need to resort to private hospitals and dispensaries, because public hospitals lack a supply of drugs. In the immediate post-reform period, there has been a rapid increase in the prices of pharmaceuticals. In nominal terms, prices of basic drugs have more than doubled and even quadrupled in some cases.

3. The promotion of self-financed health insurance

The country faces a number of real problems in health-care financing that need to be addressed. A new health-care system needs to be put in place that meets the following criteria:

(i)   improved accessibility for all segments of the population,
(ii)   improved quality of care,
(iii)   pooling of risk among larger groups of people,
(iv)   minimal administrative costs, and
(v)   restoration of comprehensive qualities of health-care services.

This section will review two health insurance systems already in operation that attempt to meet these criteria. These are UMASIDA and the Igunga Community Health Fund.

3.1 The UMASIDA health insurance scheme

The UMASIDA scheme was born out of an ILO project carried out in the informal sector of Dar es Salaam. The scheme covers about 1,500 workers (plus about 4,500 family members) who are part of five informal sector associations. It started operating in December 1995 when the five associations formed an umbrella organization known as UMASIDA (an acronym for a Mutual Society for Health Care in the Informal Sector).

By constitution, UMASIDA has been set up as a mutual association whose supreme authority is vested in the Annual General Meeting of its members. It has a supervisory board consisting of five members, each representing a member group, and an executive committee consisting of the chairperson of the supervisory board, a secretary and a treasurer. There is also a professional advisory board – consisting of a physician, a pharmacist and a lawyer – which advises on the quality of care and on legal matters. All financial transactions of UMASIDA are overseen by the executive committee in liaison with an adviser to the scheme. They have an office at one of the group's premises, and a bank account.

All beneficiaries of UMASIDA are primary members of identified informal sector groups. Beneficiaries include members and their immediate families, i.e. the husband and wife or the wife and husband and their children. In the case of polygamous families, only officially married wives and their children are recognized.

Each beneficiary is entitled to all primary health-care services at a carefully selected private health-care provider. They are also entitled to secondary and tertiary care, but this would be provided at a government health-care unit. Prenatal care, deliveries, postnatal care, well-child clinics, immunizations and chronic illnesses such as diabetes, TB and mental illness, are provided by the Government, but the cost-sharing charges are met by the scheme. All payments are made by cheque by the scheme's treasurer.

Control mechanisms

After an initial pilot phase of six months, it was found that a more effective control system was needed, so the following mechanisms were developed and introduced by UMASIDA.

(i)   *A photo identity card* which is carried by every participating member of the scheme. The card is made of transparent plastic and has on it the member's photograph, a group identity number, and an embossed seal that cannot be photocopied or reproduced. All participating care-providers know about these features so they are able to recognize forgeries. Health care is provided on presentation of the identity card. When family members come for treatment, they must present the contributing member's card.

(ii) *Sick-sheets.* Before going to the identified care-provider, beneficiaries must take the critical step of having their sick-sheets signed by the group's chairperson or secretary. This procedure brings the leaders of the groups into the control system, so that the they can check on their members' sickness and can confirm her/him as a deserving beneficiary. Issuance of the sick-sheet from the group also helps check the identity of "family members" who were not listed at the initial registration steps. Each sick-sheet also has an embossed seal that cannot be photocopied.

(iii) *Circulating invoices* are issued together with the sick-sheets, and they also have an embossed seal that cannot be photocopied. It is not possible to receive care without this invoice. Two circulating invoices are presented at the point of care. One is retained by the care-provider and one is sent back to the group. Payments are made only when both have been compared. For each visit they itemize all charges for consultation fees, laboratory and medication costs.

(iv) *Training for groups and care-providers.* All groups are given an orientation course on the need to apply faithfully the above control measures. They are made aware that any misuse jeopardizes the sustainability of the scheme and so re-exposes them to non-accessibility to the health care. Provider unit staff are also made familiar with the identity item marks, and are asked to check them before giving service.

(v) *Single source of control items.* As a further control measure, all identity cards, sick-sheets, and circulating invoices are signed by the chairperson of the executive committee. His signature is on all control items, a specimen of which is available to all provider staff at reception desks.

(vi) *Beneficiary lists.* All providers are supplied with beneficiary lists, which enable the cross-checking of names on other control items.

The health-care providers

The UMASIDA health insurance scheme makes use of private providers to meet the primary health-care needs of beneficiaries. As noted earlier, there has been a mushrooming of private care-providers in Dar es Salaam following the legalization of private practice. For a quality care seeker, it has become difficult to choose one without further guidelines. The executive committee, working with the UMASIDA adviser, has therefore laid down the following criteria for the selection of health-care providers:

(i) *The provider must be a graduate medical doctor.* This criterion was necessary because there are other qualified personnel allowed to operate private practices in Dar es Salaam. With approximately 450 private dispensaries and hospitals in Dar es Salaam, it was relatively easy to find high quality providers.

(ii) *Nurses must have diploma qualifications (Staff Nurses).* Each participating unit must have diploma-qualified nurses, as they can offer preventive, promotive and curative care, and they also have a deeper understanding of health problems in the country. Most private units prefer, however, to employ nursing cadres with lower qualifications, so as to keep costs down.

(iii) *Laboratories equipped for basic tests.* They should be able to perform Erythrocyte Sedimentation Rate (ESR) and haemoglobin tests; examine stools for hookworm, ascaris, occult blood and pinworms; examine urine for bilharzia, blood and albumin; examine blood slides for malaria and microfilaria parasites, and direct microscopy for various discharges. Ability to do culture and sensitivity tests would be an added advantage.

(iv) *Observation facilities.* Private care-providers offering short-term observation facilities were preferred, because patients with certain conditions such as fever or mild asthma do not need to be hospitalized. Eight or 12 hours observation would be adequate.

(v) *Willingness to prescribe only the WHO approved essential drugs.* In an attempt to control drug costs, the scheme restricts itself to using the WHO approved essential drugs list. Generic names are to be used all the time.

(vi) *Ability and willingness to use the circulating invoice in claiming care costs from UMASIDA.* The circulating invoice is structured in such a way that it itemizes all the possible charges that may be needed at a health-care unit.

(vii) *Acceptance bills to be paid monthly.* This condition is necessary because it enables the executive committee to verify all claims before approving payment.

(viii) *A 24-hour service.* This condition makes it possible to respond immediately to emergencies such as deliveries and child illnesses.

(ix) *Proximity to the place of work.* This requirement reduces the travelling time of group members when they need treatment.

(x) *Record keeping.* UMASIDA looked for providers who keep good records of in-patients, as such records are important for formulating promotional and preventive programmes.

(xi) *Availability of maternal and child health care (MCH).* Providers offering MCH services were chosen first, as this enables families to obtain comprehensive care under one roof.

Contributions

Premiums for this scheme are based on estimates made by the *World Development Report 1993: Investing in health* (World Bank, 1993), of US $12 per person in the developing countries for annual health-care needs, equivalent to about T.sh. 20 per day per person. To begin with, at a cost of T.sh. 20 per day, only the working members from the groups were involved in the scheme. After getting used to the scheme, immediate family members were also allowed to participate, but at T.sh. 40 per day per immediate family.

As well, at the beginning, three ways of operating the scheme were specified:

(i) *Capitation fee.* Under this arrangement a fixed rate of contribution was exchangeable for free health care by a local private health-care provider. This system was initially introduced with two private providers, who have so far been reluctant to participate because they fear that inadequate training of group members may cause overuse of services.

(ii) *Case payment.* Under this arrangement – operating in four groups – payment is made on a case- by-case merit basis. Overall costs are higher than in the capitation fee arrangements.

(iii) *Enterprise clinic.* One of the participating groups (DASICO) chose to establish its own dispensary, which is financed by collective contributions. It provides needed primary health care to members and their immediate families, with secondary and tertiary care needs being covered by the UMASIDA scheme.

Beneficiaries pay for the cost of producing their own identity card. The fund pays all costs for committee meetings, transport to visit individual groups, and stationery. The Committee does not receive any other allowances. As the scheme expands, however, a coordinator will be required, for which the fund should also be able to cover her/his remuneration.

Impact on beneficiaries and providers

(i) *Accessibility to health care.* Accessibility to full primary health-care services has been restored to all members and their families at the DASICO cooperative. This has been possible because DASICO established a dispensary within its premises (open 8 hours per day for 7 days a week), and employing a medical assistant and a nurse. Owing to its size it cannot provide secondary or tertiary health care, the latter being provided by the government health-care infrastructure but paid for by UMASIDA. Hernia operations on DASICO members at Kisarawe Government Hospital have been paid for by UMASIDA. High blood pressure investigations and treatment at Muhimbili Consultant Hospital have also been paid for by the scheme.

Primary health care for the Mwananyamala group was restored for all group members and immediate families from a contracted care-provider very close to the group's premises. The contract was terminated recently because it did not strictly adhere to prescribing drugs from the WHO approved essential drugs list. A contract with a new provider has now been signed. The other three groups, i.e. Suma, Mandela and Nasi-Tunajaribu, have also achieved universal restoration of accessibility to primary health care, with each one having contracted a provider. Secondary and tertiary care is provided at respective district hospitals. Under the scheme, occupational health education, based on observed health problems, has also been provided in all the groups.

(ii) *Quality of health care.* For all the groups participating in the UMASIDA scheme, the quality of care has improved substantially, with UMASIDA beneficiaries receiving comparatively high quality care, due partly to the recommencement of the private health sector. General quality assurance remains inadequate, but for UMASIDA all providers are screened on the 11 criteria outlined above, thereby eliminating the quacks.

(iii) *Reduction in health-care costs.* The risk-pooling aspect of this scheme has eliminated the burden on individuals and their families – hardly able to afford health care on their own – of meeting the full cost of care at a time of need. It has ensured that access to care is available throughout the year, and that the premiums paid are much lower than the actual care cost.

(iv) *Facilitating the development of quality private health care.* In Dar es Salaam, private health-care providers at all levels compete for patients. UMASIDA organized and continues to organize informal sector groups for health care. Care-providers have come to realize that being contracted by UMASIDA means that they are assured of clients and a monopoly on well-organized groups. To win contracts, private providers have attempted as much as possible to conform to the 11 screening criteria outlined. By their nature, these screening criteria ensure the development of better quality health care.

For the five groups within the scheme, the pattern of health problems has remained the same, but trends have changed over time. Substantial reductions have occurred in the incidence of (a) acute work-related health problems, (b) gastrointestinal (diarrhoea) problems, and (c) respiratory system health problems. These positive changes can be explained by the intensive training in safety and health promotion, the restructuring of premises to facilitate better air circulation, the provision of clean drinking water and the timely treatment of those who become ill.

Malaria as a health problem seems to have resisted work-based education, and is explained by the fact that most malaria infection takes place during the night, when people are at home. Since most health education as well as occupational and safety training were focused on the workplace, they did not influence areas beyond – at least not until now.

Other positive changes associated with the scheme include a 10 per cent productivity increase reported at DASICO. This increase reported by the chairman and secretary occurred in nearly all departments following the establishment of a dispensary in their plant. The explanation was that the time being wasted to seek care elsewhere was instead invested in production. The metal works department was particularly noted for increased productivity; since most cuts and acute work-related injuries are associated with metalworking, it was plausible to attribute the increase to this department.

Shortcomings and corrections

As with any other social security scheme, UMASIDA has displayed a number of shortcomings for which various corrections have been found. The main problems that have occurred so far are:

(i) *Group leaders abused the system.* As noted earlier, the group leaders are the custodians of the sick-sheets, and in some groups they gave sick-sheets to non-contributing persons. As the scheme is closely monitored, this problem was discovered early and corrected.

(ii) *Providers occasionally prescribed drugs other than those in the WHO approved essential drugs list.* This non-observance was also noted early during the regular comparison between the circulating invoices and what was actually prescribed.

(iii) *Trade names were used.* The scheme had insisted on the use of generic names, but some providers do not abide by this, in order to make more profit.

(iv) *Irregularity in contributions.* As is well known, individual informal sector workers have irregular incomes, with the result that their contributions may be delayed.

(v) *Smaller groups have problems.* Among the UMASIDA group members, smaller groups had problems in mobilizing enough funds for the premium payments, and should therefore be grouped together to reach a critical and functional number, and experience in Dar es Salaam indicates that 400 is a good critical figure.

(vi) *Limited dispensing ability.* Some provider units could not dispense all needed drugs, which forced beneficiaries to purchase drugs elsewhere at higher costs than were eventually reimbursed by the scheme.

Apart from the corrections mentioned above, the following aspects need to be reviewed and improved in the UMASIDA scheme:

(i) *The control system needs to be improved.* Photo identity cards for all beneficiaries should replace sick-sheets that are now controlled by group leaders. The current practice allows the nuclear family members to use a group member's photo identity card, but in practice it has sometimes been used for people outside the nuclear family.

(ii) *Continuous monitoring is necessary.* This requirement aims to ensure that all providers adhere to the essential drugs list and keep regular and accurate records.

(iii) *Improve the minimal awareness of health insurance.* Well-organized information systems need to be implemented to increase awareness of health insurance and its potential in enhancing the financing of the health sector.

3.2 The Igunga Community Health Fund

Adequate financing of the health sector is a prime concern of the Ministry of Health and the Government. Thus, the Ministry decided to set up a pilot scheme known as the Igunga Community Health Fund (ICHF), around the town of Igunga, in the north-west of the country. The ICHF was initiated because it became clear that the Government could not adequately finance most health-care provider units. Drug supplies, for example, last for only 14 days in most Rural Health Centres and dispensaries, so for the remaining two weeks in every month there are no drugs. The ICHF aims to mobilize communities to take greater responsibility for their health-care units, and to contribute money that will be matched by government funds, so as to finance health care adequately. Afterwards, government contributions will be phased out gradually, so that communities can take fuller control.

Currently ICHF funds contributed by individual households from the Igunga district are matched by World Bank funds, that were to finance a Health and Nutrition project. The population served is about 50,000. Each household pays an annual contribution of 5,000 T.sh. (about US$10). The arrangements are based on contributions being expected at the time of harvesting. Contributions can be paid as a lump sum or in instalments.

A District Health Board has been created to manage the fund at the district level, which has counterpart structures at the ward and village levels. These structures are designed to have full powers over the health-care system within their vicinity. They can also regulate the amount of contributions. Each contributing household is given an identity card through which it can obtain health care. Health care is provided by the Rural Health Centres, dispensaries and a mission hospital in Igunga district. Communities are free to choose to which health centres or dispensaries in Igunga they wish to go for care. Households that do not contribute will pay fully on an individual basis for care given at the Rural Health Centres or dispensaries. The poorest households, who are not able to contribute, are given free care.

Participants are entitled to all primary health-care services provided at the Rural Health Centres, dispensaries and the participating mission hospital in Igunga. They are also entitled to referral services to the district hospital and beyond. Costs beyond the Rural Health Centre and the participating mission hospital will be fully borne by the individuals concerned. Households that are able to pay their contributions are likely to use the primary health services frequently. Those who cannot afford the contribution are likely to feel stigmatized, and will therefore not use the services even though they are free. These are realities that need deeper consideration.

As far as care is concerned it is advantageous that the health-care units already know well the health problems of the area. These problems include malaria, bilharzia, TB, dysentery, typhoid, hypertension, diabetes, pneumonia and traumatic injuries like fractures.

Igunga has set up a top-heavy administrative structure. First, there is a District Health Board, and then at the ward level and village level there are executive committees, which are autonomous from the district level. At the regional level, this disproportion in structure may be further reinforced. Although it is not yet clearly stated that the various structures will be salaried, it is customary now for committee members to claim sitting allowances, which can be very expensive. One should also foresee the possible chaos that will emanate from dozens of autonomous ward-level committees giving directives to a health-care system in one district. A comparison of the main features of the UMASIDA and Igunga schemes is given in table 5.5.

A preliminary assessment

Contributions received so far demonstrate a clear acceptance of the idea within the community. Although this was slow to come at the beginning, the situation has improved, and enrolment had reached 50 per cent of the community membership by 1998. The concept is good. Its implementation, however, will need to be enriched by field experience. Currently, households are asked to contribute T.sh. 5,000 per year. Collections are made at the harvesting peak season when the financial situation is relatively better. Joining the fund is also voluntary.

The ICHF has great potential, but its operations may encounter problems for several reasons:

(i)   It relies on 50 per cent matching funds. Currently, these funds originate from the World Bank. When they are no longer available, problems may arise. Supplies to health-care units will be affected and so may the quality of health care.

(ii)   The fund is now run by local committees, but the idea did not originate in the community. It is an idea that came from outside. Imported ideas normally take time to be internalized. When the outsider leaves, the idea quite often dies also.

(iii)   For the ICHF, the issue of sustainability is critical, not only in the supply of funds and internalization, but also in ensuring that services are available. Being a predominantly rural area, Igunga only has government health-care units. Private providers are not available. Such a monopoly may affect negatively the quality of services given. If the community is not satisfied, they will stop contributing, and the scheme may collapse.

(iv)   The other districts in the country are watching the ICHF pilot scheme very closely with a view to replicability. If success is not recorded in Igunga,

Table 5.5 The main features of the UMASIDA and Igunga schemes, United
Republic of Tanzania

Features	Igunga Fund	UMASIDA scheme
Source of funds	External and internal	Exclusively internal
Autonomy	Partial	Full
Infrastructural control	External and internal	Fully internal
Services covered	Primary, secondary and tertiary	Primary, secondary and tertiary
Use of existing health-care providing system	Only government infrastructure	Private and government infrastructure
Freedom to choose provider	Limited to government providers	Choice between private and public providers
Feedback loop (to improve provided care)	Occasional	Part and parcel of scheme's activities, carried out continuously
Sustainability	Dependent on government supplying its portion	Sustainable because self mobilizing

replicability will be difficult to achieve. A potential avenue for health
sector financing will have been closed.

(v)   For the ICHF, it may be difficult to assess the impact precisely because no
baseline survey studies were done. This should be a lesson for other districts.

4.   Concluding remarks

This chapter started by examining the realities of change and its influence on
social security in the United Republic of Tanzania. It has shown how the
country's economic difficulties in the 1980s progressively eroded social sector
support while adversities related to poverty also deepened. Health deteriorated
with decreasing nutrition and reduced accessibility to health care. Illiteracy
increased due to budgetary cuts in the education sector. These were further
compounded by escalating unemployment, inadequate transport infrastructure,
poor water supplies and general insecurity in the informal sector.

Socio-economic hardship in other countries is relieved, albeit temporarily, by
a well-established social welfare network. For the United Republic of Tanzania,
this is not the case. A formalized social security system has not been established

in the country. More than 85 per cent of the population is in the informal sector. This makes a formal insurance scheme almost impossible, given the irregular and low incomes that prevail.

Still in existence, but disintegrating fast, there are certain indigenous social security arrangements, which have ensured the survival of orphans, the disabled, the elderly and those affected by natural disasters like floods, fires or drought. The disintegration of this system has left an undesirable gap behind, which has widened rather rapidly in recent years due to the fast rate of urbanization and the aging of the population. There have been attempts to redress this situation, but they have not been successful. The Government has established provident funds and other social security measures. The provident funds, however, have been ineffective due to the fact that they are in the form of lump-sum payments, they are not based on needs, they are affected by inflation and are institutionally based.

In view of the social security "vacuum" that exists in the country, there are ongoing innovative attempts to ensure that at least some social security is in place. Some of these attempts are comprehensive, while others are less so. One important development was the conversion of the National Provident Fund into the comprehensive National Social Security Fund (NSSF). The Ministry of Health is also considering establishing a National Health Insurance Scheme. This, however, will be exclusively for formal sector employees, i.e. about 5 per cent of the country's population. Other attempts to establish social security are also in place. The most recent are the formation of mutual funds and community trust funds. These have generally concentrated on health and health care only. This prioritization has a background in what has happened recently in the health-care sector in the country, which will be commented upon below.

For nearly the whole of the 1980s, government health-care expenditure in the United Republic of Tanzania decreased. At the end of 1989, it stood at only 50 per cent of its level in the early 1980s. This had negative results on the sector's quality, quantity and equity. Staff morale declined, and urgently required rehabilitation of buildings and repair of equipment could not be done. As private practice was reintroduced, there was a substantive exodus of staff from the government health-care infrastructure into the private sector. High fees charged in this sector, however, have denied the poor and most needy any access to care.

Therefore, despite comprehensive national health policies, the decreasing health status of Tanzanians is evident. Morbidity and mortality are no longer on the decline, as was the case in the 1970s. The most affected, however, are those in the informal sector. Through the help of the Social Security Department of the ILO, the informal sector in Dar es Salaam established the UMASIDA mutual health insurance scheme mentioned above. The scheme has been accepted by both the Government and people in the informal sector generally. It is also in great demand in other towns around the country. Its other advantages include facilitating private sector growth and ensuring better revenue collection at government health-care units. It also ensures accessibility to health care for the poorest of the poor. Recent international evaluation of the scheme shows that it is very popular among the poor and has a great role to play in health sector financing.

Other schemes similar to UMASIDA are the community funds which began in Igunga and which involve communities contributing to a common account that is used to finance health care.

The United Republic of Tanzania has undergone a period of economic crisis that eroded its social security infrastructure. Many attempts, however, have been made to redress the damage, some at the national level, others on a much more limited scale. All, however, aim at re-establishing a social security network. Many lessons are coming from these experiences and are being used to enrich and improve the schemes.

References

Diyamet, P. 1996. *The retiree crisis in Tanzania,* paper presented to REPOA (Research on Poverty Alleviation) meeting (Dar es Salaam).

Economic and Social Research Foundation. 1996. *Poverty Alleviation Programme in Tanzania. A research proposal* (Dar es Salaam).

Government of the United Republic of Tanzania. 1989. *Priority social action programme July 1989 – June 1992* (Dar es Salaam).

Kiwara, A.D. 1993. "Health and health care in a structurally adjusting Tanzania", in Msambichaka, L.A. (ed.), *Economic trends in Tanzania* (Dar es Salaam, Dar University Press), pp. 73–85.

Kiwara, A.D. 1997. *The emerging private sector in Dar es Salaam,* Report to the Ministry of Health (Dar es Salaam).

Kinyondo, S. 1996. Opening ministerial speech of the National Provident Fund Round-Table Consultations on the Development of Social Security in Tanzania, 17–18 December (Arusha).

Maliyamkono, T.L.; Bagachwa, M.S.D. 1990. *The second economy in Tanzania* (London, James Currey Publishers).

Meghji, Z.H. 1996. "Implementation of cost sharing and options available to improve health services for the poor and vulnerable groups in Tanzania", in Eastern and Southern African University Research Programme (ESAURP), *Tanzania's tomorrow* (Dar es Salaam, TEMA Publishers), pp. 76–87.

Ministry of Finance, Planning and Economic Affairs. 1995. *Annual Report 1995* (Dar es Salaam).

—. 1996. *Annual Report 1996* (Dar es Salaam).

Ministry of Health. 1980. *Annual Report 1980* (Dar es Salaam).

Ministry of Health. 1984. *Annual Report 1984* (Dar es Salaam).

Ministry of Health. 1986. *Budget Speech* (Dar es Salaam).

Ministry of Health. 1991. *National AIDS Control Programme: AIDS surveillance*, Report No. 4, NACP Epidemiology Unit (Dar es Salaam).

Ministry of Health. 1993. *Expanded Programme on Immunization evaluation report* (Dar es Salaam).

Ministry of Health. 1995. *Annual Report* (Dar es Salaam).

Ministry of Health. 1996a. *Guideline standards for health facilities* (Dar es Salaam).

Ministry of Health. 1996b. *Health Statistics Abstract* (Dar es Salaam).

Ministry of Health. 1996c. *Annual Report* (Dar es Salaam).

Ministry of Labour and Youth. 1997. *1996 Annual Report* (Dar es Salaam).

Ministry of National Education, Department of Adult Education. 1992. *Adult literacy in the 1990s: An evaluation report* (Dar es Salaam).

Ministry of Planning. 1980. *Economic Survey, 1980* (Dar es Salaam).

—. 1986. *Economic Survey, 1986* (Dar es Salaam).

Ministry of Planning. 1988. *Economic Survey, 1988* (Dar es Salaam).

Ministry of Planning. 1992. *Economic Survey, 1992* (Dar es Salaam).

Mkulo, H.M. 1996. *The introduction of a comprehensive social security scheme in Tanzania*, paper presented at the National Provident Fund Round-Table Consultations on the Development of Social Security in Tanzania, 17–18 December (Arusha).

Msambichaka, L.A.; Kilindo, A.A.L.; Kiwara, A.D.; Mkusa, E.L. 1997. *Economic adjustment policies and health care in Tanzania* (Dar es Salaam, Economic Research Bureau).

Shaw, R.P.; Griffin, C.C. 1995. *Financing health care in sub-Saharan Africa through user fees and insurance* (Washington, DC, World Bank).

Sivard, R. 1992. *World military and social statistics* (Washington, DC, Clarendon).

Tanzania Food and Nutrition Centre. 1995. *Poverty and nutritional status in periurban Dar es Salaam: A research report* (Dar es Salaam).

UNICEF; Government of the United Republic of Tanzania. 1990. *Women and children in Tanzania: A situation analysis* (Dar es Salaam).

World Health Organization (WHO). 1978. "Declaration of Alma-Ata", in *Primary Health Care: Report of the International Conference on Primary Health Care, Alma-Ata, 6–12 September 1978* (Geneva).

—. 1995. *World Health Report 1995* – Bridging the gaps (Geneva).

World Bank. 1993. *World Development Report 1993. Investing in health* (Oxford, Oxford University Press).

BASIC SOCIAL SECURITY IN EL SALVADOR 6

Ruth de Solórzano and Víctor Ramírez, Officials, Supervisory Board for Pensions, San Salvador

Introduction

The question of basic social security has been a major source of political preoccupation in El Salvador, particularly since the armed conflict around the 1980s. Immediately after the war, most efforts were concentrated on social assistance and the re-establishment of social services – both largely financed by external sources. Afterwards, interest shifted towards self-financing mechanisms, leading to the pension reform of 1996. However, in spite of these reforms, almost three-quarters of the labour force is not insured for old age, disability and death. As a result, new forms of social security will have to be developed that are adapted to the needs and contributive capacity of informal sector workers.

This chapter starts by reviewing the main trends in poverty, education and health (section 1), and then examines the structure and coverage of the formal social security system (section 2). Sections 3 and 4 then analyse in greater detail the health-care delivery mechanisms as well as the major characteristics of the 1996 pension reform. Section 5 reviews the opportunities for self-financed social security schemes for informal sector workers, followed by some concluding remarks in section 6.

1. Trends in poverty, education and health

Large groups of people in El Salvador live in poverty and/or do not have access to basic social services. Families are considered to live in absolute poverty if their monthly incomes are lower than the cost of the basic food basket, i.e. in 1995 about 800 colons for rural families and 1,100 colons for those in urban areas. In 1995, families were deemed to be living in relative poverty when their monthly incomes were lower than twice the cost of the basic food basket (expanded food basket), i.e. 1,600 colons in rural and 2,200 colons in urban areas. According to the 1995 multipurpose household survey carried out by the Ministry of Planning (MIPLAN, 1995), about a fifth of the population lived in absolute poverty and just under 30 per cent in relative poverty (see table 6.1).

Between 1994 and 1995 the incidence of poverty fell quite substantially – by about five percentage points. Poverty is concentrated in rural areas, where for every ten households six were in a state of poverty in 1995. The departments showing the highest incidence of extreme poverty in 1994 were Morazán, Cabañas, Chalatenango, Ahuachapán and Cuscatlán, with figures of 47.5, 47.3, 41.1, 36.3 and 35.6 per cent respectively – compared to the average nationwide percentage of 23.9 per cent.

With respect to education, El Salvador faced serious problems during the 1980s. In 1980, enrolment for primary schools was not higher than 75 per cent, while there was 16 per cent absenteeism in primary schools. In 1985 illiteracy rose to 35 per cent.

Between 1989 and 1994, the Cristiani administration introduced the Social Development Programme which led to some improvement in educational indicators. The illiteracy rate dropped to 23 per cent in 1994, but school attendance did not improve. The most important programmes implemented since the end of the 1980s include Community Participation in Education (EDUCO), which is aimed at increasing the scope and level of education of the rural population, especially in grades one to six. Parallel to this programme, there was a school meals programme designed to keep children in the educational system, and avoiding early drop-outs or absenteeism, which are the root cause of the low level of education among the population of El Salvador.

In geographical terms, the east of the country has the highest illiteracy rates, especially in rural areas (La Unión 41.2 per cent; Morazán 50.0 per cent; San Miguel 44.5 per cent; and Usulután 39.2 per cent) compared to the national rural illiteracy ratio of 36.7 per cent. However, there are also other departments suffering from high levels of illiteracy in rural areas, such as San Vicente and Cabañas, with rates of 40.6 and 47.8 per cent respectively. The best departments for this indicator are, in ranking order, San Salvador, La Paz, La Libertad and Santa Ana. This is influenced by the relatively low levels of illiteracy in urban areas.

In the health sector, the social development strategy followed in the 1989–1994 period highlighted child nutrition and maternity care programmes, to tackle dehydration/diarrhoea as the primary cause of death among children from birth to 11 months and the second for those aged 1 to 4 years. The incidence of diarrhoea is closely linked to basic sanitary conditions.

One of the most common causes of death among the population of El Salvador is diarrhoea. Statistics for diarrhoea for the whole of the country range from 5 to 16 per cent of cases of sickness among the population. The department of Cabañas has the highest rate, followed by La Unión and San Miguel (see table 6.2).

Table 6.1   Households in absolute and relative poverty, El Salvador, 1994–95 (percentages)

	Whole country		Urban areas		Rural areas	
	1994	1995	1994	1995	1994	1995
Not poor	47.6	52.4	56.2	59.8	31.4	41.5
Relative poverty	28.5	29.4	27.5	27.7	29.9	31.8
Absolute poverty	23.9	18.3	16.3	12.6	34.8	26.4

Source: MIPLAN, 1995.

Table 6.2   Percentage of persons with diarrhoea, El Salvador, 1994

Department	Whole country	Urban areas	Rural areas
Ahuachapán	7.9	12.0	7.0
Santa Ana	5.2	6.8	3.6
Sonsonate	7.6	6.1	8.5
Chalatenango	5.6	1.6	6.9
La Libertad	9.8	8.2	11.3
San Salvador	9.7	9.1	12.2
Cuscatlán	5.7	6.4	5.3
La Paz	7.2	6.3	7.7
Cabañas	15.2	8.4	17.5
San Vicente	9.2	9.8	8.9
Usulután	8.0	9.5	7.0
San Miguel	10.1	9.2	11.1
Morazán	12.5	11.7	12.8
La Unión	13.7	12.5	14.0
Total	9.0	8.5	9.4

Source: MIPLAN, 1995.

For urban areas, La Unión has the highest percentage of homes with persons suffering from diarrhoea, followed by Ahuachapán and Morazán, while of the rural areas, Cabañas has the highest figure, followed by La Unión and Morazán. These departments probably have a higher incidence of diarrhoea because of factors such as the lack of health services, lack of access to drinking water, and inadequate nutrition. The best departments, according to the survey, are Santa Ana, Chalatenango and Cuscatlán, due to the fact that these urban areas are better served than others with regard to basic preventive infrastructure.

A policy of generating projects in poor communities was implemented through the Social Investment Fund (FIS) and the Department for National Reconstruction (SRN), with the aim of creating a basic social infrastructure to reduce the social disadvantages. These programmes have led to a considerable improvement in basic infrastructure.

Nevertheless, there is still a serious lack of water supply within homes. For all departments, La Unión has the most serious deficiencies, with mains water for only 14.2 per cent of homes. This means that the remaining 85.8 per cent of homes obtain their water by other means. Of particular concern is the seriousness of the problem in rural areas in the departments of La Unión, Cuscatlán, Usulután and Cabañas, which have figures ranging from 0.7 to 5 per cent of homes with mains water supplies.[1] Cabañas and La Unión, as indicated above, are departments with a high level of diarrhoea, which may be influenced by the lack of a good mains water supply, or, which amounts to the same thing, contaminated water supplies. The departments with the best figures for the country are San Salvador (75.7 per cent), Santa Ana (50.7 per cent) and Sonsonate (46.7 per cent), which are more urbanized than the others, which is why mains water supplies are more widespread.

In summary, the above indicators show that San Salvador, La Libertad, Santa Ana and Sonsonate are the departments which have the highest level of satisfaction of basic needs. Those where the situation is worst are Morazán, Cabañas, Cuscatlán, La Unión and Chalatenango. The remaining departments, San Miguel, Usulután, San Vicente, La Paz and Ahuachapán lie somewhere in between.

2. Formal social security: Structure and coverage

2.1 Structure of formal social security

El Salvador has a social security system which can be categorized as relatively young and with a very limited coverage, in terms of both risks and persons. It consists of the following three classic social security programmes:

- The pension programme, which covers the contingencies of old age, disability and survival, protecting 26 per cent of the country's economically active population in 1996, through two social security institutions, the Salvadorian Institute of Social Security (ISSS) and the National Pensions Institute for Public Employees (INPEP).

---

[1] The data distribution by department in the Household Survey means that the sample is not very significant in some departments. The figures given may be higher, but this does not detract from the fact that these departments have the worst conditions.

- The employment injury programme, which is covered by ISSS and INPEP under different schemes, depending on the sector in which the employee works. For workers in the private sector, risks of occupational diseases and accidents are covered by the ISSS Sickness, Maternity and Employment Injury Scheme, which currently covers 19.2 per cent of the economically active population (including those who are working and those on pensions for occupational diseases). Workers in the public and municipal sector are covered for employment injury under the INPEP Disability, Old Age and Death Scheme, which covers 7.1 per cent of the economically active population.
- The health programme, which covers risks of illness and maternity for all workers who are members of the pension scheme. This social security scheme is complemented by the public health system, which provides for people with less resources who are not insured.

In addition to the population coverage mentioned above, the three programmes provide for members of the armed forces, under schemes from the Institute of Social Security for the Armed Forces (IPSFA). The Salvadorian system also has a Social Housing Fund (FSV), which administers a national contributory savings and loan scheme for housing, to which all workers in the private sector and some autonomous institutions have access.

The three programmes operate within the national social security framework and their funding comes from: (i) monthly workers' contributions, in three categories by sector of activity (employees in industry and commerce, public employees and teachers); (ii) employers' contributions (including the Treasury as employer); and, (iii) contributions by the Treasury in its own right. In addition, the system receives income in the form of interest generated by the accumulated technical reserves and other less significant revenues (mainly fines and interest on late payments).

Although the social security institutions are independent, they have close links with the Government, through the following Ministries:

- the Salvadorian Institute of Social Security, through the Ministry of Labour and Social Security;
- the National Pensions Institute for Public Employees, through the Treasury;
- the Social Housing Fund, through the Vice-Minister for Housing and Urban Development in the Ministry of Public Works.

There is little control of the administering bodies, which is the responsibility of the Court of Auditors of the Republic and the Comptroller of the Financial System. The latter, under its constitution, also controls the FSV and the IPSFA. The Presidency of the Republic appoints the Director-General of the ISSS and the Presidents of INPEP and the FSV directly.

Social security in El Salvador has aspects in common with most social security systems in Latin America, a structure of benefit schemes based on tripartite social security schemes and financing; administration rooted in non-specialist, non-profit, independent official bodies, but with strong state intervention; resources for administrative costs allocated by law; and little or no control by independent auditors.

2.2 Formal social security coverage

The coverage provided by the social security system is very limited, both geographically and in terms of population covered. Out of the economically active population of about 2 million people in 1996, the health programme covered about 500,000 contributors, i.e. little more than 25 per cent (Mesa-Lago and Durán, 1998). According to ILO estimates (ILO, 1994), El Salvador is placed among the countries with the lowest coverage in Latin America, comparable with Honduras and the Dominican Republic.

The rural population, which represents more than 50 per cent of the total population of the country, is expressly excluded from pension and health schemes, because the provision, including health, applies exclusively to urban sectors; but even for the urban sectors, coverage does not exceed 45 per cent. The 75 per cent of the workforce that does not enjoy social security protection consists of agricultural and informal sector workers; some self-employed and wage workers from the formal sector; and the unemployed.

There are other restrictions which limit coverage of the population. Under the ISSS scheme the insured's family only includes the insured person, the spouse, and children under the age of six, which is significant when one considers that the country has a population pyramid with the majority in the youth category.

The 818,000 people covered by health schemes represent only 14.1 per cent of the country's population. If to this is added the 10 per cent of the population entitled to benefits under other health schemes (members of the armed forces and others), this confirms the scant health scheme coverage, which is even lower than for the pension programme.

In total, little over 25 per cent of the active population are members of pension, health or savings schemes. Health cover is supplemented by the Ministry of Public Health and Social Security, which should in theory cover the remaining 75 per cent of the population. However, there are inherent limitations in terms of infrastructure and resources in the sector, which only allow provision, in practice, for 40 per cent.

Table 6.3 shows the coverage of social security schemes in El Salvador in 1996, including the sectors and numbers covered as well as the contributions rates.

Table 6.3 Coverage of the population by formal social security schemes, El Salvador, 1996

Social security programmes	Sector covered	Institution	Population		Contribution rates (percentages)			
			Contributors	Beneficiaries[f]	Employee	Employer	Treasury	Total
Pensions	Private sector	ISSS	380 000	29 000	1.0[a]	2	0.5	3.5
	Public employees	INPEP	110 000	27 000	4.5	4.5	-	9.0
	Teachers	INPEP	30 000	6 000	6.0	6.0	-	12.0
Employment injury	All employees	ISSS/INPEP	520 000	520 000	[b]	[b]	-	[b]
Health	General scheme [e]	ISSS	417 000	635 000	3.0	7.5	[c]	10.5+[c]
	Special scheme	ISSS	120 000	183 000	2.7	6.7	-	9.4
Housing, savings and loans	Industry and commerce	FSV	380 000	75 173[d]	0.5	5.0	-	5.5
Total population			5 787 000					
Labour force			1 981 000 (34% of total population)					
Ratio active/pensioners			8.4 to 1					

Notes: (a) Workers receiving subsidies must contribute 20 per cent of the amount of the benefit.
(b) The rate is included in the amount for the health scheme.
(c) The State must make an annual contribution of not less than 5 million colons.
(d) Value taken from the FSV report, 1990-1991.
(e) ISSS pensioners contribute 6 per cent of their pension to the health scheme.
(f) Beneficiaries are all those who, through payment of social security benefits by the insured or contributor, are entitled to all or any of the benefits for which the contribution is made.

Source: Mesa-Lago and Durán, 1998.

3.   Health-care delivery

The health-care system in El Salvador is made up of various public and private sector institutions, with differing patterns of supply and demand, different roles and a whole range of ways of interacting with other players. Currently, these institutions form a system which is not integrated, with little coordination between them and no health plan governing their operations.

3.1 Government-financed health services

Health services financed by the Government are basically provided through the Ministry of Public Health and Social Assistance (MOH), which estimates that it covers some 50 per cent of the population in terms of basic services, and 75 per cent for hospital services. In the country's rural areas, the Ministry has the largest network of services, consisting of medical posts, regional hospitals and specialist hospitals.

The health services provided by the Ministry are financed by the State from the national budget, international agencies and, in some hospitals, cost-recovery. The distribution of financing is 75 per cent from the Government of El Salvador, 19 per cent from international assistance and about 5 per cent recovered from users. In 1994, USAID alone financed some 50 per cent of purchases of medicines and inputs and some 11 per cent of the total operating costs of the MOH.

The MOH includes primary health care as one of its priority strategies. However, the enormous expense represented by hospitals means that the budget is mainly invested in curative treatment. Despite the fact that the MOH network accounts for more than half the Salvadorian health-care system, both in terms of resources and responsibility for care, this is not matched by its budget. At the end of the 1980s, the MOH provided 40 per cent of the country's outpatient consultations, 75.5 per cent of hospital cover, 38.1 per cent of the total births attended and 33.4 per cent of child health checks.

In addition to the Ministry of Public Health and Social Assistance as a provider of health services financed by the Government, there is another group of state institutions which provide health-care services, although they are not wholly or directly financed by the Government. They include 17 state institutions, the most important of which are: Bienestar Magisterial (Teachers' Welfare), the National Telecommunications Health Network (ANTEL), the Rio Lema Hydroelectric Executive Board's Health Service (CEL), and the health programme of the National Water and Drainage Authority (ANDA).

3.2 The three health-care markets

The patterns of use of health-care providers in El Salvador correlate to three distinct and largely mutually exclusive health-care markets. Users choose the type of health care in function of the characteristics of these three markets, which are distinguished by the ISSS mainly on the basis of geographical residence and cover. In addition, it is influenced by the type of demand for health service, factors such as perception of illness, motivation and waiting times for doctors, and the economic and educational level of the Salvadorian public. The three markets are:

1. People living in urban areas who are covered by the ISSS, who have the widest choice of health-care providers: the ISSS, the MOH or the private sector.
2. People living in urban areas who are not covered by the ISSS; they can choose between the MOH and the private sector.
3. People living in rural areas. This group is covered only by the MOH or the (mainly non-profit) private sector.

The choice of provider of curative treatment for the three markets was distributed as shown in table 6.4.

Given the behaviour reflected above, it can be seen that pharmacies are an important component of the supply of health services, given the high level of self-medication. In El Salvador, there are 1,004 retail outlets, covering the whole of the country.

There is also a direct relation between the use of preventive consultations and the people's level of education. The higher the level of education, the greater the use made of preventive consultations.

3.3 Productivity in health-care delivery in the ISSS and the MOH

One factor that influences users' attitudes is the travel and the waiting time for consultations. In the case of the MOH, the waiting time is quite high compared with the ISSS. A waiting time of more than 3 hours is mentioned by 44 per cent of users, while 15 per cent had a journey of over two hours to reach the place for the consultation.

As an illustration of some other measures of the average productivity of the Ministry of Public Health and Social Assistance, some comparisons with the ISSS are provided (see table 6.5).

For example, it can be seen that the ISSS has an overall average of 4.4 consultations per hour for doctors while for the MOH, in hospitals, it is 2.9 consultations per hour. Thus, the productivity for MOH Hospitals is two-thirds that of the ISSS. The other indicators can be read similarly.

With regard to costs, it can be seen from table 6.6 that the daily cost of medical hospitalization is much less than in the ISSS, only a quarter of the price.

Table 6.4 Curative treatment by provider, El Salvador, 1994 (percentages)

Market	MOH Hospital	MOH Unit/Post	ISSS	Private sector	Self-treatment[1]
Urban, covered by ISSS	—	—	22.7	8.7	68.6
Urban, not covered by ISSS	3.6	4.3	—	4.0	83.6
Rural	3.2	4.3	—	4.0	88.5

[1]Self-treatment is regarded as the situation where patients themselves, or on the advice of family or friends, diagnose their own case, and apply self-medication, directly starting a course of medical treatment, without previous consultation with a relevant professional or technician.

Source: USAID, 1994.

Table 6.5 Average productivity in consultations per hour, El Salvador, 1994

Institution or establishment	Consultations per hour		MOH productivity as a percentage of ISSS	
	Doctors	Dentists	Doctors	Dentists
ISSS: Overall average	4.4	3.4		
MOH Hospitals	2.9		66	
MOH Units	2.6	1.8	59	53
MOH Posts	1.8	0.6	41	18

Source: USAID, 1994.

Table 6.6 Daily hospitalization costs, El Salvador, 1994

Category	Daily cost (in colons)	MOH as a percentage of ISSS
Medical hospitalization		
ISSS	568	
MOH Hospital	152	27
MOH Centre	146	26
Surgical hospitalization		
ISSS	194	
MOH Hospital	190	98
MOH Centre	81	41

Source: USAID, 1994.

For surgical hospitalization, the cost of hospitals is similar, but in MOH Centres, the daily cost of hospitalization is 41 per cent of the cost for the ISSS. Also with regard to other service costs, the MOH is cheaper than the ISSS (see table 6.7).

4. Pension reform and possibilities for extension

The process of reforming the pensions system in El Salvador began around 1992 with a series of diagnostic analyses and studies on possible options for reform in the country. These diagnostic analyses revealed the fundamental problems inherent in the Salvadorian pensions system, arising from weaknesses in the design of the model. The reasons for change, indeed, are due to the original faults in the Salvadorian pay-as-you-go (PAYG) system.

4.1 Outline of the pension reform

The reform of the pensions system that was promoted by the Salvadorian Government resulted in the approval by the Legislative Assembly, in December 1996, of the new Pensions Savings System Law, with full individual funding and private administration of the funds, in which workers' benefits depend directly on the contributions credited to their accounts. This system will, in due course, replace the current state PAYG scheme.[2]

Under this law, the State allows commercial companies with fixed capital, as designated Pension Fund Administering Institutions, to provide a public service as part of the social security system. Their functions are to collect workers' contributions, credit them to each individual account, invest them collectively in publicly offered shares and deposits, in accredited formal financial markets and within prescribed limits, and administer benefits for old age, disability and death due to common risks.

Although private entities are responsible for the administration, the State has a supreme role as "institutional system administrator" through the Pensions Supervisory Department. This department must be a highly technical, specialist entity to control their operations and ensure strict compliance with the legislation. In addition, the State is the ultimate guarantor of the Pensions Savings System. The difference from the state PAYG system is that in the latter, the State guarantees the system directly, whereas in the Pensions Savings System, additional guarantees are interposed prior to any disbursement by the State.

The guarantees of the system are as follows:

(a) There is a procedure for classifying the risks of financial instruments, and if they are considered acceptable, the State allows administering institutions to invest the pension funds.

---

[2] FundaUngo proposed, as an alternative, a mixed scheme. See Mesa-Lago, 1994.

Table 6.7 Other health service costs, El Salvador, 1994

Goods and services	Unit cost (colons)	MOH as a percentage of ISSS
Outpatient consultations		
ISSS	42	
MOH Hospital	41	98
MOH Centre	43	102
MOH Unit	26	62
MOH Post	32	76
Average cost of x-rays		
ISSS	47	
MOH Hospital	28	60
MOH Centre	33	70
Average cost of laboratory test		
ISSS	14	
MOH Hospital	6	98
MOH Centre	9	41

Source: USAID, 1994.

(b) Investment limits for funds are laid down by law, in the form of ceilings or maxima for each generic type of instrument, within which each administering institution may determine its own policy for profitable, low-risk investments.

(c) The financial instruments in which the funds invest must be held in safe keeping by specialized institutions, specifically authorized in accordance with the Stock Exchange Law for custody and deposit of securities.

(d) The accounts of the Fund must be maintained entirely separate from the assets of the administering institution, so that the workers' assets can be clearly established. Thus, an administering institution may become bankrupt, but not the pension funds.

(e) It is stipulated that administering institutions must generate at least a minimum return from the funds, and this simply refers to the average returns of all funds over a determined period.

(f) A profit equalization fund is established in each fund, to cover the obligation to achieve a minimum return, when an administering institution invests at higher returns than those required.

(g) Administering institutions form, from their own resources, an asset designated as a special guarantee contribution, which must be invested in the pension fund itself, to support the guarantee of minimum returns.

(h) When the obligation to achieve a minimum return cannot be covered by the profit equalization reserve and the special guarantee contribution, the administering authority must apply its own capital, which is regulated by law, and its own assets, which grow as a function of the size of the fund which it administers and the number of members in it.

(i) Lastly, the State exercises control over all the above requirements through the Pensions Supervisory Department.

The objectives of a process of change such as this are major social objectives: to provide better pensions for future generations and provide a minimum level of guarantees to pensioners. In addition, under the constitutional principle of equality before the law, it seeks to harmonize conditions and benefits for employees in the private and public sectors.

4.2 Opportunities and obstacles to greater coverage

As the new Pensions Savings System allows voluntary and optional entry, it offers opportunities for greater coverage for the self-employed, and for non-resident Salvadorians, farmworkers and any other Salvadorians who wish to insure against the risks of old age, disability and death.

For example, agricultural cooperatives, which were originally totally denied access to the ISSS, may enter the formal system quite easily under the new legislation. In fact, there are cases of associations of farmworkers, cooperative or otherwise, such as "Asegure su Futuro" (Assure your Future), an organization with some 40,000 members, that have expressed their interest in becoming pension fund administrators with the support and trust of their members. In addition, the more than one million Salvadorians living abroad could provide for their retirement, disability or death, by joining a pension fund.

However, the main constraints remain. These are of a structural nature and depend on the nature of the Salvadorian labour market, where more than half the economically active population works in the informal sector. However, with the reform, the possibilities of informal sector workers entering the formal sector of social security are no longer prohibited by law.

5. Towards the self-financing of social security in the informal sector

The approval of the Pension Savings System Law in December 1996 may be the beginning of a series of changes in the field of social security. As noted in the previous section, the reform will benefit much of the income-earning population, but leaves out a large section of the population which is excluded because of its inability to pay contributions. However, this means that, by having a contributory pension system which provides adequate cover for those in the formal sector, the State can take up its role of financing pensions for those who are not protected, and they are the group requiring its contribution and attention. The second priority on the agenda should be health, which requires reform to improve provision of services and reduce costs.

In order to reach the adult population excluded from the pension system and improve health care would require enormous expenditure. About 2 per cent of GDP is allocated to the pension system and health care. This percentage is well below that allocated by other countries under these headings. Indeed, any attempt to implement a programme of welfare pensions for adults without incomes would require massive fiscal reform, so as to raise the taxes evaded year after year by contributors who are easily able to pay. Unless this is done, it is unlikely that any new programme could be implemented or existing ones extended.

However, at some levels of the informal sector, it has been possible to design welfare programmes using a form of mixed financing – subsidy and contributions from the community – which has to some extent improved coverage. Examples of this type of project are given in sections 5.2 and 5.3. They also seek to show that there are ways of organizing people so as to carry out joint programmes under the banner of social security which will benefit the informal sector.

In addition, occupational schemes in private and public sector companies are constantly being increased, covering both pensions and health, as a priority. Generally, people covered by these plans are also covered by the State's health and welfare schemes, but where there are private schemes in companies, they relieve the demand overload in public health establishments, resulting in better services to the customer.

5.1   Social security needs and contributory capacity of the informal sector

It is difficult to imagine that groups in the informal sector could have much ability to contribute, but what is clear is that, with adequate organization, access to social security programmes can be improved, especially health and housing. The contingency of old age is apparently not an immediate concern or they simply think that in the future someone will take care of them. A survey for the ILO-PROMICRO project (1997) on the contributive ability of micro-entrepreneurs, measured by profits achieved, showed that there is a fairly large number of micro-entrepreneurs with high incomes who are willing to pay for private old-age and health services. However, it also emerged that the majority of micro-entrepreneurs have very low incomes, which makes them unable to pay the contributions required by such services.

The above survey drew two important conclusions: the public system has not found ways of significantly extending coverage to micro-entrepreneurs who, although they are income-earning economic actors, have been relegated to the welfare sphere. Up to now, there have only been a few limited efforts by some organizations of micro-entrepreneurs to try to provide some kind of social security cover.

A sector as heterogeneous as micro-enterprises cannot be tackled by designing a single intervention strategy for social security. It is a sector which may be the subject of policies and programmes of various origins. For instance, there are some micro-enterprises which, although few in number, have high income levels, and could participate in forms of social security provided by the private sector. There are also other segments which could associate to reduce costs and allow access to social security insurance. In the case of health insurance – which is the most expensive – they could try forms which allow integration of central and local government measures, together with voluntary organizations (PROMICRO-OIT-PACTEM, 1997).

5.2 The savings and loans cooperative for market women in Santa Ana

The Savings and Loans Cooperative Association for the Women of Municipal Market No.2 in Santa Ana, a limited company with variable capital (ACACSEMERSA R.L.) has been registered in the National Register of Cooperatives of the Salvadorian Institute for Cooperative Development (INSAFOCOOP) since 1965. It has some 2,500 members and its capital consists of their contributions.

(a) *Type of risk covered.* ACACSEMERSA provides its members with health cover through soft loans and insurance and savings protection in the event of the death of the insured member or her family.

(b) *Type of providers and users.* The service provider is ACACSEMERSA and the users are the members and the respective beneficiaries. To be a member, and thus to enjoy the benefits provided by the organization, women must be aged over 16 and under 60, be proposed by two members of the cooperative, pay a contribution from income of 81 colons per year and meet certain solvency requirements (such as a confirmation of income, in the case of a private or public sector employee, or a certificate of solvency from the administration, in the case of a trader in the municipal market, together with trade references).

(c) *Conditions for access to benefits.* In all cases, there is a basic condition for access to the organization's benefits and services, which is to save at least the value of a share, 10 colons, every month. The following specific conditions apply:

i. In the event of death, provided that the member's contributions are paid up to date, there are two types of protection for the member and her beneficiaries:

- For an annual payment of 20 colons, the cooperative pays the bene-ficiaries the sum of 2,000 colons on the death of the member for funeral expenses, and in the event of the death of any of the member's family, the sum of 1,000 colons.
- The beneficiaries receive an amount of twice the sum saved by the member, up to a maximum of 24,000 colons.

ii. Health cover is by loans to members, as follows:

- Loan to obtain glasses, for the member, family or friends, for a maximum term of 10 months, at a fixed annual interest of 12 per cent.
- Dental benefit, consisting of a special loan for all members and family who wish to obtain dental services, for a maximum term of one year at a fixed annual interest of 12 per cent.
- Loans for purchase of goods and/or services to improve the member's living standards, including health needs. If the loan is up to 4,000 colons, the maximum term is 30 months, and if over 4,000 colons, 36 months. The interest rate is 24 per cent per year, calculated monthly on the outstanding balance, and the maximum loan is five times the balance of the member's contributions.

   To qualify for such loans, the following documents must be submitted: photocopy of identity card, certificate of solvency from the administration and guarantee.

(d) *Type of cover.* In the main, the members of the cooperative are traders in the Santa Ana Municipal Market, who are not covered by any of the formal social security institutions. In this regard, the health cover by means of loans, and the death cover are unique. In the case of members employed in the private or public sector, the cover operates as a non-exclusive complement to the statutory social security benefit.

(e) *Funding mechanism.* In this case, the protection is entirely self-financed by the group of cooperative members, who through their monthly contributions, entry fee and extra savings have succeeded in establishing a fund which covers their needs for financing and special protection against death through funeral insurance and savings protection.

(f) *Administration.* ACACSEMERSA R.L. directly administers benefits to improve the social and economic welfare of its members. The governing bodies are the General Assembly of almost 2,500 members, an Executive Board consisting of five members and a Supervisory Board of three members. Services are administered by 21 employees: seven in administration, one social worker, two financial analysts, three loans staff, five collection staff and three accountants.

5.3 The Maquilishuat Foundation

The Maquilishuat Foundation (FUMA) is a national NGO, established in the mid-1980s to work specifically in the health field. Nowadays, it also covers adult literacy, street children and gender questions, although with a lower presence in the health field.

(a) *Type of risk covered.* The Foundation primarily covers health risks, using a model consisting of eight components: acute respiratory infections, diarrhoea, women's reproductive health (pregnancy and planning), perinatal health, community planning, growth and development in children from 0–5 years, immunization and environmental health. All the components contain a single nucleus focusing on priority care to mother and child (maternity and infancy programme), as a prime means of tackling or preventing the highest risk diseases.
(b) *Type of provider and user.* The Maquilishuat Foundation, a private non-profit organization, provides services directly through previously trained community promoters. These services have been extended to the departments of San Salvador, San Miguel, Sonsonate and La Libertad, which were determined from a diagnostic analysis to be areas of deficiency in terms of access to health services.

As a result of the diagnostic analysis, leaders were selected to organize the provision of medical services, and after a comprehensive training course accredited by the MOH, they will serve as trainers at the community level. The main area of provision is based on bringing problem-solving close to the places where the problems arise.

Demand was defined and established by a study of areas defined as having deficiencies, on the basis of criteria such as: no MOH presence, extremely poor users, resident in rural areas. It was also laid down that demand should be in places inaccessible due to lack of infrastructure: poor roads, long distances to travel to health units, posts or clinics.
(c) *Conditions for access to benefits.* At present, in addition to meeting the eligibility criteria defined above, users are asked to make a token monetary contribution, so that the programme is not seen as mere social assistance. In addition, it is a condition of access to health benefits that beneficiaries keep their appointments for health-care services.

161

(d) *Type of cover.* The various components of FUMA's mother and child programme provide care for some 30,000 beneficiaries. As described in the types of cover, and taking into account the criteria for selecting communities and beneficiaries, the health cover provided by FUMA is unique, since those who receive the health care do so from a single provider. The programme covers four departments and, specifically, communities in rural areas.

(e) *Funding mechanism.* To finance the components of the health programme, the Foundation called on the resources available in the Mother and Child Health Programme (PROSAMI) provided by USAID, as well as from Medical Service Corporation International, an NGO from the United States. The amount currently required to finance the programme totals 1,800,000 colons, which is used to provide medicines and to pay promoters' salaries and programme administrative costs. An effective plan to recover costs from the recipients of the service was introduced, producing 50,000 colons in 1995.

PROSAMI was recently transferred to the External Financing Technical Department (SETEFE) in the Ministry of Foreign Relations, and bodies which are financed under this programme must comply with the access rules of this body. According to FUMA officials, this has resulted in longer delays in "customer" care by the Foundation.

(f) *Administration.* The health programme is directly administered by FUMA through promoters and doctors working for the Foundation, with the support of the community authorities.

Some disadvantages which have arisen in this respect should be highlighted. First, there was USAID's decision to move the entire PROSAMI programme to SETEFE which made the network of NGOs financed from PROSAMI resources depend on MOH supervision. Secondly, as a result of the former, this transfer meant that the Foundation fell under the supervision of a state body and thus entered the world of bureaucratic restrictions which slow down the arrangements for delivering services to recipients. A clear example of this is the MOH's prohibition of promoters supplying antibiotics, permitting only doctors to do so.

In any case, the Foundation's experience of administering this model of health care has had its successes. The incidence of pneumonia, as principal cause of death, has declined by 12 per cent. Dehydration has fallen and thus diarrhoeal diseases are being controlled. Practising midwives have been trained in handling complications with births. The diagnosis and treatment of diseases of mothers and children have been modernized.

The FUMA health programme has developed the capacity to provide the basic range of health services, with levels of efficiency which compare favourably with the state system. The cost to FUMA of providing this service is 53 colons per annum per patient.

5.4 Promoting self-financing

A whole range of organizations in the non-formal sector are seeking through self-financing to provide protection against various circumstances that are not covered by formal care schemes (FundaUngo, 1997). The contingencies covered by these organizations and institutions include disability, old age, death, illness and maternity. In addition, other types of need can be covered, such as housing, education, funeral expenses and assistance to families on the death of a relative.

The non-formal social security network can be characterized as having a planned organization, in cases where there are well-defined administrative or operational structures, or natural organization, when driven by the need to survive, as within a family. We shall refer to these types of organization below, with emphasis on those which predominate in El Salvador.

(a) *Extended family.* This natural way of organization to meet future risks can take charge of the education of the children, land and housing for the whole family, and thereby share the joint task between generations. Generally, the children take responsibility for the parents when they reach an advanced age, thus transferring income between generations. In rural areas in El Salvador, it is very common for young people to take care of the contingencies of old age for their parents. However, parents in an extended family have previously worked to earn this benefit, by generating income to cover basic social needs.

When the children grow up, many of them migrate to urban areas in search of work, while others, using savings made by their parents, decide to travel to the United States, Canada or Australia. The phenomenon of family remittances explains, in large measure, how families[3] that do not have access to the formal security system can cover contingencies such as disability, illness and old age. Moreover, with the remittance income, they can pay for education and housing, so that the family cycle continues and protection is strengthened between past, present and future generations.

(b) *The organized community.* When the social services provided by formal systems do not meet demand, the need arises for the community to protect itself against disease, lack of education, housing and other matters. The armed conflict in El Salvador, mainly in the 1980s, forced many communities to organize against such adversities and so, from the local community, emerged people's doctors, paramedics and nurses as well as people's teachers in non-formal schools. Nowadays, in El Salvador, this type of organization has been

---

[3] It should be explained that the phenomenon of remittances is not confined to extended families, but it is very important; 46 per cent of households receiving family remittances have five or more members in the household, according to the Household Survey.

improved with the assistance of non-governmental organizations which have directed or channelled resources to cover certain social security needs.

(c) *Religious institutions.* The churches have also been channels for resources or a means of organization to achieve certain forms of protection for the population, mainly against disease and food shortages. However, rather than being a social security plan, programmes run by these institutions had the main objective of tackling issues of poverty, thus falling into the category of social welfare programmes.

(d) *Entrepreneurial organizations.* The most common form of protection outside the formal social security network is the organization of occupational plans or protection funds within enterprises, both public and private. Generally risks associated with disability, age, illness, maternity and others are covered by contributions from employers and employees. Resources are thus used to provide benefits which are not part of a social security programme. In some instances, this type of organization links the programme's benefits with those provided by the formal sector. In most instances, the employee obtains benefits additional to those he or she receives or will receive under the formal system. Historically, the main way in which this type of organization has been created is through trade union pressure to obtain a beneficial collective agreement. Within the institutional framework of the public sector, this type of benefit has created distortions in the labour market, by discriminating in favour of certain privileged groups, to which the State allocates much greater resources, although other alternatives would be of greater social value.

(e) *Mutual funds.* Mutual funds have been a traditional form of organization both for groups which have access to formal social security and those which do not. The organization arises in connection with a particular profession or sector. In El Salvador, for example, there are two mutual funds, one connected with the legal profession and the other for those working in education. If the origin of mutual funds is related to public sector activities, they almost always receive an initial subsidy from the State, which serves as the primary financial basis for the programme.

(f) *Cooperative associations.* While cooperative associations start out with specific objectives, it is not unusual to find aims concerned with the social and economic needs of their members. Members make voluntary contributions to a common fund which serves to cover a variety of contingencies, such as illness, funeral expenses and education among others, depending on the scope of the programme designed for such purposes.

The agrarian reform in El Salvador, for example, opened up the possibility that such organizations might feel the need to protect themselves against such expenditure and, in an informal manner, to seek appropriate ways of doing so. For instance, cooperatives have an in-house doctor or clinic or contract medical insurance, depending on the size and income of the cooperative. They may also have resources to finance members, for investment in education or housing construction.

(g) *Non-governmental organizations.* In El Salvador, the Government's lack of attention to fundamental problems of the people led, mainly during the conflict, to the proliferation of NGOs. Many of them include provision for social security risks in their objectives. Thus there are NGOs which specialize in tackling poverty, providing the poor with access to health, education and housing. In other cases, these organizations have a more diversified structure and allocate resources to income-generating programmes for the target population. An example of this type of programme are the Communal Banks, which allow the poor access to credit for small businesses.

A fundamental characteristic of this type of organization is that the service is targeted at an established demand, meaning that the beneficiaries are organized in some way to receive the benefits. But the main achievement is that the NGOs manage to match supply to a demand already present in the community.

6. Conclusions

Poverty in El Salvador is a widespread problem which affects thousands of Salvadorian families, mainly in rural areas and in certain departments. Practical experience has shown that when projects are carried out within the framework of a well-defined social policy, the problem can be tackled and the persistence of the phenomenon can be reduced. Educational programmes certainly do not immediately reduce poverty, but it is very likely that a generation which has greater opportunities for education will be better equipped to face the future than one which did not have such opportunity. El Salvador's social development strategy since 1989 was initially a reaction to the negative effects of the structural adjustment programme that was being implemented, and which caused temporary social imbalances. However, it later launched a medium-term component, involving more far-reaching programmes so as to address the problem of structural poverty. Even if progress has not been spectacular, for a country which suffered from armed conflict for more than 12 years, it must be encouraging that even in the worst cases, the poverty indicators have not worsened. There is no doubt that 1989 marked the beginnings of a basic social security system, with more direction and cohesion than any other social plan introduced in the past.

The health services financed by the State are the backbone of the country's health system. The provision of such services through state institutions, which do not always have adequate budgetary provision or additional means of generating income to provide an efficient service, makes people somewhat distrustful in accepting the health service provided by the Government. The case study of the Maquilishuat Foundation, FUMA, suggests the possibility that the State could entrust the provision of health services to third parties, such as NGOs, and that the main function of the State would be to finance and supervise the service.

Another important lesson shown by the FUMA health programme is that the closer the service provision is to the users, the greater is the political impact of the policy. However, it has to be recognized that a programme of this nature cannot be self-sustaining, because the users to whom it is addressed have little purchasing power. Nevertheless, the cost-benefit results to the community in the endeavour to contribute to keeping the programme "self-financing" are wholly to the advantage of the local beneficiary population, and also to those who continue to be treated in MOH centres, which can provide a better service to those not covered by the NGO schemes.

The coverage of formal social security services, specifically pensions and health insurance, is relatively low. However, a number of factors – including the ending of the armed conflict, the country's relative social and economic stability, and the introduction of the new law on the Pensions Savings System – may generate a process of change in the economy and thus in the pattern of employment, which will allow more workers to insure themselves against contingencies such as death, disability, old age and illness within formal social security programmes.

However, it must be borne in mind that the main constraints on the expansion of coverage do not stem from existing models of social security, but from the fact that they are contributory, requiring monetary contributions that not everyone in El Salvador can afford, precisely because of the conditions of poverty and informality.

References

FundaUngo. 1997. *Red de seguridad social no formal* (San Salvador).

ILO. 1994. *ILO News. Latin America and the Caribbean. 1994 Labour Overview* (Lima).

Mesa-Lago, C. 1994. *Changing social security in Latin America. Towards alleviating the social costs of economic reform* (Boulder, Colorado and London, Lynne Rienner Publishers).

Mesa-Lago, C.; Durán, F. 1998. *Evaluación de la reforma de pensiones en El Salvador: Antecedentes, objetivos y perspectivas* (San Salvador, Fundación Friedrich Ebert).

Ministry of Planning (MIPLAN). 1995. *Encuesta de hogares de propósitos múltiples 1994–95* (San Salvador).

PROMICRO-OIT-PACTEM. 1997. *Seguridad social y microempresa en El Salvador* (San José, Costa Rica).

USAID. 1994. *Análisis del sector salud* (San Salvador).

SOCIAL SECURITY FOR THE INFORMAL SECTOR IN BENIN

7

Bernardin Gauthé, Consultant, Paris

1. Existing social security arrangements

1.1 Formal social security coverage

The formal social security system in Benin consists of a general scheme administered by the Benin Office of Social Security (OBSS) and a special scheme for civil servants and military personnel. The two schemes cover not more than 5 per cent of the active population, and are very limited and selective. This state of affairs is linked to the fragmented nature of the national economy, with a predominant informal sector. Moreover, the two schemes do not provide their members with sufficient benefits to meet their needs.

The Benin Office of Social Security covers family allowances, employment injury risks and retirement pensions for workers covered by the Labour Code. The National Retirement Pension Fund (FNRB), which is separate from the OBSS, administers pensions for civil servants. Recently, a complementary pension fund was created, designed to improve the living standards and welfare of retirees, particularly for wage-earners in the public and private sector and for the self-employed. The Ministry of Labour is responsible for overall supervision of the schemes, while the OBSS administers them.

In practice, the OBSS general scheme applies to wage-earners in the private sector, local government workers and private individuals governed by the Labour Code. It is mainly financed by contributions paid by employers and employees. The contributions vary for employees and assured persons depending on the type of benefit. The system covers six of the nine branches defined in ILO Convention No.102 – namely old-age benefit, invalidity, survivors', family, maternity and employment injury benefits – but omits unemployment benefit, medical care and sickness benefit.

The state-run civil service scheme applies to personnel in any of the regular civil service departments or the army. It is financed by the State from public funds and covers family allowances and pensions. There are medical insurance and employment injury benefit provisions, but in diffuse forms; under the provision for medical care, the civil servant is reimbursed 80 per cent of the costs, except for medicines.

1.2 Social assistance

On the formal level, social assistance for vulnerable groups in Benin is provided by several public departments and national and international NGOs through specially targeted programmes. The Department of Social Affairs (DAS) has set up national social welfare promotion centres, 88 of which are now operating, as well as social action centres in the main hospitals, schools and even judicial departments. However, this social assistance is very limited, if not totally absent, due to lack of resources.

However, the legal framework is effective in organizing and regulating help for people in distress. Help is in the form of non-reimbursable grants to people in need who have inadequate means or none at all as a result of a temporarily critical situation. Grants are at the discretion of the Ministry of Social Affairs. There is no appeal against any decision on social welfare grants, and assistance may never be permanent or for life.

The actions of NGOs are most evident and effective in the area of social integration. There are several organizations working with remarkable success to combat social exclusion. This particularly applies to religious organizations, which today play a leading part in protecting and integrating marginalized groups in the urban and rural areas. These organizations are involved in health, education, nutrition, and even financial and material help. Their action has increased with the devaluation of the CFA franc.

Nevertheless, the various social assistance programmes have had limited impact on reducing poverty. Several constraints prevent the implementation of a truly effective social assistance policy for marginalized groups:

(i) *lack of adequate and reliable information about specific groups.* There are still no quantitative or qualitative studies of the various vulnerable groups, and such research might permit really focused action.

(ii) *lack of an operational institutional framework* to coordinate the work of the various international agencies engaged in combating poverty and integrating marginalized groups. The actions undertaken are sectoral and/or specific, which leads to duplication of effort in the field and waste of energy.

(iii) *inadequate human, material and financial resources* in the state bodies concerned. Most of the state bodies involved in social affairs lack adequate human, material and financial resources to handle the tasks to be carried out (Ministry of Labour, 1994).

2. Social security and the informal sector

2.1 The informal sector: Concepts and trends

The multi-criteria definition of the informal sector suggested by the ILO in its report on Kenya (ILO, 1972), a concept which could perhaps be updated, nevertheless has the merit of defining the fundamental characteristics of informal micro-enterprises:

- ease of entry,
- utilization of local resources,
- family ownership of local resources,
- small-scale activities,
- highly labour-intensive technology,
- education acquired outside the school system,
- unregulated competitive markets.

Clearly, the diversity of forms of the informal sector is a key point. Without going into detail, we can distinguish three main categories in the sector:

(a) *The informal subsistence sector* includes all small-scale trades which involve little or no capital (car washers, shoe-shine workers, itinerant vendors). These are often itinerant trades which do not require any kind of premises. They generate low incomes and are often only an additional family income. They are sometimes carried on short-term, while waiting for other work. The flow of new migrants is governed by these trades, as is the social integration of the unemployed in family or ethnic host structures. It may also involve household trading activities, site labour etc.

(b) *The traditional rural craft sector* (also found, more rarely, in urban areas) is a category for which it may even be asked whether this can be called an informal activity. While production volumes are small and the technology is of low capital intensity, the organization of the trade is often advanced, either through effective corporative structures or because of their monopolies in the trade (blacksmiths in Senegal and Mali, sellers of statuettes in Senegal). The free entry and flexibility which characterize the informal sector are very limited for such activities. However, under certain conditions, these structures can develop into small and medium-sized enterprises (SMEs), which is inconceivable in the case of the previous category. The Moroccan carpet industry and, to a lesser degree, leatherwork are illustrations of this potential evolution.

(c) *The competitive informal sector* offers goods and services which aim to compete with modern products. For most of these activities, the degree of competition is weak due to great differences in the quality of products and services. Generally, therefore, the informal and the modern sectors aim at different customers. However, some enterprises in this category that have reached a certain level in terms of equipment, maintain coherent management and improve their product quality can compete strongly with the modern sector.

2.2 Self-financing schemes

In social practice, "tontines" are regarded in Benin as a financial institution and means of mutual aid. It seems above all to be a way of encouraging saving, and can be perceived as a form of social insurance. There are also mutual benefit societies in Benin, which collect money from their members and return it in the form of investment and operating loans for their businesses, or as social development loans. There are two sorts of mutual benefit society – health societies and loan societies – which are, in effect, enhanced tontines.

Cooperatives are generally defined as mutual aid groups, often made up of farmers, craft workers, etc., from the same village or district and with the same objective of social security for their members and their families in case of illness, accident, death or other risks, through a fund created by their members' monthly contributions. Cooperatives work on a larger scale, and include mostly rural and urban craft workers, and to a lesser degree those in the informal competitive sector.

These various organizations differ widely in form, depending on the number of members, the regularity of payments, etc., and the permutations are almost infinite. They are real social security systems both in the way they operate (with contributions and benefits) and their objectives (to cover against social risks). These tontines, mutual benefit societies and cooperatives combine social solidarity and economic efficiency, without, however, being governed by the profit logic as an absolute value.

There was a time when the savings collected appeared not to be distributed widely enough in the form of loans. This was explained by an emphasis on security and social behaviour in relation to savings (hoarding and sheltering of money) rather than the economic logic of accumulation (financing operating and investment costs). Today, however, thanks to the success of the most dynamic mutual societies, cooperatives and tontines, notably SASAKAWA 2000, there has been a change in attitudes towards lending.

Although created in the fertile experience of savings and informal loans, mutual benefit societies and tontines have still managed to introduce novel practices, adapting the way they operate to the enterprise economy. Three major innovations should be mentioned: the introduction of the notion of interest; the essential use of credit in the operation and development of the enterprise; and the introduction of social and professional relations to encourage self-help organization through the management of savings and access to services in support of production.

Some trade unions and cooperatives have begun to make their members aware of the need to create mutual health societies. These groups have funds, from tontines or contributions, pooled to assist women in case of illness (purchase of medicines, financial aid), but these initiatives are still very limited.

One should also take note of a tightening of neighbourly bonds and mutual aid between members, for these organizations rely on mutual trust and a territorial base. They are a means of promotion which is well suited to the needs of their members. The services that they provide are highly appreciated, which is a measure of their social and technical viability. Moreover, the cash in circulation in these organizations encourages the hope that the extension of social security to the informal sector will promote a flow of a considerable amount of hidden savings into the official economy. Improvements in the strength of these organizations can thus be a factor in local development.

These informal structures are attempts to counter the problems faced by people in their daily lives. The extremely important role that they play and their responses to people's problems are a challenge to a security social system which aims to cover the informal sector. The viability and success of such a project depends on the relevance and effectiveness of the proposed solutions. The challenge is to put forward attractive and realistic proposals.

Given the social and economic problems which a large section of the country's population face today, it is a matter of urgency to create a basic social security system for the whole population. It must be a basic system which provides insurance for everyone, without it being dependent on membership of a particular occupation. That is one of the obstacles to the extension of the formal system.

2.3 Social security needs

The majority of workers in the formal sector can make regular social security contributions, generally with a long-term outlook. Since they can save for their retirement, formal social security systems often concentrate on old-age pensions.

The social security needs of vulnerable groups and the informal sector have diversified due to the increasingly precarious economic situation and the inability of administrative authorities to meet the legitimate expectations of the least advantaged. Paradoxically, one can see a vitality and economic dynamism linked to the Benin spirit of making do. In reality, what is missing is a structure which can look after people in health and other social security benefits. The growth in the informal sector, and its percentage of the active population, engender more and more needs which remain unsatisfied by the formal framework, which is in any case inadequate.

The situation of agricultural populations remains worrying at certain periods, since with little money, these people find it difficult to feed and house themselves properly. This situation leads to disease among the most sensitive groups (pregnant women, children, the elderly). Disease is the result of a combination of factors of dirt, lack of hygiene in housing, i.e. living conditions in which infection and parasites are endemic.

Women find such living conditions hard to endure, forced as they are to help in the fields and do the housework. For children, apart from health problems, there is the problem of schooling. The parents' lack of means to pay for school materials interrupts children's normal education, which leads to lower attendance at certain times. Elderly people are looked after by their families. However, in rural areas where there is a fairly massive exodus, the elderly must go on working to a fairly advanced age.

In Benin's informal urban sector, the inventory of needs expressed by people during surveys (GTZ, 1995) puts health as a first priority; and choices primarily reflect the health of children and mothers as the most sensitive concerns among such populations. This is followed by the need for children's education. Assistance with schooling was a frequent demand among respondents. Certainly, the cost of education is a heavy burden for traditionally large families. Added to these two priorities is the need for long-term benefits, to cover retirement and inactivity through illness. Family allowances are mentioned in some towns.

For the informal subsistence sector, the main issue is how to cope with daily life, where needs are limited to very few items – eating and bringing home a little money is the goal. Motivating and sensitizing workers in this category to make any provision for the future seems very difficult, even if, as elsewhere, the problem of health arises. However, it should not be assumed that none of these people, such as vendors in particular, would be ready to organize social security for themselves.

The problem is different for rural or urban craft workers. They are much better organized, and their needs are more comprehensive. Over and above health cover and assistance with education, analysis of their priorities reveals a concern to take account of pensions. This reflects identification with the wage-earning model. The same preferences are found among workers in the informal competitive sector.

3. Health protection

3.1 Access to health care

Despite the political will and the urgent need to improve the state of health nationwide, health indicators remain alarming in Benin. This can be explained by the difficult financial and economic situation experienced in Benin in the 1980s. Furthermore, structural adjustment, with its drastic budgetary constraints, forces the State to curb allocations for health and social affairs. With a constantly declining health budget, from 8.8 per cent of the national budget in 1987 to 3.3 per cent in 1992, people remained poorly served in terms of social contingencies. However, there has been an increase in the health budget since 1995, to 4.8 per cent of the national budget.

According to the UNDP Human Development Index for 1996, Benin is ranked as one of the poorest countries: 162nd out of 173 countries surveyed. This is confirmed by a host of indicators on demography, income, employment, education, health, food security, nutrition and the environment. This poverty is primarily felt by vulnerable groups such as women and children, uneducated young people, the destitute, unemployed and demoralized graduates, farmers with little income, and those living in isolated and unhealthy areas.

Health indicators concern provision of services and public health. The availability of health services, both in terms of personnel and infrastructure, shows a disparity between urban and rural areas in Benin. According to Ministry of Health statistics, the number of people per doctor for the whole country was some 18,000 in 1992 compared with the 10,000 recommended by the WHO.

In rural areas, there was only one doctor for every 42,000 people. The regional distribution of infrastructure (hospitals and hospital centres) reveals a concentration in the main towns and department capitals and in the south of the country, where the population is relatively dense. This raises the question of geographical accessibility.

To analyse financial accessibility and assess the effect of payment for health care on use of health services, a survey was carried out in 1989 in six villages in Benin, one from each of the six provinces, whose health centre operated the Extended Vaccination Programme (EVP) and primary health-care strategies.

People who had been ill during the two weeks before the survey were questioned about what medical help they sought and the expenses incurred. Households were classified *a priori* into three socio-economic groups based on housing conditions, means of transport, the economic activities of the household and any membership of a tontine (local savings scheme). The survey covered 2,099 people (see table 7.1).

The average expenditure was 500 CFA francs per person, but there were significant differences depending on the place where the treatment was provided.

Table 7.1 Distribution of median expenses in CFA francs for a period of illness, by
type of treatment and socio-economic group, Pahou-Benin, 1990

Socio-economic group		Health centre		Other than health centre		Total
		Only	With other	Financial reason	Other reasons	
High	Median CFA	500	1 700	150	500	500
	Number	20	119	193	236	568
	%	(4)	(21)	(34)	(41)	(100)
Average	Median CFA	1 000	2 500	175	500	500
	Number	65	211	408	346	103
	%	(6)	(20)	(40)	(34)	(100)
Low	Median CFA	600	3 000	100	300	400
	Number	61	100	201	139	501
	%	(12)	(20)	(40)	(28)	(100)
Total	Median CFA	600	2 500	150	500	500
	Number	146	430	802	721	2 099
	%	(7)	(20)	(38)	(34)	(100)

Health centre only: persons going only to the health centre.

Health centre with other: persons who went to the health centre and another place (e.g. private clinic).

Other than health centre: persons who went somewhere other than a health centre for financial reasons (traditional medicine, etc.).

Other reasons: persons who went somewhere other than a health centre for non-financial reasons.

Source: International Children's Centre, 1990.

The cost for the health centre (600 FCFA) was of the same order as the average cost for all treatment centres (500 and 600 FCFA). However, where health centres and other places were both used, the cost of treatment was much higher, from 600 to 2,500 FCFA. People who said that they did not use the health centre for financial reasons spent a similar amount to those using the health centre (600 FCFA). However, those who said that they did not use health centres for financial reasons (802 people) spent less on treatment than those who used health centres (150 FCFA compared with 600 FCFA). Those 802 people account for 38 per cent of the total sample. The socio-economic category of households seems to have little influence on the choice of place of treatment and the expense incurred, but people in the low socio-economic group (12 per cent) use the health centre more frequently than those in the high socio-economic group (4 per cent).

Finally, the percentage of individuals who said that they did not use health centres for financial reasons is the same for all socio-economic categories. That may mean that other factors than actual ability to pay enter into the decision, notably the use of self-medication and traditional medicine.

The 1989 survey seems to show that the cost of treatment in EVP/PHC centres is similar to other places of treatment. Some people did not use the centres for financial reasons, but as this proportion was independent of socio-economic status, it suggests that families give priority to expenditure other than on health. Only 201 people in the disadvantaged group (40 per cent of that group and 10 per cent of the total) did not attend the centre for financial reasons linked to a genuine inability to pay.

3.2 The Pahou experience: CREDESA

CREDESA (the Regional Centre for Development and Health) was established under the Pahou Health Development Project (PDSP) so as to obtain a better idea of the interaction of health and development, and to use health as an entry point for basic integrated development. Based on the Primary Health Care (PHC) strategy, its overall objective is to identify models for low-cost service available to the people, with their participation.

The main results of CREDESA/PHC include:

- a community financing system which largely inspired the Bamako Initiative, via a seminar for practitioners from other sub-regional centres at CREDESA;
- a community-based information system, used by members of the community; and
- an analytical framework for community participation and some indicators to measure community participation.

All these programmes were designed to facilitate access, as indicated above. Geographical accessibility may be improved in two ways, either by creating local centres or by providing regular transport between the population and treatment centres. In Benin, the first approach was favoured, i.e. local centres, with a wide distribution of human, material and financial resources of doubtful effectiveness. The introduction of health zones is an approach which could produce solutions to the current problems. Apart from the essential drugs policy, there has not been much experience of or consideration given to financial accessibility. According to Djigbèhoudé (1995), some health units may have different means of financing health care. For example, medical insurance could be based on the following principles:

- Free treatment for insured patients hospitalized in the case of sudden illness.
- Subsidy of 75 per cent for care during normal pregnancy or treatment planned in advance. Preventable illnesses cannot be subsidized.
- Possibility for people who are not insured to call on these services, but they would have to pay the full cost.

However, an experiment of this type presupposes a good information system, central management and rationalization of treatment. In reality, several factors influence the use of health services in Benin. In a study carried out in 1993, several determining factors were identified (Djigbèhoudé, 1995). These were:

- self-medication,
- perception of illness and pain,
- ignorance of treatment available in health centres,
- organization of services, and
- multiplication of treatment centres.

In essence, all these factors make it even more urgent to create a new system of medical insurance for the people.

3.3 The potential scope of medical insurance

One of the main problems in introducing a social security system for the informal sector is not the lack of organization among permanent or casual workers who are not covered (because the various associations, cooperatives and trade unions to which these workers belong show the opposite), it is rather the absence of a functioning administrative structure. The structural means exist for collecting contributions and managing a social security system, but these innovative new structures require a clear definition of the roles and means of paying benefits and contributions.

The crisis affecting all social security systems in Africa, characterized by suspension of payment, constitutes a formidable obstacle to extension. It engenders distrust among workers for the system proposed by the OBSS. Reforms are therefore essential in order to extend the formal system to other categories of worker, given that the present system is so selective and unfair. These schemes should primarily target the current inadequacy of the benefits paid by the OBSS, which are limited in scope by restrictions that have failed to keep up with the dynamism of the informal sector.

There is a very strong desire among the target groups for the creation of special options for workers both in the formal and informal sectors, designed to cover health care and education of children.

4. Conclusions

In 1980, the OBSS set up pilot projects with a view to extending the social security system to rural areas. The experimental structures chosen for the project were agricultural cooperatives created and organized by the Regional Action Centres for Rural Development (CADER). However, these cooperatives did not last long because of the untried nature of the proposed schemes. Since then, the planned extension of social security to rural areas has foundered due to the lack of an experimental base.

Today the State should encourage any initiative aimed at broader coverage of social security. However, the State's role would not be to guarantee the financial viability of new forms of social security outside the OBSS, but to create the legal framework in which they could operate. Technical support could be provided by social security officials and international organizations such as the ILO. The social partners and NGOs would be involved at the organizational level. Insurance experience, notably that of the Société Nationale d'Assurance et de Réassurance (SONAR) could also be useful.

In fact, all the elements required for developing an enlarged social security system for other workers are in place, covering health costs and perhaps even education. The needs are real, there is effective political will for such a change and the capacity of the target populations to contribute is substantial.

It is therefore feasible for workers in the informal sector to set up a social insurance scheme, through collective action, to cover their most basic needs. Indeed, this capacity has been illustrated by the work of associations, tontines, mutual benefit societies and cooperatives.

Against this background, there is a need to test new schemes through pilot projects. The results of these pilot schemes will facilitate their replication in other regions, and will certainly be useful for the State's social protection system. The workers to be targeted in the trial phase will be, first of all, those in regular employment in the informal sector who are not covered and the self-employed; and secondly, some categories of the informal sector that can be integrated as part-time workers, based on their ability to contribute as a group. Individual membership for these categories would not be desirable, because the success and viability of such projects rely essentially on social pressure and discipline that are essential to the proper functioning of a group. When there is a dispute or any abuse of benefits, the group could exert a positive influence on the individual and take appropriate measures.

References

Djigbèhoudé, O. 1995. *Benino-German Primary Health Care Project* (Cotonou, GTZ).

GTZ (Deutschen Gesellschaft für Technische Zusammenarbeit). 1995. *Benino-German Project* (Cotonou).

ILO. 1972. *Employment, incomes and equality. A strategy for increasing productive employment in Kenya* (Geneva).

International Children's Centre. 1990. *Children in the Tropics* (Paris).

Ministry of Labour, Employment and Social Affairs. 1994. *National Social Development Report* (Cotonou).

POLICY RECOMMENDATIONS 8

Wouter van Ginneken, Senior Economist, Social Security Department, ILO

In most low-income developing countries, not more than 10-25 per cent of the working population and their dependants are covered by statutory social insurance, mainly for pensions and sometimes for health-care costs. Extension and reform of the statutory social insurance system could reach about another 5–10 per cent of the working population, i.e. most of the so far non-covered regular workers and some casual wage-workers in the formal sector. At the other end of the income scale are the 30 per cent of poor households who can probably only be helped by tax-financed social assistance, social services and poverty alleviation measures. In between these two groups are the bulk of the working population (about 40–60 per cent) – above the poverty line but not eligible for or not interested in statutory social insurance – who have some contributory power and are interested in contributing to social insurance programmes that are tailored to their needs.

The first challenge of a comprehensive social security policy is to reach the majority of the aforementioned working population, with social insurance schemes specially designed for them, that are effective in protecting against poverty, while at the same time promoting productivity and employment. Workers are willing to contribute to special insurance if they feel that they will get value for money, if the benefits correspond to their priority needs and if the system that administers the benefits is trustworthy.

The second challenge is the promotion of cost-effective social assistance aimed at certain groups within the 30 per cent of households that live in poverty. The effectiveness of social assistance schemes depends to a large extent on their design, and – in a general sense – also on the overall willingness of society to show solidarity to those who in most cases have left the labour market, such as old-age pensioners, widows, orphans and disabled people.

The third challenge is the reform of statutory social insurance schemes and their extension to larger groups of regular and casual workers.

Finally, the collaboration of all social security partners is necessary to design and carry out a comprehensive social security policy. The partners involved are, of course, first of all the working people and their families themselves, sometimes represented by trade unions, cooperatives and NGOs. Employers play an essential role where wage workers are concerned. Insurance companies and social security agencies are a third group of partners. The Government also needs to be involved and committed at all levels, to provide sustainability and consistency to the whole structure of social security.

1. Promoting contributory schemes

The contributory schemes reviewed in the case studies are organized by a variety of associations or organizations, such as producer and employer organizations, cooperatives, credit associations and self-help groups. Sometimes, there are some intermediate carriers such as trade unions, NGOs and private insurance companies. Most schemes are limited to small groups of workers, so that the administration costs are relatively high. The analysis of these contributory schemes has also shown that there are two fundamental requirements for setting up a successful contributory scheme: (i) the existence of an association based on trust; and (ii) an administration that is capable of collecting contributions and providing benefits.

Important implementation and design issues of social insurance packages are affordability and meeting the priorities of workers, but there are a number of other issues that need to be analysed so as to establish conditions for replicating and extending such schemes. These include:

- dependence on the input and charisma of one person or group of people;
- dependence on external funding for the scheme's long-term financial viability;
- an evaluation of the implicit costs and the capacity of the scheme's administrators, who usually are not remunerated;
- the possibility of pooling resources among different schemes;
- the possible link-up with private insurance companies and/or social insurance agencies.

1.1 Health insurance

All the case studies have noted that people increasingly pay out of their own pockets for health care. This explains why access to health care is the main social security priority for most workers in the informal sector. All the case studies also plead for greater efforts by the Government to finance primary health-care services and enhance the spread of public health infrastructure, especially in rural areas. There is also a clear case for the extension of health insurance, both for raising additional finances so as to increase access to medical services and for enhancing their quality. A review of a few health insurance schemes operated in the informal sector shows that they are most successful in a wider context of health provision and/or other development activities. With regard to contributory schemes, it is therefore necessary to:

- experiment with various financing mechanisms, either through NGOs or through community- or area-based schemes, both with regard to primary and secondary health services as well as to hospital costs;
- evaluate the experiences of current schemes, in terms of financing, administration and beneficiary satisfaction;
- experiment with, and evaluate, basic hospitalization packages introduced by private health insurance companies, such as the Jan Arogya Bima Policy in India (see Chapter 2).

1.2 Life and disability insurance

The various case studies have shown that – among the long-term benefits – informal sector workers are most interested in coverage against death and disability. Some self-employed workers in the informal sector do have such cover in the context of credit programmes. However, more generalized life and disability pension systems tend to be supported by the Government, in terms of administration, policy advice or subsidies. In India, such programmes have not been so effective, which may be explained by a lack of contributory power, a lack of awareness and information, a lack of administrative commitment and the low amount covered by the insurance. It is therefore important to aim for higher participation in the programmes.

However, the employment injury insurance scheme for township and village enterprises in China seems to have been successful (see Chapter 3), mainly because of the persistence of the Ministry of Labour and Social Security. This scheme provides employment injury benefits, reimbursement of medical care cost, as well as disability and survivor benefits. Full employment injury insurance contributions are made by employing units at an average of 1 per cent of the total payroll. In sectors with a higher incidence of employment injuries and occupational diseases, the rate is higher. The rate is readjusted each year within a maximum range of 40 per cent, according to the occurrence of employment injury cases.

1.3 Special government-supported schemes

These special public schemes are usually financed by government subsidies or by an earmarked tax, and they are administratively and financially distinct from the scheme for formal sector workers. The "labour welfare funds" in India (Chapter 2) are an interesting example of this approach. They cover specific groups, such as *beedi* and construction workers, provide a wide range of benefits and are financed by a special tax on output.

The existing welfare funds could be improved in the following ways:

- concentrating on a limited number of benefits, some in return for specific contributions from workers;
- allowing greater participation of workers in the definition of what are their priority social security needs;
- rationalizing the administration of the funds.

Special schemes could also be considered in countries with many domestic workers. Such employment is stable, in general, with limited turnover. Simplicity would be an essential feature of such a scheme. A flat-rate scheme may be advisable, perhaps using the system of stamps and contribution cards. Similarly, special schemes could be established for agricultural workers through a levy on produce and for construction workers by a levy on the overall construction site contract. Occupational health is yet another neglected area that can be appropriately addressed through welfare funds.

1.4 Extension and replication

Most of the contributory schemes for informal sector workers are organized on a occupational or sectoral basis. They generally provide a good base for generating the necessary trust that has to be the foundation of any social insurance scheme. For their extension and replication, it is necessary to set up an umbrella organization that can provide administrative and technical support to small-scale systems. In Chapter 5 this was demonstrated by the UMASIDA health insurance scheme, which could grow into a professional organization with a so-called "beehive" structure, that would enable informal sector workers' organizations to affiliate rapidly.

Another option for extension and replication is to experiment with area-based schemes which aim at full coverage within an area, and are mainly run by the (local) government in collaboration with a wide variety of possible social security partnerships. They can contribute to the reduction of administration costs and can be designed so as to include local participation and control. And, most importantly, coverage could be extended to other areas relatively quickly, because governments would be able to replicate the schemes on the same conditions.

2. Fostering cost-effective social assistance

The case studies have shown that statutory social assistance schemes exist in Benin and the United Republic of Tanzania, but that they are not fully implemented. In India there are contingency-based social assistance schemes for the old, the disabled and for widows, while China has a general social assistance programme, both in rural and in urban areas. The studies generally complain of low coverage ratios, i.e. relatively small numbers of people who receive benefits compared to those who are entitled. In China for instance, 3 million people receive benefits while 13 million would be entitled to them. These low coverage ratios are first of all explained by the lack of tax revenues, but also have to do with the complicated administrative arrangements to deliver the benefits. There are three implementation issues that merit special attention.

(i)   *It is essential to determine criteria for eligibility.* The so-called means tests can be based upon various criteria, such as consumption, income and/or assets. Other tests are also applied, such as residence, nationality and the availabilty of potential family support, as well as the availability for work and training. In India for example, the application of both the income and the "Niradhar" (presence of an adult son) status of a pensioner leads to ambiguities and administrative problems. Statutory social assistance programmes have conventionally emphasized the notion of relatives' responsibility to require family members to care for dependent relatives. However, the notion of relatives' responsibility has relied on a punitive rather than incentive approach, and it fails to recognize that in many poor countries, relatives are themselves often too poor to assume additional responsibilities.

Another issue concerns the types of institutions that need to be involved to determine whether someone is eligible or not. In China and India, local government officers decide on eligibility, but it may also be worth considering the use of community-based procedures. In general, it is best to leave the determination of eligibility to the lowest level of administration (at the Panchayat or block level in India for instance), but in participation with the local community so as to guarantee maximum transparency.

(ii) There are *various tasks at the state and central levels* that require better implementation, such as:

- assessing what are the best modes of payment,
- designing a rigorous poverty assessment method that will be the basis for fixing budget ceilings at the district level,
- defining a mechanism by which benefits can be adjusted for inflation.

(iii) It is necessary to *link up social assistance programmes with other anti-poverty programmes,* such as employment guarantee and food security schemes. There is significant scope for coordinating social assistance with other promotional anti-poverty measures. Pensions and survivor benefits to widows can be combined with training and loans to improve their earnings. Maternity assistance can be linked to pre-natal and post-natal maternal care, to institutionalized deliveries and to family welfare. Pensions for the physically disabled can be linked with rehabilitation therapy and suitable employment.

3. Extending and reforming statutory social insurance schemes

Efforts to extend statutory social insurance protection will ultimately depend on the priorities of the non-covered workers as well as on their contributory power and that of their employers. It can be expected that insurance against medical costs is a first priority for these workers, particularly in a situation in which the Government performs a small role in providing medical care. Old-age pensions will probably be mainly of interest to regular workers, since they have a longer planning horizon and a more stable income pattern than casual workers.

With regard to pensions, the Chinese example is noteworthy in that a clear distinction has been drawn between the mandatory pension schemes for urban workers and the pension scheme for rural workers and rural migrants to urban areas, which is government-supported and provides for the voluntary participation of such workers. Moreover, there are considerable variations in the benefit and contribution structures of pension schemes for different groups of workers in urban areas. With regard to health insurance, the Chinese are experimenting with a system that pays the workers' half share of contributions into an individual savings account that is first used for reimbursement of medical costs. The employers' half goes into a social pooling fund, which finances additional reimbursement when the total medical care costs for the year exceed the sum of the amount held in the individual accounts plus 5 per cent of the total wage of employees. If the maximum medical care costs exceed a ceiling (which varies from one locality to another), the excess is not covered by the social pooling fund. Enterprises may set up supplementary medical insurance funds, to cover higher costs, but in most cases have not done so.

Any enlargement of coverage under the statutory social insurance scheme can only be achieved with the concurrent improvement of its administrative capacity and governance. However, with respect to specific issues related to the extension of coverage, the administrators of social security systems often find it difficult to deal with the special circumstances of the self-employed and casual wage workers. When statutory social insurance is extended to smaller enterprises, each new employer has to be identified, and then registered, educated and persuaded to comply with all the scheme's rules relating to the registration of employees and to the mode and timing of the payment of contributions. In the case of casual workers, contributions are difficult to secure, and maintaining up-to-date and correct records is administratively complicated when such people work intermittently and irregularly for different employers. There is also a conflict with the underlying concept of replacement income, if the income to be replaced cannot be determined easily.

The extension of coverage in a mandatory scheme should depend on the capacity to enforce it. Where a country has decided to broaden the scope on a mandatory basis without a supporting administrative infrastructure, the solidarity and redistributive basis of the scheme may be threatened, and insured persons may strategically plan their contributions so that they maximize their benefits from participating in the scheme. An example is provided by the Philippines, where the Social Security System scheme was developed to provide universal coverage, but was restricted in its enforcement by a combination of public sector restraints on resources and a soft compliance policy.

Given the variety of countries, with regard to the level of economic development and the range of social security institutions, it is difficult to propose general policy conclusions. It may be possible to distinguish two types of developing countries. The first consists of middle-income countries, some of whom have well-developed social security institutions. Such countries could aim at covering the population as a whole through the extension of the statutory social insurance programme. Secondly, there is the large group of low-income countries, where a rapid increase in social security coverage may only be achieved through setting up social insurance schemes directly financed and managed by informal sector workers. However, for both types of countries some of the following conclusions may be suggested:

- Consider a reform of the statutory scheme to facilitate partial membership by the self-employed, domestic workers, agricultural workers and those with a regular income from informal sector activities.
- Strengthen the administrative capacity of the statutory social insurance schemes, particularly as regards compliance, record-keeping and financial management.
- Undertake education and public awareness programmes to improve the image of the statutory social insurance system.
- Extend coverage within a prescribed timetable to all persons working as employees except those in special groups such as domestic servants, family workers and casual workers.
- Create special benefit schemes that suit the needs and contributory capacity of non-covered groups.

4. The role of the social security partners

In most low-income developing countries, the time is not ripe for the formulation of a comprehensive social security policy, because so little is known about the opportunities for social insurance in the informal sector. Most workers in the informal economy are self-employed, i.e. they create their own employment, and by implication will play a greater role in the financing of their own social security protection than wage-earners in the formal sector. Since social security is expanding its scope from the world of formal sector wage employment to that of casual labour and self-employment, new social security partners, such as cooperatives, NGOs and women's organizations, will have to be included in the process of social security financing and management. Much more experimentation will have to be undertaken in this area to see which types of schemes would meet the priorities of workers and which can be replicated on a large scale. In the area of social assistance, new ways have to be found for cost-effective delivery mechanisms, while there are usually only limited opportunities for extension and reform of the statutory social insurance schemes. Thus, at the end of this book, it is appropriate to think of the roles of the various social security partners and to formulate some critical conditions under which they can help to implement a comprehensive social security policy that will achieve social security protection for the excluded majority of workers and their families.

4.1 The Government

The Government is the ultimate guarantor of the sustainability of social security programmes, as it has the power to regulate their design and it possesses resources and the administrative infrastructure to regulate its implementation. The Government is also in the best position to ensure that isolated experiences can be replicated in other occupations, sectors and areas. As noted in Chapter 7, one important function of the Government would be to define the legal framework for efficient and transparent operations of contributory schemes. Moreover, in collaboration with international agencies, such as the ILO and ISSA, national governments need to encourage research into the functioning of contributory programmes and provide technical assistance to foster the development of such programmes.

Administrative segmentation has been a major cause of the lack of focus and thrust in social security policy. In India for instance, the Ministry of Social Welfare has the general responsibility for social security and social insurance. The Ministry of Labour is concerned with social security legislation for the so-called organized sector, as part of the "welfare of labour". Unemployment insurance is also a subject assigned to it. Policy relating to life and general insurance is the responsibility of the Ministry of Finance. On various other aspects of social security, the Ministry of Health and a number of Ministries dealing with industries, mines, plantations, etc. are involved. Similarly, in the states of India, social security policy and administration are fragmented among different departments: General Administration, Labour, Social Welfare, Women's Welfare, Health, etc. Given this situation, it is necessary to create appropriate integrative, coordinating and consultative structures at the central and state levels.

As part of the ongoing restructuring of government administration in China, a new Ministry of Labour and Social Security was created in 1997. The new Ministry represents a unified social security institution which has taken over the insurance operations previously carried out separately by the Ministry of Labour, the Ministry of Personnel, the Ministry of Civil Affairs and the Ministry of Health. In El Salvador, it is interesting to observe that the recent pension reform did not originate from the Salvadorian Institute of Social Security (ISSS), but from the National Pensions Institute for Public Employees (INPEP).

It is beyond the scope of this book to enter into detailed options for administrative reform. What is important is to start by recognizing that concentration and focus need to be created in one place in the Government with regard to policy formulation; programme design; monitoring and evaluation of implementation; data, analysis and research; and interaction with employers, employees, NGOs and the academic community.

Apart from the need for integration, there is also a clear trend towards decentralization. In India, the experience with the Central Welfare Funds and the National Social Assistance Programme has shown that the central Government cannot ensure proper supervision and design, while an increasing part of such work has to be left to state Governments. In addition, the local community councils, such as the Panchayats and Nagarpalikas, should be fully involved in social security administration. Several advantages can be expected from decentralization: reducing overheads; effective targeting; transparent, responsive and accountable delivery of benefits; mobilization of resources for supplementing benefits; and most importantly, creating a basis for communitarian solidarity.

4.2 The social partners

The social partners could play an important role in the extension of social insurance benefits to regular workers not covered so far, as well as to casual and contract labour employed in formal sector enterprises. The social partners, and in particular the trade unions, are encouraged to negotiate on extending the coverage to workers in small enterprises. Training and awareness-raising, followed by collective bargaining and consultation with the Government, would be the ideal road to greater coverage.

Trade unions and employers could also play a major role in setting up new social security funds at the state or provincial levels – such as for construction workers – and in experimenting with area-based social insurance schemes. The trade unions would ensure that the benefits provided correspond to the priorities of workers, while employers' organizations could convince their members to comply with their contribution obligations.

4.3 Insurance companies and social security agencies

The example of India has shown the advantages of the involvement of insurance companies or social security agencies, in that they already have a well-functioning administration. However, the administrative costs claimed by such companies and agencies could be much higher than those incurred by smaller NGO schemes. It is, therefore, recommended that comparative studies be made of the relative cost-efficiency of NGOs on the one hand, and the companies and agencies on the other. To reduce administrative costs, it may be worth considering the use of NGOs as insurance agents working for companies and agencies on a commission basis.

4.4 Non-governmental organizations

NGO action for the informal sector is generally based on a comprehensive concept of development and social security. NGOs have a good understanding of the particular needs and priorities of their client groups and with them have developed institutions and policies that are quite different from what the Government is used to and/or can cope with. In the social field, NGO action often integrates the traditional social security measures with complementary ones in the fields of primary health care, child care, housing and targeted social action. In the economic field, more security can be achieved through self-help and self-employment, resulting in an enhancement of income and creation of productive assets. This not only helps to reduce, to some extent, the need and cost of conventional social security measures available, but also makes a positive economic impact by enabling the poor to actively participate in and contribute to the economy of the nation. The NGOs have only very recently started to set up contributory schemes. They therefore require technical assistance for the design of such schemes, as well as support structures needed to improve governance, such as through training, data banks and research facilities.

5. The role of the ILO

The ILO's future role in the extension of social security coverage is potentially very great. It will, first of all, have to help informal sector organizations to establish and maintain their own social insurance schemes. It will also have to assist governments and social security agencies to design and carry out policies to include those people who have not been covered so far. A substantial amount of solid research and experimentation will be required to back up these technical assistance activities. Moreover, new standard setting by the ILO could provide a powerful incentive for governments and their social partners to commit themselves to strategies and policies for the extension of social security coverage.

5.1 Research and experimentation

Little is known about the possibilities for informal sector workers to set up their own social insurance schemes, and various experiments are also called for in the area of social assistance. Thus, what could be called "action research" is needed in this area of ILO activity. It would be a form of participatory research, at the grass-roots level, and in collaboration with NGOs and other groups from civil society. The aim of such research would be to find practical and innovative answers to the problems, as seen through the eyes of the informal sector workers themselves. Such research should also be documented with great care and in great detail, so as to permit replicability between different countries and circumstances. This approach would also imply close collaboration with other international organizations, such as the WHO and UNICEF, because health insurance is a key social insurance priority for informal sector workers.

Another research activity would be the analysis of social expenditure patterns by governments and informal sector households. Trends in public social expenditure indicate to what extent low-income households have access to much-needed social services. Expenditure patterns of informal sector households will reveal how much workers already contribute to informal social security arrangements and what they spend on vital life areas, such as health, education and savings. Such information could be obtained from household and similar surveys, and would provide a basis for estimating contributions that households could make to the social security financing of health care and pensions.

Finally, it would be highly relevant to compile an inventory of current experiments to extend social security coverage. This research should focus first on existing social insurance schemes for informal sector workers, and in particular on health insurance. In addition, researchers should carefully document and analyse efforts to extend the coverage of social assistance and statutory social insurance.

5.2 Technical assistance

The main aim of ILO technical assistance is to strengthen the capacity of governments, social security agencies, social partners, NGOs and insurance companies to design and implement social security schemes for the informal sector. This capacity can be strengthened by experimenting with pilot activities, as mentioned in the previous section. The ILO could assist with carrying out feasibility studies, with the aim of assessing how and under what conditions these pilot activities could be successfully implemented and replicated. On the basis of experience gained with these activities, the various social security partners could then also be trained and helped to formulate their own policies and activities with regard to social security for informal sector workers.

A second aim would be to assist the governments with the formulation of a comprehensive social security policy. With regard to social assistance, it would have to formulate a minimum package of social assistance that is affordable and coherent with other anti-poverty policies. In the field of statutory social insurance, the ILO could provide technical assistance to the administration of social security in areas such as organization, coordination and legislation. The ILO could also give advice on ways to improve the participation of all the social security partners in policies to extend social security coverage.

5.3 Standard setting

Most social security Conventions of the ILO focus on wage-earners in the formal sector. However, since the beginning of the 1990s some instruments have begun to formulate standards on social security for workers outside the formal sector. For example, the Home Work Convention, 1995 (No. 177), stipulates that national laws and regulations in the field of maternity protection should apply to homeworkers. In addition, it proposes that social security protection can be achieved for homeworkers through extension and adaptation of existing social security schemes and/or through the development of special schemes or funds. The Job Creation in Small and Medium-Sized Enterprises Recommendation, 1998 (No. 189), proposes to review labour and social legislation to determine whether it meets the special needs of such workers and can be extended to them, and whether there is a need for supplementary measures, such as voluntary schemes and cooperative initiatives.

Since these standards cover only specific groups of workers, it is desirable to generalize their applicability to all workers, and in principle to the population as a whole. The ILO could therefore consider formulating new standards on the extension of social security. Such standards could: reaffirm the right to social security as included in the UN International Covenant on Economic, Social and

Cultural Rights; seek commitment from governments and their social partners to elaborate and carry out strategies for extending basic social security protection; and adopt statistical indicators for measuring progress towards universal coverage. In addition, standards could provide recommendations on guidelines to design, manage and administer social security schemes and to develop national and international policies and strategies.

The adoption of such standards could galvanize governments, social actors and the population at large into action, so as to achieve basic social security protection for the excluded majority – and indeed for all inhabitants of our planet.

INDEX

Page numbers in *italics* refer to tables

United Republic of Tanzania 98-9, *99*, *100*, 123
insurance 5-6, 23, 32, 180, 188
  China 77
  group schemes 26, 48, 52-4, *53*, 61-2, 181
International Covenant on Economic, Social and
  Cultural Rights 2
International Labour Organization
  Home Work Convention, 1995
    (No. 177) 190
  Income Security Recommendation, 1944
    (No. 67) 4-5
  informal sector definition 169
  Job Creation in Small and Medium-Sized
    Enterprises Recommendation, 1998
    (No. 189) 190
  Medical Care Recommendation, 1944
    (No. 69) 5
  Philadelphia Declaration 2
  research and experimentation 189
  Social Security Department 1, 2
  Social Security (Minimum Standards)
    Convention, 1952 (No. 102) 5
  standard setting 189, 190-1
  technical assistance 189, 190
invalidity 5

Jacquier, C. 23
Jan Arogya Bima Policy (India) 54, 61, 181
Jenkins, M. 15, 96

Kane, P. 21
Kinyondo, Sebastian 123
Kiwara, A.D. 110, 117, 119, 130, 131
Korea, Republic of 14
Krishnan, T.N. 60

land, as security for old age 10, 12, 105-6
Latin America 1, 8, 150
life expectancy *3*
  United Republic of Tanzania 118, *120*
life insurance 10, 26, 181
  ACACSEMERSA 160
  India 41-3, 52, 65
literacy rate 2, *3*
  El Salvador 146
  India 39-40
  United Republic of Tanzania 119, *120*

Madihi, M. 97
malaria *19*
Malaysia 12
Maliyamkono, T.L. 118
Maquilishuat Foundation – FUMA
  (El Salvador) 161-3, 166

maternity benefits 5, 7, *7*, 10, 184
  India 41-3, 45, 51-2
  United Republic of Tanzania 100-1
means tests 5, 183
medical costs insurance *see* health insurance
Meghji, Z.H. 117, 126
Mesa-Lago, C. 8
microenterprises 8, 158-9
Midgley, J. 7-8, 16, 21, 28
Mkulo, H.M. 123
Mongolia 28
Mozambique 12
Msambichaka, L.A. 118, 119
mutual benefit societies 9, 20, 21
  Benin 170-1
  El Salvador 164
  United Republic of Tanzania 122

National Provident Fund (United Republic of
  Tanzania) 95, 97, 123
  expenditure patterns 100
  extension 103-4
  improvements suggested 110-11, *112*
  poor mobilization 11, 107-8, *109*, 113
National Social Security Fund (United Republic of
  Tanzania) 95, 96, 112, 121, 123
  extension 109-10
  improvements suggested 15, 111, 113
natural disasters 10, 122
non-governmental organizations (NGOs) 9
  Benin 168
  China 94
  contributory schemes 26, 34, 180, 186, 188
  El Salvador 161-3, 164, 165
  health insurance 181
  India 55-60
  social assistance 27
  United Republic of Tanzania 98, 110,
    122, 124
nutrition 40, 118, *120*

occupation-based schemes 12-13, 31, *32*
  El Salvador 158
old-age pensions 5, 6-7, *7*, 10, 30
  Benin 2, 167
  China 9, 81-7, 90-2, 184
  contributory schemes 25-6
  India 9, 50, 52
  as priority 98, 102, 171, 172, 184
  United Republic of Tanzania 2, 11-12,
    105-6, *107*
old people *see* elderly
orphans 6, 11, 30, 120